Call *the* Roll

by Thomas R. Moran

ISBN Number: 0-9667989-5-3

Library of Congress Number: 00-193427

Printed in the United States of America
Sharp Printing
3477 Lockport Road
Sanborn, NY 14132

Cindy, Colleen, Kevin, Bridie and Mike,
I LOVE YOU GUYS.

Table of Contents

Foreword

Many of my acquaintances have told me that I can really tell a story and usually it is with just a touch of BULLSHIT. Well, I intend to tell you my story of fourteen years of government, politics and personal experiences as Chairman of the Wyoming County Board of Supervisors and Java Town Supervisor.

I want to show you that 99.9999% of the public officials that I have encountered, are working for the good of the people. I also intend to illustrate that 99.9999% of the residents of Wyoming County are honest, hard working, nice people.

This book will be an in-depth account of my experience of the political events from 1986 through 2000. As you know, I was a Town Supervisor for fourteen years and Chairman of the Wyoming County Board of Supervisors, for four years. This book not only provides the history behind the decisions but also why and how those decisions were made. The title could be " Who's Who in Local Government ". Those people who set, supported and even opposed policies are all recorded here in black and white. It also provides an insight how small town politics can influence towns, counties and individuals. Some of the stories are humorous and some not so humorous. It will take you, the reader, into the smoke filled back rooms of Albany, Warsaw and even Java. But more importantly, in this age of apathy and mistrust of government, it will empower readers to draw their own conclusions based on historical facts. I believe it truly is a lesson in history, yet also a profound lesson in human nature.

I thank everyone who helped but especially Helene Schlick. Helene even questioned the Jesuit education that I received at McQuaid. Helene graciously agreed to edit this book for grammar problems, of which there were many. She was extremely patient with me. Unless you have ever attempted to edit a book, especially written by a Jesuit-educated man, you can not imagine the amount of time and effort that Helene put into this book. I thank her and I also thank Jim. God only knows how many dinners he had to prepare for himself because Helene was so absorbed in this book. Thanks, Helene.

Many people have asked me who I am dedicating this book to. I have put a tremendous amount of thought into that question. Obviously, my entire family deserves it. They went through the same experiences that I did. I love them dearly for it. I could not have possibly accomplished what I did without their support. In fact, I would not have been able to write this book without them

That being said, I wish to dedicate this book to all the elected and appointed local officials of this great state. They experienced the trials and tribulations that are depicted in this book on a regular basis. Those fine individuals deserve your praise. Next time you encounter a local public official, say thank you to them. You will make their day !

I hope you enjoy this book. I know that I have enjoyed writing it.

Chapter 1

Genesis

My days as a political activist actually began in April of 1966. I was a senior at McQuaid Jesuit High School in Brighton, N.Y. Brighton was an affluent suburb of Rochester and McQuaid was a relatively new Catholic High School. Now, let me tell you what 1966 was like.

Lyndon B. Johnson was president and Hubert H. Humphrey was vice president. The war in Viet Nam was going full scale and Medicare was about to be put in effect on July 1, 1966. The Supreme Court had just heard and ruled on a case called Miranda versus Arizona. That case and the subsequent ruling gave more rights to the accused. The top television shows were Get Smart, Batman, I Spy, and Mission Impossible.

I was not your typical honor student or even an above average student. Instead, as one teacher told me, I was a " social butterfly ". I should tell you about my part time job after school and on Saturdays. Does anyone remember the S&H Green Stamps or Top Value (TV) Stamps ? Well... I worked at the TV Stamp Redemption Center in Henrietta at Southgate Plaza. I loved that job and the local store manager was my idol. My God... can you imagine anything greater than being a manager of a TV Stamp Redemption Center? Not me. My job was to work in the stock room, bringing the claimed merchandise to the front desk. I also bundled up all the little books that people had worked so hard to put together. Keep in mind, that you were given one stamp for every dime that you spent at the gas station, department store or the grocery store. Sometimes they awarded you double stamps. WOW. Anyway, then you had to go home and lick the stamps and put them into a book. When you saved enough books, you went to the local redemption center to claim your merchandise from a great catalogue. Now, I am quite sure that anyone raised in the sixties has a smile on their face.

McQuaid is a Jesuit High School. Most of our Teachers were Jesuit Brothers. They were different. Jesuits constantly are demanding that you think. They did teach me well in that regard. In Theology class, as you entered the room, you were greeted by two huge signs. : " God is Dead " and " Religion is Absurd "

Amazing huh ? After all that, twelve years of religion, years and years of being an altar boy, and yet today, I still am a practicing Catholic. More on Catholics later.

McQuaid had a senior lounge on a sub-ground floor. It really wasn't the basement but it wasn't the first floor either. They had tables, chairs, a pop machine and a juke box. On the juke box, you could request songs like, " Strangers in the Night ", " Hang on Sloopy", " Michelle " or my favorite," Monday, Monday " by the Mamas and the Papas. Only seniors were allowed in the lounge. If you had a smoking permission slip signed by your parents, you were also permitted to smoke in the lounge. In April of 1966, the Prefect of Discipline, Mr. Casey, (a Jesuit brother) issued an edict that there was to be no more smoking in the senior lounge. How dare he! What were we to do? Remember, Mahatma Ghandi and Reverend Martin Luther King would never have stood for action like that. The students at Berkeley were " sitting in " protesting the War. Why not right here at McQuaid?

Gerry Curre, Dennis Clemente, Davey Fisher, Ed McGee and some others organized a sit in for mid morning. Every senior joined in. By noon, no seniors were in class. We were all sitting in the hallway outside of the lounge. We were not going to disperse until the smoking lamp was on and there were assurances from the Administration that there was amnesty for all. Finally, before the end of the day, our Jesuit educators gave in to our demands.

That was the beginning of politics and activism for me. After that, it was all down hill or maybe I should say uphill.

I will fill you in a little more on my life in the sixties. I attended Monroe Community College for about one year. I say attended very loosely. I rarely was in class. Instead I had a great time for a year. It was my first big mistake. I was young and foolish, you might say.

In October of 1967, I applied for a job with the New York Central Railroad in Rochester. They started me that midnight. My first job was called a " puddle jumper " . Every night, I had to physically walk the entire railroad yard off of Goodman Street and record every freight car's initial and number. In 1967 there were still plenty of hobos and big rats in the railroad yards. Many times they'd jump from a boxcar and scare the living beejesuz out of you. Anyway, this was another job that I loved.

Probably because my father and grandfather had both worked on the Railroad.

I was promoted to management and was transferred to Philadelphia, New Jersey and Buffalo and some other places in between. What I am trying to say, is, that I did about every type of job on the railroad. I supervised and was responsible for the data processing from Rochester to Niagara Falls. I was a trainmaster in Jersey and Buffalo, responsible for the safe and timely movements of trains. I was also a crew dispatcher and customer service agent in the union.

Speaking of the union, I was also a Legislative Representative for the Transportation Communication Union (TCU). I was on labor management, safety and even quality management teams. I became very, very active in the Union. Well rounded, huh? I'll be telling you some railroad stories along the way.

Then, in 1978, my life changed forever.

Chapter 2

Sweet Cindy

For personal reasons, I am not going into my divorce in 1975. I had custody of my two children, Colleen born in 1969 and Kevin born in 1972. Two astonishing things occurred at that time. Number one... I had custody of my children, not the mother, and number two, I was working full time on the Railroad.

I was in management when we first split. In railroad management you worked twelve or fourteen hours a day and usually six days at a stretch. If you were lucky, you could put in a half day on Saturday or Sunday. One night in New Jersey we had a serious derailment in the yard. I had been on duty since about 10 P.M. and finally at about noon, we cleared the wreck and the yard was back in operation. The Terminal Superintendent came to compliment me on a job well done and also to tell me that I didn't have to come in that night until midnight. Pretty big of him, huh? This was not going to work with the kids so I elected to go back into the union ranks. The railroad was tough on management. They expected total dedication.

Now, it was not such a bad thing having the kids. Personally, I loved it and I hope I did a good job. There were some tense times and there were times that I am sure that I failed them. But it also opened doors for me socially. Many single women felt in awe, or at least somewhat sorry for me. I had a great time as a single father. That all changed on March 17, 1978.

I have always celebrated St. Patrick's Day to the fullest. In 1978, I was living in south Buffalo. Three of my Railroad buddies, Tom Humphrey, Paul McQuillen and Jimmy Robinson and myself met at the Buffalo Irish Center on Abbot Road for lunch. From there we hit a couple of Irish bars in the South Buffalo area and headed downtown.

We landed in a bar named Brinkworth's on Main Street. Blue Cross had its offices across the street. About 5:00 P.M. all the women from the offices came in. After all, it was Friday, March 17th. Immediately upon seeing Cindy, I fell in love with her. Really. I spent the entire evening trying to convince her that I was the right guy. When she was ready to leave, I asked her to go out and she said " call me ". I told her that I did not have her phone number and she responded that she was listed in the telephone book. From the first moment my eyes were on her, I was sure that she was Irish. Green jumper, green eyes etc. Then I asked her last name. ZIELINSKI !!! Oh my God, I had been wooing a little Polish girl on St. Patrick's Day. May the leprechauns forgive me.

Well, she didn't want anything to do with me at that point. She thought that I was nuts and that I was just " too fast " for her. Fortunately for me, her roommate convinced her to go out with me. The following night, I took her to a St. Patrick's Day party at the Knights of Columbus in south Buffalo. At that time, the south Buffalo Irish actually celebrated from March 1st through March 31st. It was like Mardi Gras in New Orleans or Times Square at New Years. It was just awesome.

Cindy and I were married on February 17, 1979 and moved to Java that summer. Cindy took to Kevin and Colleen and they could not wait for the wedding to have a real mom. You don't see too many great relationships between step mothers and step children. Now, the Zielinski family didn't know whether to accept Cindy and her new instant family or not. But, prior to our move to Java, I went out on my days off and helped with the farm chores and what not. I was also invited to participate in a euchre game down at the Java Center Tavern. Mike Zielinski and Tim McCormick (his best buddy) thought they were going to take me and Uncle Lum Zielinski for easy pickings. It didn't happen and I was accepted from that day forward.

And so we were a happy, young working family commuting back and forth to Buffalo every day. I really didn't have much time for politics then. I was active in the newly formed Java Center Fire Company and was a coach for the Little League team that Kevin was on.

So what the hell happened ?

Chapter 3

Huh?

Kevin was first diagnosed with asthma at about the age of three. He was on medication and frequently needed emergency room treatment. Occasionally, Kevin was even admitted to the hospital. In 1983, he was eleven years old and was having a rough winter with his asthma. He was in and out of Wyoming County Community Hospital on a regular basis. The pediatrician worked out of Warsaw and we all liked him. I won't tell you his name because he has left the area. Anyway, on one trip to the ER, the doctor asked me if I had thought about taking him to Children's Hospital in Buffalo. What ? Is the doctor actually stating that he and/or the hospital can't treat a young asthmatic? He scared the hell out of us and we began taking Kevin into Children's. They also recommended that we attend an " Asthma Clinic " in Williamsville that would help explain asthma and how the family should cope with it. That went on for about eight weeks. Cindy and I would rush home from Buffalo, pick up Kevin and head back into Williamsville. All because our county hospital suggested we go elsewhere. In the spring of 1983, Kevin was admitted to Children's Hospital for several days as a result of an acute asthma attack. Upon his discharge, the staff recommended a respirator that Kevin could use to prevent or minimize an attack. The medication would be inhaled by use of the respirator. I asked how much this would cost and the doctor told us not to worry because the State of New York provides them at no charge. In fact, they had them on hand at Children's. Great !! I proceeded to the Pharmacy Department with the prescription and new hope for Kev. The clerk was completing the application when she asked me what county Java was in. I replied that it was in Wyoming County and hearing my answer she tore the application out of the typewriter and threw it in the waste basket. She then informed me that Wyoming County did not participate in the Asthma Program funded by the State. " Why not ? ", I asked. She told me I would have to find the answer to that.

When I arrived home, I immediately telephoned our Town Supervisor, Vince George who had been Java Supervisor and a member of the Wyoming County Board of Supervisors for fourteen years. I explained what had happened and asked him why! Vince said he'd check it out and get back to me.

The next day I was off and to my amazement a County car pulled in my driveway. The young lady identified herself as a case worker for Wyoming County Department of Social Services. She had been contacted by Vince George and was told to see me. I told her my story but also added that in no way would I qualify for any social service program because of my income. She had never heard of the Asthma Program but suggested I call the health department. I telephoned and spoke with Suzanne Stopen, the Director of Public Health. Ms. Stopen informed me that there were numerous programs that were available to the County which the County elects to participate in or not.

Now, why did I have to make all those calls? Shouldn't Vince either have known or at least used his influence to obtain the explanation ? Not only was I exhausted from all my inquiries, but then, I learned that if I was a Buffalo Bill living in Erie County, and making millions, my son would qualify for a free respirator. But because I was a Railroad employee living in Wyoming County, I was required to purchase the machine myself.

I started calling old Vince. A few days went by and he finally got back to me. I said, " what the hell is going on in Wyoming County, first the hospital and the doctors suggest I go to Erie County and now you can't help me." For those of you that don't know Vince George, I'll try to sum him up. Let's put it this way, Vince gave me a twenty minute speech and never mentioned the respirator, just how good he was and how busy he was. Ask him what time it is and he'll tell you how to build the watch. For Christ's sake.

I began to worry about our Town Supervisor. Was he OK ? Maybe he was in office too long. I didn't know. Something sure was weird though.

Chapter 4

Campaign Number One

Throughout the summer of 1983, I met many fantastic people. I asked them if I should run for Supervisor. They all encouraged me. Folks like Frank and Joan Minkel who owned the Outlander Restaurant and Bob McCormick, a farmer in Java Center. Bernie George, a retired Justice, well liked and well respected also encouraged me as did Don and Bonnie Clark from Java Lake. In September, I decided to run against Vince at the Democratic caucus.

Java, like many Towns in Wyoming County and New York State conducts a caucus to determine who is going to be the endorsed candidates for Town offices. Winning the endorsement is simply a case of who brings the most people to the caucus. It was no secret that I was going to run. But, I don't think Vince ever realized the support that I had.

Bernie George offered to drive me that night and walk in with me. The caucus was scheduled to be at St. Patrick's Church Hall. There were more Moran supporters present than George supporters. However; Vince and his friends were running the show. Paul Keenan, Bill Kerwin, Dan McNulty and Dick Schwab put their heads together and decided that the caucus should be started at the Town Building, have a recess and then reconvene back at the Church. When Bernie and I got back in his car, we just looked at each other. Are you kidding me ? Dirty politics in little old Java ? So... we drove from the church to the Town Building and then back to the church. All the while that was happening, little Paul Keenan was on the pay phone outside out of the tavern calling Vince's supporters. Paul is vertically challenged. The delay worked and I lost the caucus by five votes. At least that's what they told me. That night, I vowed I would never have anything to do with the Democratic Party, again. That next day, I became a registered Republican.

The following night, I was nominated by the Republican Party and accepted. Here we go !!!

I campaigned hard. I went door to door. I had Bill Paxon's help. Bill was our N.Y.S. Assemblyman at that time. I had a good time. I was everywhere. My motto was " Time for a

Change". It was the cleanest campaign that Java would ever see again. By election day, I think I had met every one in Town.

There are two election districts in Java, one administered at the North Java Fire Hall and the other at the Strykersville Fire Hall. Tradition calls for the candidates to be at their polling place when the polls close and the results are read aloud. In 1983, the entire entourage then went to the Central House, North Java Inn, Outlander and finally Java Center Tavern. The victor always bought the drinks. The results were in. Vince George beat me by 12 votes. I was on cloud nine. Never, ever did I dream that I would come that close. I congratulated Vince and also mentioned that John Kennedy had lost his first election bid. Ha Ha, I just can't ever let anything go without a smart remark. Cindy and my father-in-law, George Zielinski were with me. We walked across Route 98 to the Central House. No one, and I repeat no one, offered me a drink. Fine, you don't have to hit me with a sledge hammer! We headed to the Outlander. Now, because of Frank and Joan, the Outlander was like my campaign headquarters. On the ride, I looked at Cindy and she was crying, George was crying in the back seat. I was happier than hell. The Outlander was simply mobbed. When I opened the door, dead silence. Everybody stopped talking and began to clap their hands. There I was, a loser, and these people were giving us a standing ovation. That was a moment that I would remember and cherish forever. Pete Kline, Neil Baumgartner, Paul Killillee, Don Bowen, and I have to say, Joanne Krauss were also there.

The fun and good times that we had in the beginning of my political career were just unbelievable. Here are a couple of cute stories. Bernie George was one heck of a man. They called him the "judge". Bernie tended bar down at the Java Center Tavern (JCT) during daylight hours. He was also an ardent euchre player. One rainy, cold Friday night, Cindy and I stopped for a beer on the way home. Bernie worked till 6 PM. At six, Bernie mentioned that he did not have his car and asked if Cindy would mind giving him a ride home. Of course, Cindy didn't mind. At about eight o'clock, I was beginning to miss Cindy and wanted to go home. She had the car and hadn't been back since taking Bernie home. He only lived around the corner. Mike Chassin was tending bar and said they were probably playing cards at Bernie's house. Norb Hoyt said that he heard that Cindy's Uncle Leonard and Bernie's wife Jean were all playing euchre at Bernie's. So.. Stupid me, I called Bernie. Bernie answered the phone and I asked if Cindy was there. He shouted into the phone, " If you can't keep track of your wife and don't know where she is, don't ever call here looking for her!!! " Norb drove me home. About 11 pm, Cindy pulled in and yup, she was playing cards with Bernie, his wife Jean and Uncle Leonard. The next day, Saturday, I stopped in the JCT. Bernie said, " So did you ever find your wife last night? " I said, " Oh yeah, she tried to get in the house at eleven o'clock at night. Bullshit! No wife of mine is going to be missing for five hours and get in my house. She slept in the car last night ". You should have seen his face drop. He didn't know me well enough to know if I was telling gospel or pulling his leg. I left almost at once. Then, on Sunday, leaving church, Jean asked me, " So, I heard you had some problems at your house, Friday ? " I replied, " No problem, Cindy came home late and slept in the car ". Bernie has since passed on and God Bless him but I don't remember if we ever told him the truth.

You will never meet better people than Frank and Joan Minkel. And this is a generational thing. Because their kids, Elaine, Bobby, Ken, Doug, Donna and Jay Schofield, Nancy Herman and Renee, Rachel and yes, even little Jay, (who some say stole my campaign signs. Did you, Jay?) are great too. Frank and Joan ran the Outlander. Frank is a real fiscal conservative in every aspect. In the winter, he would rarely turn the heat on . About the only time it was warm was when Joan was there. Any other time, you could hang meat. During deer season several of us stopped for lunch. We all ordered cheeseburgers. Paul Rogacki asked for a slice of onion on his. When we got the bills, Paul's was ten cents more. Paul asked what the ten cents was for. Frank said a slice of onion is ten cents extra. The very next day, we were back. Paul ordered another cheeseburger and Frank asked if he wanted a slice of onion on that. Paul said, "no thank you." When Frank served the cheeseburger to him, Paul reached in his hunting coat took out an onion and cut off a slice with his hunting knife. It was very hard to pull one on Frank, but Paul did. Frank was easy too. Judge Bill Horton was in one night and asked Frank if he could charge a six pack of beer to go. Frank answered, "Of course." The next night Bill returned six cans of beer, in a grocery bag. Not the price of beer, but six cans of beer. I was there and I told Frank, to let me know when I owed a case and I would go to the discount store and return it to Frank.

I was usually off on Monday and Tuesday and sometimes other days during the week. I always worked week-ends and holidays on the railroad. Well, one morning on my day off, Cindy ordered me to be home and cook a good chicken dinner. No euchre, she hollered as she got into the car. Remember, this was my Saturday off. I did some yard work and went to the Outlander for a couple of beers. Sharon Schultz and Don Bowen were just finishing lunch and Joan asked if anyone wanted to play euchre. I said that I could for a little while as I had to cook dinner or face Cindy's wrath.

Well, about 3:30 PM, I decided I'd better go. Joan did not want the game to end. She told me to run home, put the chicken in a roasting pan and bring it back. Of course, I did as I was told. Joan not only cooked the chicken but she threw in a vegetable and potato. We played cards till the last possible moment. I rushed home with my prepared dinner, set the table, and Cindy drove in the driveway. She was both elated and shocked.

I don't think she knew what happened until poor Joan passed away, years later.

Chapter 5

The Eye of the Tiger

I really thought my political life was finished. After all, I gave it my best shot and came close. In the summer of 1985, Joanne Krauss, Pete Kline, the Minkels, the McCormicks (Don and Bob) and many others convinced me that I should give it one more try.

Well.. I thought I campaigned hard in 1983. Java was still two to one in favor of the Democrats and here I was trying to get elected as a Republican. This time, I was serious. I had a huge team of supporters and we all worked hard.

There were pens, signs and advertisements in the local papers. I went door to door with Bob McCormick, Joanne, Frank Minkel and Bonnie Clark. Door to door is not easy. It's a real pain in the ass. I did pretty well at the end. I carried the biggest milk bones you could buy for the mean dogs. Bonnie was probably my first campaign manager. Bonnie had made arrangements to meet at my house and then go to my father-in-law's barn on a Sunday morning in September to paint up some signs. Cindy had home made strawberry jam for them, along with Bonnie, Gayle Grandits and a couple of other women who were supposed to be there.

We waited and waited and finally, I went down to the barn alone. You'll see that I am not known for my patience. I painted some sheets of plywood all white. Then, as only I can do, I painted " Tom Moran " on the signs. What I mean by saying as only I can do is, I am not a neat printer, writer or painter. When Bonnie and Gayle saw those signs, they had a fit. They did allow me to keep one as long as I agreed to put it up on a back road.

Speaking of signs, that same fall we were at an Oktoberfest at Beaver Hollow in Java Center. This was before Paul Snyder and Beaver Hollow as we know it today. This was when there was just a concrete block building and lodge. Some young entrepreneurs were trying to make a go of it. This was like the grand opening for a place that never did open. They had a band, food and even a mechanical bull for those so inclined to ride him. There was a table of my supporters sitting by the band.

In came Vince George and he was feeling no real pain. Humble Vince came right over to our table and sat down. We all had " VOTE TOM MORAN " hats on. First thing he said was, " I probably shouldn't be here because I don't have one of those silly hats on". No one replied. "But I probably shouldn't be here because I'm not a UNION man. I wouldn't belong to a union for all the money in the world". I then spoke up and said that I belonged to a railroad union because like many employers, it was mandatory. It was mandatory both ways. Not every employer is a fair and open minded employer. There are many cases where you simply MUST have a Union. At that he directed his wrath to Paul Rogacki. Now Paul too, was a union construction worker. Paul had a " Moran " sign at the end of his driveway. Vince asked him, who the hell painted that sign. Paul responded that it was Walter, his teen age son. We could not believe the next statement that came from Vince. Vince asked Paul, " And just what type of an institution did he just get out of ? ". Paul jumped out of his seat and was about to charge Vince when we subdued him. Nancy, Vince's wife escorted him out of Beaver Hollow. It was unfortunate but I guess it really showed the true colors and how desperate things were becoming for the old guard.

Java had only one Republican Supervisor in the last twenty five years and that was Ed Redding. There was another classy gentleman. Ed and his wife Irene were among my favorite supporters. I visited them several times for advice and good intelligent conversation. I always and still do admire Ed. Ed was convinced that if I worked hard enough, I could defeat Vince.

My campaign agenda focused on the youth of Java because they are the number one natural resource of any town. I also advocated that we should no longer accept mandates from the state. Back in 1985, I was quoted in the Arcade Herald, 10/31/ 85 issue... " I feel this is a critical period for local government. The State is attempting to push far too much legislation and other regulations upon the Towns ". Imagine! I even impressed myself when I gave that statement to the paper.

Again, I was everywhere. At weddings, picnics, firemens carnivals, chicken Bar-B-Que's, church etc. The Outlander Restaurant had a sound machine playing on Saturday nights then. I was working 3PM till 11PM at the railroad. Cindy and I would go there after I came home. Jay Johnson, a good friend and fellow softball player, would always request the song, " The Eye of The Tiger " from one of the " Rocky "movies. That's what I had, the eye of the tiger. I wanted to be Supervisor and I felt that I was very close.

I was so confident that I had a meeting with the local director of labor relations at the Railroad. Mr. Don Dillon issued a letter to me stating that I could have reasonable time off without pay for fulfilling my duties as an elected official. I was working 3 to 11 and even 11 PM to 7 AM with days off during the week. Our daughter, Bridie had been born on April 26th. Things were good and getting better !!

I had another huge plus on my side. Mike and Arlene Witkowski, owners of the famous Hungry Mike's Resort on beautiful Java Lake, were big time supporters. Mike was also running for election as the assessor. They agreed to host the election night party.

On NOVEMBER 5, 1985, ELECTION NIGHT !!!, Java voters elected Tom Moran as Town Supervisor. That year, we did it right. We went to the Central House, North Java Inn, JCT, the Outlander and finished at Hungry Mike's at Java Lake. I even called Ed Redding at about midnight to give him the news. He was so excited, he got out of bed, dressed and came to Hungry Mike's for a drink. What a celebration! Unbelievable! Amazing! We partied till 6 AM.

Tony Prezyna, of Strykersville fame, knocked on the door at about 8 o'clock, with a bottle of Canadian whiskey in his hand. Tony insisted that I have a shot of whiskey with him. I refused and refused and finally relented and had ONE with him. GEEEEZZZZZ!

I attended the December Board of Supervisor's Meeting in Warsaw. But.. boy I wasn't prepared for our Town of Java's Board Meeting two days after the election on November 7th. The Town Board at that time was Mark Hopkins, Dan McNulty, Don Roche and Fran Brunner who was also leaving on 12/31/85. That was also the night that the 1986 Town Budget for my administration was adopted. We had heard through the Java grapevine that the new people better be in attendance because Vince and the boys were going to try and pull something. First mention of a storm came when they were discussing the 1986 salaries. My good buddy, Mike Witkowski defeated Carl Graves for the assessor position. Dan McNulty said and I quote, " A couple of years ago, one assessor didn't do anything.

We're probably going to run into the same thing, this year. Ed (Redding) and Toni (Bazer) are going to do all the work while the OTHER GUY is doing nothing." That was a fine howdy do. And Mike Witkowski was there with me. Dan suggested they lower the assessor salary. Fran (?) Made a motion to lower the salary. From $2,000 to $1500 and it was seconded by Don Roche. Mark, Dan (?) And Vince all voted no and the motion was defeated. Mark Hopkins offered a compromise. He suggested lowering it to $1,750 per year. All ayes. Mark then questioned the raise in the 1986 budget for Supervisor that was increased by $500 from $4000 to $4500. Vince said it was " quite a jump " and then rambled on and on about how the County NEVER hires anyone at the old salary. The new person always received less until they prove themselves. Yeah, right, Vinny !! Mark asked me, what I thought. I said something like, I can't believe you guys are stooping this low but it is your decision this month and I have no choice but I AM KEEPING NOTES!! No further comments followed and the 1986 Budget was adopted. Nice people, huh ?

So now you know how it all started and why.

Chapter 6

Hello Politics

On January 2, 1986, I was seated as the Town of Java Supervisor at the Wyoming County Board of Supervisor's and held the Town's annual organizational meeting that evening. Wyoming County has sixteen towns unlike the majority of New York State counties that have county legislatures, Wyoming still governs with a Board of Supervisors. Each Town Supervisor sits on the County Board. Whereas a county legislator may represent two or more towns or parts of towns, the Supervisor is closest to the people. The Supervisor deals directly with the people. Of the many negatives of a county legislature, the old " pass the buck " mentality is probably the worst. In a legislature, the towns and villages may very well be subject to unfunded mandates, cuts in aid and experience a general disregard or even disdain, by county legislators toward local towns and villages. The Board of Supervisors, with its make up of Town Supervisors, would be cutting its own throat if it didn't support the Towns and its interests.

I had attended several county board meetings during the fall, but I was still not prepared for the pomp and circumstance of the ceremony. Kevin and Colleen attended the meeting with me. The Board Meetings are held in the courthouse, second floor, in Warsaw. All the Supervisors are seated at desks in a semi-circle, alphabetically. The Chairman, Clerk to the Board, the Deputy Clerk and County Attorney sit on raised platforms in front of the members.

In 1986, there were four new Supervisors to be seated. Alexandra Lane from Warsaw, Geraldine Luce from Orangeville, Ed Hamilton from Genesee Falls and myself. I was the only new Republican. Procedure called for the current Supervisors seated on either side of the newly elected supervisors to escort them on their arms to their desks. I was escorted by Norm Smith from Middlebury and Bernard (Barney) Erhart from Gainesville. Barney was also the colorful Chairman of the County Democratic Party.

It was still a pretty awesome feeling. Even the kids were impressed. What the heck was Dad getting involved in ?

Then came my first Town Board meeting, I actually had an agenda and called the meeting to order with the Pledge of Allegiance to the American Flag. Councilman Dan McNulty asked if we were going to do this at every meeting. I responded in the affirmative and stated that Java was in the United States, I was an American and I felt we should always open the meeting in this fashion. Vince George never had any real format for the meetings. They would start at 7:30 P.M. and sometimes not conclude until midnight. Most of it was small talk.

The Town Board was made up of Dan McNulty, Mark Hopkins, Don Roche and Bob Kibler, who also had just been elected. Our relationship at first was tense and I'd like to believe that it improved greatly in the next two years. But Danny would never forgive me for beating Vince, the icon of Java Democrats. Oh well.

The best campaign promise that I ever made was that if elected, I would issue a monthly newsletter to inform the public what was happening at the Town and County level. I issued my first one on January 3, 1986 and my last one on December 15th, 1999. These newsletters not only informed the residents but they also assisted me a great deal. In fact, I'm using them as my notes for parts of this book. One time and only one time, Councilman McNulty suggested that I should NOT be using the Town copier for the newsletters. In the next Newsletter, I mentioned that and Dan never brought it up again.

1986 was a very unsettling time for the Town and myself. Frank Minkel told me after the election, " Be careful, be very careful ". Remember the November 1985 Meeting?

On January 1st, I visited the Town Highway garage. There was Ron George working under a truck, trying to put it back in running condition. I told him that I heard that we didn't have any trucks on the road. Ron said, " Not right now, but Arcade, Sheldon and Wethersfield are helping out and we should be alright by tomorrow." Ron George and the Highway Employees were not given the resources or respect to do their job. I was going to try to change that.

At the Board meeting in January, I learned the Town only had enough money to meet the payroll. On top of that, NO BILLS had been paid since October. We ended up paying over $24,000 in 1986 for 1985 bills. This is all documented. I wondered if the Democrats were up to sour grape political retaliation at the expense of the taxpayers. I had to wait for Marge Lefort to collect the taxes so that we could pay those bills.   The $24,000 deficit and the additional $12,000 in the premium for the Town's liability insurance immediately meant increased property tax for 1987.

I also became aware of just how slow all government works; not just the Federal and the State governments but all governments including Wyoming County and the Town of Java.

Bob Kibler, Mike Witkowski and myself attended the New York State Association of Towns Annual Meeting in New York City in February of 1986.   Bob and I were focusing on all the Zoning and Planning sessions. Holy smokes ! Java was not in compliance with the U.S. Constitution. Java had one Zoning/Planning Board. This was a conflict because if a party, with a zoning issue was denied, they had no place to appeal to.

Together, we brought home tons of literature and supporting documents. We immediately began to work on a master plan and amending our zoning ordinance. Boy, oh boy, was I excited. I contacted the County Planning Board, Stu Brown, the County Planner and others for their assistance. I kept emphasizing that we couldn't drag our feet. The Town Board, Planning Board and the new Zoning Board of Appeals met for almost THREE YEARS. Finally on November 4, 1988, the new zoning ordinance was adopted. Imagine if the Declaration of Independence took that long. We'd still be bloody Englishmen!! Cheerio, pip pip, old chap.

I also learned early in 1986, what a real pain in the ass, the North Java Water District was going to be . Talk about whiners. I'll have a separate chapter for those fiascos or "clusters" at a later point.

In the County, Ross Roberts was elected as Chairman and Jim Foley from Bennington was chosen as Vice Chairman. There were sixteen committees and so every Supervisor was a Chairman of a Committee. I was appointed to the "all powerful" and "influential" Planning Committee as a Chairman. I say that without ill feelings. After all, a new Supervisor is fairly busy in his/her Town the first year or so. The Planning Committee at that time, only had Planning under its jurisdiction.

Alex Lane, Geraldine Luce and Rita George all attended the new Supervisor's school in January held in Rochester. So, I guess you could say that we were all fellow students of the class of 1986. What an honor. Well, I do have to point out that I have the utmost respect for Alex Lane and always admired and respected Rita.

On September 9, 1986, at a County Board Meeting, the new kid from Java, requested that the County share its sales tax revenues with the Towns. Oh, Oh! The Chairman referred me to the Taxation Committee for their review of my proposal. I suggested that the County just share the unappropriated revenue that they receive. In 1986, Wyoming County collected 1.5 MILLION DOLLARS more than they budgeted for. Why not share what they didn't anticipate ? If anything, it would have resulted in better budgeting. In any event, I was told thank you for your proposal and we'll think about it. (Remember, what I said about all governments working slowly).

I was also appointed to the Sheriff's Committee. Sheriff Capwell and Under Sheriff Ron Ely gave those interested a tour of the jail. It seems the Board had been talking for ten years about building a new one. For those of you who had never seen it or visited it, I like to call it an " Old Roy Rogers type jail ". If you don't remember who Roy Rogers was, then just imagine those old cowboy movie jails. And.. really that's what it was. The bars did not go all the way to the floor because the floor was uneven. They had one small portable TV on a shelf at the end of the hall. The "Library" consisted of an old end table with about six books from the 1940's on it. I realize that's what jail is supposed to be.. But we also had guards attempting to keep it and themselves safe too. In fact, at that time there was only one guard on the third shift (midnight to eight). Those issues were on the back burner. The State Department of Corrections continued to issue violations to the Sheriff because the Department of Corrections(DOC) felt that the jail was not suitable for both guards and inmates. The DOC oversees every correctional facility in the state. If they condemned or closed the jail, the county would have to board their prisoners out to another facility. That was a very expensive proposition. The sheriff did a great job satisfying the DOC as long as he did.

On November 12, 1986, the Board created a NEW POSITION called Commissioner of Community Health Services at a salary of $1.00. No, that was not a typo. The salary was ONE DOLLAR PER YEAR. WHY ? Phil Murray, who was the Mental Health Director, was going to be appointed to the new position. Several of us questioned the need for this at the meeting. The position of Director of Public Health had been vacant and they were hoping that this new position could help in the transition when the new Director was appointed. Jim Foley, Vice Chair, remarked that the public health and mental health departments were sharing a building and " ... within a month, they're going to be fighting unless one person is named to be in charge of the building. " Ron Herman said Mr. Murray asked for the title. " It will look good on a resume ", said the Wethersfield supervisor. I still don't get it, but it passed with only George LaWall, the new Supervisor from Sheldon, Alex Lane, Geraldine Luce, Ed Hamilton, Barney Erhart and myself casting negative votes.

And then in October of 1986, Norm Kehl, the Supervisor from Sheldon disappeared. Yes, he just vanished. Apparently no one, including his wife Carol knew where he was. I remember George LaWall calling me and asking what to do because Norm left. " What do you mean, he left? ", I asked. Now, I still don't know where the hell he went, and I really don't care. But I was a little disappointed with him for leaving the Town in a lurch. In November George was seated as the Supervisor from Sheldon. I got along great with this great gentleman.

This was my welcome to big county politics.

Chapter 7

North Java Water District Step One

For the first six months of 1986, Cliff Sheer, the North Java Water District Superintendent along with others, were crying about repairs and new lines that needed to be installed on Perry Road. Select Interior Door, a local business in North Java ,with Bob Gibson attended several Town Board meetings to plead their case. Joanne Almeter also requested new lines due to poor water pressure.

Cliff and I attended a couple of New York State Rural Water Association's seminars that summer. We learned that there was a program available through the State called " Self Help ". The Rensselaerville Institute of Albany sponsored it. In the State government , it fell under the Secretary of State's jurisdiction. Gail S. Shaffer was appointed as Secretary of State under Governor Mario Cuomo. The Program had begun in 1983, when the Department of Environmental Conservation (DEC), Public Health and the Department of State joined forces in an attempt to reduce the costs of water projects for small rural, financially distressed communities across New York State. Well, man , did I ever take this to the limit. I thought to myself, what a great idea ! And we always have the technical and professional advice of the entire State of New York to fall back on.

Ed White was the Western New York representative who coordinated the efforts of the Health Department and the DEC. Ed came to a couple of the public meetings in North Java. It was planned to complete Perry Road and ask for financial assistance for Route 98 from Wethersfield Road north to the Family Mart.

We had received estimates of up to $50,000 to complete just the Perry Road section. George Flummer of the N.Y.S. Rural Water Association was a fantastic resource. The Self Help People never showed up. That includes Ed White, Gail Shaffer, the DEC, the Health Department. No One. I was working 11 PM till 7 AM on the Railroad in Buffalo. As soon as I got home, I would change and go to the site in North Java for the day and it was also World Series week. So... I didn't get much sleep those two weeks, but we did get the project done October 22, 1986. Joe Dupre of Centerline Gravel was the General Contractor. The entire project was less than $20,000. That meant the Water District only needed to borrow $16,000. Of course, Joanne Almeter's line was never installed the right way. Should anyone be surprised?

I wrote to Congressman Jack Kemp, Assemblyman Paxon, Senator Volker and even Governor Cuomo asking for financial help for Route 98. Nothing. Hang on and you'll hear more about the Water District.

Chapter 8

Getting Stronger

1987, was a very good year. The Town's financial condition finally improved and became stable. The County began a study to determine whether to build a new jail or renovate the old one. Can you believe that and the Town of Java was still wrestling with zoning.

Julie Hackett, the long time Town Clerk resigned in July to relocate to the south where her husband, Don had been transferred. Julie was a Republican. Not knowing what the process was for filling a vacancy, I called the Secretary of State and the Association of Towns. The appointment to fill the vacancy had to come from the Town Board. Usually, it was pointed out the successor comes from the same political party. The Java Republican Party Committee recommended Donna Schofield as Town Clerk. The appointment passed 4-1, with Dan McNulty voting in the negative. Dan thought we should have advertised it more thoroughly. Yeah, right.

Gradually, the Town Board became more active in State politics. We were sending our Assemblyman Bill Paxon and Senator Dale Volker resolutions which affected Java and Wyoming County. We were actually being heard. In the County, I continued to ask for a share of the sales tax revenue.

Mike Moran, my youngest son was born on September 18, 1987. And... about the same time, I decided to run for re-election as Supervisor. Charlie McCormick was nominated by the Democrats to be my opponent. Now, Charlie was a regular attendee at the Board Meetings. For those that don't know Charlie, I'll try to be kind. First, Charlie is a very intelligent human being. However; I can't go much farther, than that. He is easily mislead. He is also the extreme opposite of well-groomed and dapper. Do you get my drift ?

Anyway, the election was held and I trounced poor Charlie by 459 to 175. That told me that 70% of the people of Java were satisfied with my performance over the first two years. I must also inform everyone about Java politics. Dan McNulty mailed a nasty little piece to all the residents of Java, a few days before the election. McNulty was apparently part of the 30% that was

dissatisfied with my performance. Dan wrote to all residents..
" We need to get our town board back in the control of the people
who really care about the future of the town. " That is really the
core of the problem. There are many, many biased people in
Java who believe if you are not born in Java, you are forever an
outsider and you don't care about the future of Java. I never
could understand his closing statement.. " Please help make Java
an even better place to live, not just a place to park. "

Maybe that's how they view us " Outsiders " as just parking
in Java temporarily. Get a grip for Christ's sake. I will point to
hypocrisy many times in this book. Those critics of "outsiders"
are the same ones who milk the Town taxpayers for every dime
they possibly can. I'll give you examples of that later.

I should also mention the great budget battle of 1987, in the
County. I was the Chairman of the Planning Committee.
The Wyoming County Tourist Promotion Agency came under
my jurisdiction. The Agency had only been created a couple of
years ago. Elaine Semlitsch was the executive director.

Prior to that, the County and its tourism businesses had no
inter-action with each other. Believe it or not, Wyoming County
was the only county in the state that was not participating in the
" I Love New York " campaign. Isn't that strange considering
Letchworth State Park, the Arcade and Attica Railroad, the
historic Village of Wyoming and all the campgrounds that are
located in Wyoming County?

Anyway in 1985, the Agency was created. I believe the entire
budget at that time was $10,000. Obviously, they could not do
much promoting or marketing with $10,000. The State came out
with a matching funds program, whereby for every dollar the
County puts in, the State would match. The reason for their
generosity was that tourism was the second largest business in
New York next to Agriculture.

Ross Roberts, Howard Payne, Alex Lane and myself were
very supportive of the Tourism Agency and their efforts. There
were others who were not.

Elaine was working from her home, supposedly on a part
time basis. I knew better. Elaine made calls to businesses and
individuals, attended various tourism shows, attended all
the Agency Meetings, worked with the State and other counties
and came to our County Committee meetings. I think it was in
1987, that Wyoming County published our very own first
Tourism Brochure.

In 1987, the Agency requested about $40,000 for the year 1988. Oh my God !!! Finance led by Urlin Broughton, Jim Foley and Barney Erhart shot it down to $25,000 in the Budget. The increase was to pay for the brochure, have the State kick in an extra $15,000 and actually pay the Executive Director a part time salary.

Elaine, Ross and myself attended the Finance Committee in October. "No way," they all said. But... if you need more money in 1988, you can always come back and ask for it. Sure, I can pray that I will win the lottery tonight, too.

At the Budget Public Hearing on November 24, 1987 we did the unthinkable and went out of bounds. The Budget Hearing is very unique from all other Board of Supervisors meetings. Resolutions are allowed to be presented up to 10:00 A.M. that day. Usually, they must be presented about five days prior to the Meeting. Ross and I decided to call a Planning Committee Meeting to request an additional $5,000 in funds for Tourism. It passed committee with Alex Lane, Howard and myself voting in favor and of course Jim Foley opposed it.

This resolution was far more than just another resolution. We were telling the Finance Committee that we were not pleased with their budget and we were going to force them to appropriate more money. What nerve!!

At the budget hearing, I introduced the resolution. All hell broke loose and Elaine was asked to explain the need and exactly where the additional money was going to be spent. The resolution was passed with Foley(R), Broughton(R), Rita George(D), Barney(D), Norm Smith(R), Ed Hamilton(D) all voting no. I always found it peculiar that Ed Hamilton from Genesee Falls voted no on additional funds for Tourism. Ed worked for New York State at Letchworth State Park. Was he trying to abolish his own position or look like a fiscal conservative who was still at the public trough?

In any event, I thus began my second term. All the incumbent Supervisors were re-elected. However, Geraldine Luce resigned in January, 1989. She served one term and a couple of weeks and quit. I lost any respect I had for her at that point. Here was a woman, who wanted to change things. She was committed to the people, at least that's what she always said. And then she up and quit. What the hell Geraldine? Couldn't you stand the heat? Thought it would be easier to throw stones from outside? It is, isn't it? You don't have to do anything. There's an old adage, - if you don't do anything at all, no one can criticize you. You just keep writing and keep thinking people care about your opinions.   Yeah, right !! And then she stuck Orangeville with Roy Haller.

Chapter 9

The Democrats Walk Out

In March, 1988, the Board of Supervisors agreed to move forward with plans of constructing a new jail. But where would we build it? The sites that were being considered were :

1) the site next to the courthouse that would require the purchase of several homes by the County. Warsaw Supervisor Alex Lane was opposed to this site. She had received petitions from residents opposing the downtown site. Alex was concerned about the historic nature of the Courthouse and what a new jail would do to that. She urged us to vote for the hospital site.

2) a site directly behind the Wyoming County Community Hospital but also directly in front of the Rochester Southern Railroad line. Some Supervisors were concerned about a possible derailment that could effect the jail. Also of concern, was the access road (Duncan Street) beyond the Hospital.

3) adjacent to the fire training center on Wethersfield Road. It was the center of the County and as the Sheriff pointed out, all the communication devices were already there. However, there was no sewer or water and the State Department of Corrections had problems with that.

4) a site north on Route 19, where Wal-Mart and Tops are now. There really was no serious effort to consider this site. It was more valuable and suitable for commercial development.

Anyway, on May 11, 1988, a Resolution was brought to the full Board of Supervisors to build at the hospital site. It was narrowly defeated by 1,080 to 913 and actually an eight to eight vote among the supervisors. All resolutions voted on by the full board are based a weighted vote formula. The number of weighted votes for each town were calculated by the previous census, based on population.

The Board did contract with MRB Engineers and Architects out of Rochester to provide some direction. Believe it or not, we all debated and dragged our feet, delayed a decision for another year. Finally, on May 9, 1989 a Resolution was approved to build a new jail on the Main Street site. But... we were not done.

As a side note, it is my contention, that the new jail issue caused a rift between two fine Supervisors. Ross Roberts was our Chairman. Ross is a true gentlemen who simply commands respect and admiration. I cannot say enough good things about Ross. However, he was Chairman during very tumultuous times. And after the jail issue, he not only had to contend with Barney Erhart and the Democrats, he now had to deal with Urlin Broughton and some of the Republicans. Urlin was a very conservative Supervisor. He was knowledgeable, soft spoken and very helpful. Urlin was the Supervisor who advised me to keep a notebook, because "down here in Warsaw," people tend to forget what they say. Well, thanks Urlin, now I have plenty of notes to help me in writing this book. But Urlin could also be cantankerous.

For example, at the May 1989 Meeting, Urlin offered an amendment to the Jail Building Resolution. The Resolution was for the construction but " NOT TO EXCEED $5.5 MILLION DOLLARS". Well, how can you do that? What if it comes in at $5.6 or higher? Do we now have a half completed building? Things like that were what Ross had to put up with. I guess that I admire him even more, knowing that. Ross was a man of convictions and did what he believed was best. Keep in mind though, Urlin was gathering support.

The County Budget for 1989 was another story. The Budget called for a <u>40% tax increase</u>. Imagine! Shirley Holbrook and Urlin Broughton insisted it was due mainly because of an error by Griffith Oil in sales tax distribution of about $1.6 million. At the budget hearing, myself along with Alex Lane, Burdette Randall and Howard Payne begged Urlin to reconvene the Finance Committee for the purpose of considering using more of the surplus to reduce the tax increase. Urlin did agree and returned after a 15 minute recess to say, " I'm afraid that's not being realistic. If this were a one year deal, then it would be realistic." HUH ? But I thought he and the treasurer said it was mainly because of an error of $1.6 million in sales tax? Anyway, the four of us were joined by Ed Hamilton and we voted no on the Budget. It passed 1,157 to 752. That was the closest budget vote in my fourteen years.

Now, Urlin had the support of Barney, Alex Lane, Rita George, Ed Hamilton (Democrats) and Republicans, Jim Foley, Norm Smith, Roy Haller, and of course himself. Ross had Gus Petri, Howard Payne, Ken Lowe, Ron Herman, George LaWall and myself. Usually, the Party in control (Republicans) determined the Chair and Vice Chair appointments at a private caucus sometime in early December. Not in 1989!!!

We must have had three or four caucuses and could not come up with a consensus. I was always behind Ross because, first, I thought he was doing an extraordinary job and he was a Republican. Urlin also a Republican, on the other hand, chose to align himself with the Democrats, as did Foley, Smith and Haller.

On New Year's Eve, I received two telephone calls. Burdette Randall from Castile wanted to come to my house on New Year's Day to discuss the Chairmanship. I agreed. Barney Erhart was the other call.

Barney's was really amusing. " Hey kid, I'll tell you what we're gonna do ". He then offered me the Chair of Finance if I supported Urlin Broughton. I said, " Now let me get this straight. You are the County Democratic Chairman and if I do as you say, and support a fellow Republican, you will make sure that I get to be the Chairman of Finance, is that right? "

"Yup," he says. I then said, "You've got to be crazy, who the hell do you think you are," and then Barney hung up on me.

On New Year's Day, when Burdette came over, I told him the story and we agreed that Ross was going to be our choice. On January 3rd, the votes came out exactly the way they are listed above. Some of us were extremely upset about fellow so-called Republicans, Jim Foley and Norm Smith for aligning with the Democrats. It's even more ironic now that Foley's bed partner is the Chairperson of the Republican County Committee. I wonder if Carole holds it against him. I doubt it. Roy Haller is another story, anyway. Norm Smith was my neighbor on the Board. I sat right next to him. In his defense, I always knew where he was coming from. Norm was informed, intelligent and very loyal. He and Urlin were very good friends. So, I can understand his position.

In any event, I immediately became a more involved player. Ross appointed me as Vice Chair of the Finance Committee. Now that's the kind of gentleman, Ross is. Foley supported Urlin and Ross gave him the Finance Committee Chair. I wonder if Foley ever felt guilty. Probably not. I was also appointed to the powerful County Officers, and Sheriff's Committees.

Then came the big walk-out, protest, job action or whatever you want to call it. Let's call it the Sally Wing Issue. Sally Wing was the Civil Service Officer for Wyoming County. At times, she could be a royal pain. However, she did know her job. On the downside, she did not try to make new friends or keep old ones.

There were no simple answers to questions put to her. She would go on and on and on and never give a straight answer. Everybody was after her. Most of the Department Heads, the Supervisors and probably half of the county. Sally had major opposition from Urlin, Foley, Barney and his Democrats and the Treasurer, Shirley Holbrook. Sally did cause her own problems at times. Her re-appointment was up and brought to the floor on Valentine's Day, February 14th, 1989. I was totally sick of listening to all of the constant bickering and speaking for myself and George LaWall from Sheldon, we thought it better to NOT re-appoint her than to have six more years of in fighting. Let's cut the problem from the county. So... Sally's re-appointment was defeated 918 for, to 1075 against. It was actually ten towns to six towns in actual votes.

Consequently, we had to advertise for the Civil Service Officer and conduct interviews etc. So, by God, we did. I was on the County Officers Committee that did the interviews that spring and summer. In the meantime, Sally remained on the job and did do her best to change and mend fences. In any event, after all the applications and interviews were completed, we had ONE CANDIDATE that stood head and shoulders over the rest. SALLY WING.

The Committee voted to re-appoint her to the position and it was now time to bring it to the full board. Keep in mind, that the Board was already divided between Barney and his rabble and Ross and the Republicans.

October 10th, 1989, a day that will live in Wyoming County's History ! The Board was in full attendance with no one absent. Mr. Herman, Chairman of County Operations introduced Resolution 89-217 that would re-appoint Sally Wing as Civil Service Officer. The Resolution was read by the clerk as all resolutions are.

Then, Barney Erhart stated, " I'd like to ask Mr. Herman if he has the audacity to withdraw this resolution or let it stay on the floor. I have been on this Board for about 28 years , I have never seen a resolution yet that caused so much disruption in the county. My telephone started ringing this morning from people that don't even work for the county or have anything to do with the county of why we are letting this resolution carry. And I ask you, will you withdraw this resolution or do you still want to leave it on the floor? "

Mr. Herman replied , " I'm going to leave it on the floor."

Imagine, Barney asked Ron if he had the audacity to withdraw it. HUH ? Then as he always did, Barney mentioned the telephone ringing off the wall. He apparently received more calls than anybody else on the Board. No one ever called me about the resolution. If someone didn't have anything to do with the county, how the hell did they know it was even on the agenda? I remember one other time, Barney was up on his soap box about getting all these telephone calls. He could see that I was less than convinced. Barney said to me, " Yeah, I even got calls from people in Java, Moran." " Wait a minute Barney, people in Java are calling you long distance about county issues rather than me? " But that was Barney. A real show boat.

Anyway, after Ron said the Resolution is going to remain, Barney then said, " Thank You. Good-Bye. I am leaving the Floor".

Now what upset me the most was that Barney led this walk out included by Urlin Broughton, Rita George, Jim Foley, Ed Hamilton, Norm Smith, Roy Haller and Alex Lane. That meant eight Supervisors remained and eight had left. Eric Dadd, the County Attorney then spoke and said that we may not have a quorum and we should schedule a special meeting. The Special Meeting was then held on October 16th with again only seven of us. (Howard Payne was legally excused as he was out of town on county business)

The eight that walked out had met prior to the meeting. They even retained Richard A. Dollinger, Esquire, as an attorney to question the Board's action. They NEVER confronted any of us with their concerns or a potential compromise to resolve the issue. No! They just wanted to grandstand. And, Foley, Norm Smith and Roy Haller pandered to and followed Barney's lead. And worse, they tried to sneak through a bill for their attorney's fee. HAHAHA.

For the 1989 County elections the Town of Java had two hot issues. One was serious and the other was downright silly.

On the corner of Routes 78,77 and 98 in downtown Java Center there was a house called the " Hart House". In about 1979, The Town took ownership of the House to allow for more parking and future expansion. At that time, the owner, Merrill Hart, was granted life use of the house. About 1987, Mr. Hart went to live with relatives out of the area. The Town Board was concerned with not only the maintenance but also the potential for liability. After all, it was a vacant house that was an enticing playground or worse. The Town now had responsibility for upkeep and maintenance of the house.

It was built in 1829 and was considered to be the oldest house in Java Center. The Java Historical Society wanted to have the necessary repairs done and to eventually use it as a museum type of facility. Local contractors inspected the building and all agreed that the house should be gutted, rewired, get new plumbing, a roof and siding. The Historical Society obviously did not have the financial resources to complete such a project. The Town Board considered it and we had several public hearings to hear the public views on this. The only other alternative to demolition was actually moving the house to another site. In 1990, we asked the Landmark Society to evaluate the house and give us a report. At that time, we were considering using it with a multipurpose method. The Town Assessor, Town Historian and the Society could all use the building for their needs.

Jim Yarborough , an architect from the Landmark Society, came back with his report and dated the house at 1845. So it did have historic significance. The Board scheduled another public hearing to discuss the matter. The estimate at that time was $40,000 to $50,000 to have the necessary repairs done and work completed. At the August 2, 1990 town board meeting, a motion was made by Bob Kibler and second by myself to lease the Hart House to the Java Historical Society for $1.00 per year. Bob and myself voted yes, Ron McCormick, Don Roche and Dan McNulty all voted no and the resolution was defeated. In September, I was directed to contact Jack Fisher our County Fire Coordinator to have a control burn of the Hart House.

On October 17, 1990 a "control burn" was conducted by the Strykersville and North Java Fire Companies and the Hart House was gone in a puff of smoke. Pat Vadney, a reporter with the Arcade Herald, summed it up best... " Neighborhood children sat on the curb across the street , as if waiting for a parade to begin.... While .. 'It's sad to see history go,' said John McGinnis who lives on the northwest corner of the intersection. " I think most people, including myself, were very sad that night and it was not one of my proudest accomplishments as Town Supervisor. Opposite of that sentiment was Dan McNulty, who in the same issue of the Herald, said, " I hope this is the last time we'll see mention of the Hart House in the paper ".

In February of 1990, the Java Historical Society became owners of the old grange in Java Village. The Town then committed to paying rent for space for the Town Historian. So all was not lost.

The silly issue I mentioned before was one of a personal nature. Ken and Lee Unger operated a legal campground on Route 78 in Java Center. Right in the middle of this campground, was a 1.04 acre parcel. It had a house/garage on it until 1982 when it was destroyed by fire. Anna Wolfe of the Buffalo area and a regular season camper of the Ungers, bought the parcel from Robert Gilman, in 1986. In 1989, Ken Unger registered a complaint to the Town about illegal camping by Anna Wolfe. It seemed that the Ungers and the Wolfes, while Mr. Wolfe was still living, were the very best of friends. But... then Anna Wolfe bought the property. Why Ken did not buy the property is anyone's guess. In any event, Ken and Lee and their friends came to every Board Meeting to complain. And, naturally when they complained, so did Anna Wolfe and her sons. There were allegations by both parties. Ken Unger was allegedly spreading raw human sewage on nearby fields. There were claims of no clean water or restrooms, etc. by the Wolfes.

After months of meetings and legal fees, Anna Wolfe was granted a variance to utilize her property as a camp site for her immediate family. That's the trouble with small town zoning. It can be much too personal. This little silly issue tore two families apart and Ken tried to bring the Town into it and was somewhat successful. Then some of those folks go to church and appear to be so goddamn holy. For Christ's sake, that pisses me off. Just imagine how God, a Republican, feels.

Then in 1989, it was election time again.

Chapter 10

1989 Elections

Shirley Holbrook was retiring and would not seek re-election as Treasurer in the fall election. Many names were thrown into the hat, mine, Marty Mucher, John Edwards, Michelle Millen, Ray Luce, and Martha Richardson from Java. The County Republican Committee met and all candidates were invited to attend and speak. The County endorsed John Edwards, a good choice by the way.

Martha Calmes Richardson was from Java and was the bookkeeper at Reisdorf Feed Mills in North Java. Martha decided to run as an Independent. Everyone else endorsed John except Ray Luce. Keep in mind that Ray was and is a registered Republican, but Geraldine, his wife is a registered Democrat.

Ray Luce was a Town Supervisor from Orangeville for eight years and then was appointed to a gravy position as Administrator of the County's Workers Compensation Plan. This appointment could not have been possible without the support of the Republican Supervisors. In " gratitude " for that support, Ray ran against John Edwards, the endorsed Republican and was supported by Jim Foley and other so called Republicans. Luce ran on the Democratic ticket and was buried in the general election by John Edwards. Way to go, John!

You can see that the Republican Party was not helping itself. Fortunately, the Java Democrats did not run anyone against me. Mark Hopkins decided not to run as a Councilman and Ron McCormick was elected in his place. Bob Kibler and Donna Schofield were both re-elected.

Also victorious in 1989, were Supervisors Jim Schlick, Bennington, Bob Bowles, Castile, Arnold Cox from Middlebury and a very, very classy lady from Sheldon, Irene Glaus.

Guess who else was unopposed? Roy Haller from Orangeville!!

Chapter 11

The Big Leagues

Sometime in early December of 1989, I was painting Mike's bedroom walls when Howard Payne, the Vice Chairman of the Board of Supervisors called me. Howard and I got along very well from the beginning. He really helped me in my first year or two. Anyway, because Ross had decided to step down as Chairman, Howard wanted to give it a shot and asked if I could support him? Absolutely! Anybody except Barney and his damn Democrats. Great and he wanted to know if I would be willing to serve as Vice Chairman under him. Are you kidding me? There I was, with only four years as a Supervisor and I was being considered as Vice Chairman. What a tremendous honor!!!

Well, of course Urlin threw his hat into the ring to run against Howard so we went around again. Only this time, Barney did not have Jim Foley or Norm Smith on his side. Ole Roy voted with the Democrats again. Ron Herman voted twice so his counts were voided and Howard won as Chairman. Ross Roberts nominated me as Vice Chair and Barney nominated Alex Lane. Another vote. Yours truly was the next Vice Chairman of the Wyoming County Board of Supervisors.

Not only was I Vice Chairman of the Board but I was also the new Finance Chairman, and a member of the County Officers, Taxation and Planning and Economic Development Committee. As Chairman of Finance, I was also to sit as the Supervisor's Representative on the Hospital Board of Managers.

I was going to be a very busy boy but I was also about to receive another political lesson and another lesson in human nature. Looking back in early 1990, I still am in awe of the situation.

Chapter 12

Cable Television Hits Java

One of the most colorful people that I have ever met, arrived on the scene in Java in early 1990. Allan Skelly from RCH Cable out of Cinnaminson, New Jersey approached the Town of Java and advised us that he was ready to build a cable television system in not only Java, but also Bennington, Sheldon, Eagle and Pike, and Darien in Genesee County.

Mr. Skelly told us that he was an attorney licensed in New Jersey and some other states. He always drove to Wyoming County. I believe it was a Mercedes or BMW. He attended our Town Board Meeting on April 5th, 1990.

By that time, I had been in contact with the New York State Cable Commission and Carol Jamison who was the municipal consultant for our area. Allan Skelly would have to apply with the Commission for authority to provide the Cable TV. At the same time, we all (all the proposed towns) would be required to submit requests for proposals (RFP) to every Cable System operating within a twenty five mile radius. There were 11 such systems. Carol and the rest of the staff at the Cable Commission did not have any faith in poor Allan.

Guess what? The towns all did their share but old Allan did not. The Java Town Board was so enthused about the prospect that at our next meeting, we passed a Resolution to authorize the Supervisor to submit the necessary papers, notification to Cable Operators and even form the Town's Cable TV Committee.

In July, we had heard from Carol Jamison and she advised us what was to be done. On July 11th, Java was on the agenda for the State Cable Commission to have a waiver granted. That meant we could go for alternative procedures that were supposed to be easier and faster. If the supposed waiver was granted, the town would issue requests for proposals for providing cable service to the town to all cable TV systems. We would have a public hearing. There would be a representative from the Cable Commission, on hand to help sort out all the proposals. The State Rep would advise us of the pros and cons for each cable company and then the town board would ultimately award a franchise to one.

The franchise agreement could vary a little. At that time the going rate for the town's share was 3% of the gross receipts of the cable TV system. Allan had already promised us 5% and a studio manned in town to broadcast local events of interest.

The State Cable Commission provided us with the proposals that I sent out. The deadline to have them back was September 3, 1990. Carol Jamison would be on hand to help us out. The public hearing to consider and possible award a franchise was held on October 9th. Two Cable Companies were present. Allan Skelly of RCH and Ronald Trybushyn, Kathy Connelly, David Testa and Nick Glangualano from then Cabelvision out of Batavia.

Cablevision emphasized their longevity and dependability. They would pay the Town 5% of their gross receipts. They expected to build and provide service to about 60% of the Town. They needed to see a housing density of at least fifteen(15) homes per mile. Their monthly rate would be $14.95 to customers.

RCH and Allan Skelly offered 5% of the gross and their rate would be $9.95 per month. RCH would build at least 77% of the Town. Allan said he could do that because RCH owned their own construction company rather than contracting it out. RCH would also establish a local office in Java with local residents trained as employees.

The next process was to sort out both proposals and submit our choice to the State cable Commission. The State Commission would analyze the system both financially and technically. This could take several months. But wait, there's more..

We held another special meeting on November 13, 1990. I had heard some disturbing rumors about RCH and so had requested Tom Fendick, our Town Attorney to be present. Allan Skelly was there but no one from Cablevision came. Allan Skelly indicated that he had run into some problems at Bennington's Meeting. RCH had offered a map of the homes to be included and so had Cablevision. But Cablevision came back with another map that included more homes than RCH and Bennington awarded the franchise to Cablevision. After all that was our real concern. Who could provide the service to the most homes?

The question was asked of Mr. Skelly about the financial condition. Where were the financial statements? He said that was not a problem. He would even be willing to put up a $500,000 bond to ensure his commitment. We told Skelly to have a letter from a financial institution that committed the funds to

Java for building a cable TV system. Mr. Skelly said he would have it by the December 6 meeting.

The December meeting came and we had not received anything more from Allan Skelly. However, there were many residents who wanted to know why we were dragging our feet. After a long discussion, the Board awarded the Cable franchise to RCH Cable pending financial statements and commitments. We then forwarded our choice to the State.

Then Allan Skelly fell off the face of the earth. And more.. The Sheriff's Office called me and asked about him. It seems that on one of his trips to visit us, he stayed at Byrncliff and paid them with a bad check. Oh Boy. Wasn't that great? I called the equivalent of the Cable Commission for the state of New Jersey. Boy, you talk about cloak and dagger. As soon as I inquired about Allan Skelly, I was asked for my telephone number and told that someone would call me back. I gave them my number and sure enough, the phone rang. " Why did I just answer the phone, 'Hello'? Why didn't someone answer the 'Town of Java, may I help you?'", the caller asked. I told the caller that he was calling my home phone and that I was a part time Supervisor and no one would ever answer the phone in such a manner. Anyway, all he would tell me was that Allan Skelly did NOT operate any cable system in New Jersey, but they did know of him. Anything else, they just could not provide without more background. I told you at the beginning that he was colorful. Now Bennington's cable system was being built and the rest of us were S.O.L.

The Board agreed to pursue it again and lo and behold if another cable system wasn't interested in Java, Sheldon, Eagle and Pike. Grassroots Cable out of Exeter, New Hampshire. Bob Felder was the owner of Grassroots. Here we go again. We asked for proposals again and again, only Cablevision and Grassroots submitted any.

Again, Cablevision highlighted their years of providing cable to the western New York area. Bob Felder pointed out that he was the principal owner and no one had to climb the corporate ladder for answers. He was the man. There was a thirty day period of waiting and the Town of Java awarded the franchise to Grassroots. Again, this award was based on the fact that Grassroots was providing cable to more homes than Cablevision.

Then in May of 1992, I received a letter from Carol Jamison from the State Commission with bad news. She included a recent article from a Cable TV Publication that indicated Grassroots was in deep financial trouble. They no longer had the equity to allow them to borrow any more money. Cable TV was done in Java again.

It was later in 1993, at the Association of Towns Meetings in New York City that I learned what Allan Skelly was all about. He was trying to secure " Finders Fees" for the towns in Wyoming County from Grassroots and any other Cable TV System. I guess you can't blame him but he sure did cause undue anticipation and lots of unnecessary work for some. I personally gave up any hope of cable and went out and purchased a satellite dish.

In November of 1993, we were again approached by Cabelvision to provide Cable TV service to Java. We agreed to hold a public hearing on January 13, 1994. At that Public Hearing, Councilmen Ron McCormick and Don Roche expressed their opinions that the town should not enter into a long term contract with Cablevision. Don Roche, in the Arcade Herald of 1/27/94 said " he understood that NYNEX was planning to make cable TV available for everyone." Really, Don, where did you hear that? Thank God we didn't hold our breath. Finally, on March 8, 1994 the Town of Java agreed to award the franchise to Cablevision out of Batavia.

In May of 1995, Java actually had Cable Television. Praise the Lord!

It only took five years. See, I told you government works very, very slowly.

Chapter 13

Desert Storm

As you all should remember, Desert Storm and the war with Saddam and Iraq began on January 17, 1991. Where were you when the bombing started?

I was on a Safety Committee for the Railroad. We had annual meetings in Albany. The idea was to obviously prevent accidents and have all employees return home in the same condition that they arrived in at work. The safety Committee operated like a total quality management team and I think it was successful. In fact, I mirrored the railroad concept for Wyoming County. Jack Fisher was our safety Officer and he did a splendid job.

The Safety Committee was meeting at the Holiday Inn on Wolf Road in Albany. I flew to Albany with an old railroad buddy, R.W. (Goose) Garry. Goose was not real good at being away from home. He had not made any reservations and there was no room at the Inn for poor Goose. He asked if he could stay in my room for ONE NIGHT? " Sure", I said but only one night.

That evening we were having a sandwich in the Sports Bar at the Holiday Inn. The bombing began by order of President George Bush. The bar was so crowded that we could not hear the television. We decided to go to the other bar, Fender's in the Holiday. It wasn't too bad, and we did hear what was going on in Iraq.

It was kind of quiet at Fender's, so when the door opened up, everyone looked to see who was coming in. One time, the door opened, and who was it except.... Jim Schlick, Supervisor from Bennington. I then remembered that the County Highway Superintendents were having their meetings at the Holiday Inn. Jim's mouth dropped about six inches toward the floor. He came over to me and asked what was I doing there. I snapped back that Howard Payne sent me down because he had heard that Jim and Gary Weidman (County Highway Superintendent) were both spending too much money and both were misbehaving. Jim believed it for about 30 seconds.

That was my first experience at the Highway Superintendent's Meetings. I learned that there were about 25 hospitality rooms and you should never have to spend a dime.

In subsequent years, I looked forward to attending them and always viewed them as a perk. After all, we did not make much money and if we had a chance to travel, actually learn something to bring back home, and have a good time, why not ?

That trip with Goose, though? As I said, he didn't travel much. He actually made the bed and picked up for the maid. On top of that, he'd bitch at me for being a slob. If you knew Goose, he could get under your skin, know it and keep it up all day and night. On the commuter plane flying back home to Buffalo, he was on a roll with that stuff. Keep in mind, it was a commuter plane so everyone on board heard every word that he was saying. He was ranting and raving about me leaving towels on the floor, not making my bed etc. Then he said to me, you probably didn't even leave a tip for the maid, did you? He said he left a $5 bill on the night stand as his tip. I said, "really, I thought that was my five, so I picked it up". He never knew if I was bullshitting or not.

Speaking of inexperienced travelers, Janet Zielinski went to New York City to the Association of Towns Meeting one year with Bill Horton, John Meyer and myself. She brought her own towels, soap and wash cloth. I told her that that was all provided by the Hilton. She got all bubbly and excited about it. The next morning, she mentioned that she thought it was great, that the Hotel also provided snacks and beverages. I said, " Oh, oh , that honor bar in your room is monitored and you have to pay dearly for every item you take." Then one night, we are all at the hotel bar and she was talking up a storm with about four guys that were not with the Towns. She and they were laughing and joking and just having a great time. Finally, Janet came over to us and we got on her about not introducing us to her new found friends. She said, " you don't even know who those gentlemen were, do you? They are all movie producers, " she piped up. Oh great, nothing like a gullible naive Town Clerk. They were movie producers, alright ! I have more stories to tell about trips to New York City, but I will save them for later.

1991 began with my re-election as Vice Chairman and continuing on as Chairman of Finance. Then Governor Cuomo released his proposed State budget. What a job he did on Towns and Counties. Java had had enough with more taxes.

Right away in January, we went on record opposing any further state legislation that would impose additional burdens on the property owners of Java. The resolution also stated that the Java Town Board challenged the Governor and all elected and appointed State Officials to take a voluntary salary cut of 10%. The Board also agreed that all elected and appointed Officials in the Town of Java would take a 10% cut, if the State Officials did the same. We sent the resolutions to the Governor, Senator Volker, Assemblyman Reynolds, and Speaker Miller. We received replies from all except Mario Cuomo. That really irked me. Granted, Java is not a big Town, but I felt that resolution was sent by 2,200 New York State Residents and our Governor chose to ignore it. The State cuts amounted to over $55,000 to Java. That figure at that time was 25% of all property tax collected. Substantial. Another road trip was needed.

The Association of Towns was sponsoring a Supervisor's Forum in Albany in early March. Howard Payne, Frank Smith from Yorkshire and myself attended. The three of us rode together. There were several sessions and I attended all of them. After one, I was talking to Kevin Crawford, the Association's General Counsel and telling him about not only my frustration with the State but also the lack of acknowledgment from the Governor. Kevin said, go on over and see the Governor right now. OK !

I walked across the street to the Capital building and went to the elevator to get to the Executive Chambers where the Governor had his office. A state policeman confronted me at the elevator and asked where I was going. I told him, "to see Mario." Upon exiting the elevator on the second floor, another state trooper, another question and again I said I was there to see the Governor. Room 213, I think. I opened the door and there must have been ten young ladies working at desks. "Can I help you?", was their resounding cry. " Certainly, I'm here to see the Governor", I said.

One young lady asked if I had an appointment.

" Of course not, I didn't know I was coming over here until about 10 minutes ago", I said.

" What is it pertaining to? ", she asked.

" I want to know why the Governor of New York State is trying to crush Java and still refuses to talk to us, " I said raising my voice a bit.

" You really need to talk to Laura Chassin, she's the Local Government Representative for the Governor ", she responded. I said, " fine, could I see her? "

" Do you have an appointment to see Laura? ", she asked knowing the answer or at least I hoped she knew the answer.

" Now.. That's quite a question, " I said. " Of course not, I never heard of Laura Chassin until just a minute ago and in addition to that, if I didn't have any appointment with the Governor, why the hell would I have one with someone named Laura Chassin? ", I was getting pissed off.

A big door opened and a woman asked me if she could help me.

" I doubt it. I'm here to see the Governor. And... I'm beginning to wonder if he even exists, hell, maybe Mario Cuomo is just another hoax, like the Easter Bunny, Santa Claus and the second shooter at the Kennedy assassination ", I yelled back at her.

She then said, " I am Laura Chassin, would you please come in".

I repeated my whole sob story to Laura. How I had personally sent Mario letters, resolutions and not once did I ever receive a reply. She thought that perhaps my staff mailed them out in error. My staff? Now that was a joke. I told her that she was looking at the whole staff. I didn't have any staff.

Bottom line, Laura just could not understand how something like this could ever happen. She promised me it would never happen again. In fact she asked if I would be so kind to see that she would get a personal copy, in the future. Of course. And.. We DID receive an acknowledgment for every letter I sent to him. Not bad, for the Supervisor from Java.

I don't know how Mario felt about solid waste, but garbage was another hot issue in 1991.

On June 6th, 1991, the first Solid Waste Committee for the Town of Java was appointed with Willie Limburg, Gary Boorman, Peggy Meindl, Janet Beechler, Charlie McCormick, Bill Close, Debbie Kirsch, Sue Stephan, Dick Fisher and myself all serving on it.

We were to look at the adoption of a recycling law and the feasibility of joining the County in a county-wide curbside pick up program. The benefit of a county-wide pick up was initially two fold. One, it should be cheaper for the residents and two, it should clean the county up. If the Town did not provide curb side pick up of garbage, it was left to the residents, as an option. Some actually contracted with a local hauler, some took their garbage to work or some other place with a dumpster. Some joined with neighbors for a group pick up at the expense of the hauler and some did nothing.

In other words, as Don Roche said, " I have a special place for that ".

" Oh yeah, where would that be, Don? ", I asked.

"Well, I spread it with the manure from the barn and everything is OK.", Roche replied.

" Well, how about the aerosol cans and the plastic containers, Don? ", I asked him.

Anyway, in Java we had one huge problem besides being locked into a five year garbage program. We had Java Lake and its private roads. The Contractor, BFI would not pick up on private roads. They also had no provisions for seasonal pick up. End of argument. Java then began looking at the idea of having a transfer station.

Chapter 14

Java's Transfer Station

So, the Solid Waste Committee met and met to discuss first, the Recycling Law that every municipality had to have adopted by September of 1992. What happens if we didn't? The landfill operator was not permitted to accept your garbage. So we decided that we'd better pass a recycling law.

As I've said previously, Wyoming County was looking into this idea of a county-wide curb side pick up program. The Solid Waste Committee was very busy. It was probably one of the best working committees that the Town had. They actually worked and made decisions. Oh... some got upset when they could not get their point across to the Town Board, but all in all it was a great committee. Maybe it was the personal chemistry that made it work. We had the funniest comedian that Java could offer, Dick Fisher. Dick is a pleasure to be around and I don't think I've ever seen a sad face or even a frown when he was in a room.

Now, many years ago, there was a restaurant on Transit Road in Clarence called the Boston Sea Party. On a particular Saturday night, Dick and his girlfriend at the time, Rainy Farrant, Pete and Eileen McNulty, Mike and Debbie Zielinski, Bernie and Jean George, Don Bowen and his girlfriend, Sergeant Riggleman, Tim McCormick and his girlfriend, Kate McNulty and probably some others all went into the Boston Sea Party for a great meal. It was a smorgasbord of all you could eat seafood.

After the meal, someone mentioned that we should go to the " GO-GO " joint on Clinton and Transit, I think the name of it was Mr. C's. So, about six of us headed out. We did agree beforehand that if Mr. C's was closed, we would go to a night club that had entertainment called the Four Stallions. I was in the first group to get to Mr. C's and sure enough, they were closed. The first two cars then proceeded to the Four Stallions for some dancing and drinking.

We were there about ten minutes, when the band's lead singer made an announcement that there was an emergency phone call for Doctor Thomas Moran! I immediately smiled and went to the bar. The bartender informed me that they do not accept telephone calls unless it truly is an emergency. He gave me the phone and I said hello. It was Dick Fisher on the other end. Dick was at Mr. C's. They were open and they wanted all of us to come back. But this time, the bartenders and bouncers were watching and listening to me. I said something like, " OK, prep him for emergency surgery and I'll be right there. " I thought the joke was over and that should satisfy everyone.

I went back to our table, and let everybody in on the joke. At about that time, the waitress came over and asked if we needed anything more. Of Course, we did!! I ordered another beer and really got a dirty look, from the bartender. How the hell could I have another beer and go to the hospital for an emergency operation, I'm sure he wondered. After I finished the beer, I went to the men's room and was followed in there by one of the bouncers. While I was standing at the urinal, he said, " So, you have an emergency operation, uh? " " Yup", I said " but nothing too serious ". Then he wanted to know where I went to medical school. I blurted out " Syracuse ". Good answer, I guess because he said that was great and wished me good luck in the operation. When we walked into Mr. C's, there was Bernie George cleaning his eyeglasses with his handkerchief. Jean was telling him he was a damn fool. What a guy.

As you can imagine, a politician really needs some recreation time to relax and kick back. I loved to play cards (Euchre) with Dick Fisher and the boys at the Java Center Tavern (or Sad Dog Saloon) or the Outlander or anywhere else. Some people refused to play euchre with our group because they thought we were cheating. We were just fast. Come on, no thinking about it, either you got the cards or you don't. I could go way back and say Bill Roche, Bernie George and now Bill Becker will actually try and talk you out of a hand.

Even today, you can always find a crappy old card game at the Sad Dog Saloon. Every afternoon, Lum Zielinski, Norb Hoyt, Bill Converse, Charlie Minkel and others are ready to play at the famous words, " Got time for one set?"

When Mike Chassin (no relation to Laura) ran the Java Center Tavern (JCT) there were card games at all times. Usually he and I were partners and we normally beat up on Mike Zielinski and Tim McCormick. They could not beat us. I hate to think of the money that we took from those two. And.. They were not quiet games, you had to slam your hand or knuckles on the table. We taunted each other and gave out high fives for success.

Back then, we might have time for only one game because we were snowmobiling or something else. Let me tell you about riding snowmobiles back in the early 80's. I had an old, and I mean it was old then, John Deere 340 sled. I bought it used and the guy's dog had eaten the seat cushions. So you had to ride on the frame. It was not electric start and had no reverse. In fact, many times it did not start period!

Mike Chassin and I prided ourselves in our ability to cope with the conditions. We WERE NOT WIMPS OR WUSSES ! We wore baseball caps, sneakers, jeans and regular winter coats. Not even carharts. Hell no. Of course, we didn't go 80 or 100 miles per hour either. In fact, we putted around and were usually passed by everyone in the group and then some. But.. When we got to a place, we were ready for a beer. We didn't need ten minutes to get undressed and then find a place to store all your crap. And.. When we wanted to leave, we put on our gloves and left.

Back to euchre and my " time off "from politics. I have played and seen every thing in euchre. I played for $1.00 and I have played for many dollars. I even played in a game at the Outlander with Paul Rogacki, Ray Kozlowski and a young girl from Holland, N.Y. Jeannie Dillon. Ray and I were partners and Paul and I were playing for a buck a game. Not Raymond. He and Jean were playing for the nest. If Ray lost, Jean would be able to live with him for a week. The bet got as high as six weeks until Ray and I finally won. You see, that was the ultimate punishment for Ray. He did not want to live with anyone.

There was even more euchre during deer season. But.. There was euchre at any time of the year. Some days were just better than others. The best games were the spontaneous ones. Some partners were better than others. My buddy, Bill Horton and I rarely won a euchre game if we played as partners. I think the only team we could ever beat consistently was Spike and Irene Glaus.

Ice fishing was fun, too. Hank Bauder, Paul Rogacki and Cliff Stephan and I would go to either Silver Lake or Conesus most of the time. Once in a while to Cuba Lake. It was imperative that we stop at Silver Springs. First there was Jones's, then the Kenwood and finally the Country Gentlemen. Now, most of them are gone.

Here's one good, true ice fishing story. Remember, I told you about Tony Prezyna? Well, he was not only a good euchre player but he was an avid, and I mean avid, ice fisherman. One day, we were fishing Silver Lake. It was below zero and I was having a heck of a time keeping my hole open and the bait from not freezing. We were using oak leaf grubs. They're only about an inch long but they are about as round as an inch. Very juicy. Anyway, Tony is just bringing fish in one after another. I walked over to him and asked how he was keeping his grubs from freezing and breaking apart when you try to put them on the hook. Tony reaches into his mouth and brings out a couple of grubs. I said GEEZUZ, you gotta be crazy. Tony says, no you rinse them off in the water and just be careful not to accidentally bite them.

It takes a different type of character to ice fish. I mean, you sit on a little box and pray that you are going to catch a perch or some other pan fish. But there are always people on the ice. Just take a look the next time you go by a frozen lake and see how many are "hard water" fishing. Now, you can buy a pop-up shelter for about $300 that will keep you as warm as a bug in a rug. But... I still use my ice fishing box with a little Coleman stove to keep my butt warm and cook grilled cheese sandwiches. My son, Mike, is just starting to get into it and he now has his own little ice fishing box that he helped build. Mike can't explain why he likes ice fishing either.

In any event, it still is a sport that is relatively inexpensive and you don't have to travel far for. After all, what else are you going to do in a Western New York winter when you're a politician? God, they were good times. Maybe it is male bonding or something. But we sure did have a lot of laughs. I don't think I'll even get into the deer season stories yet.

As you can see, all that hunting, ice fishing and card playing made me a better negotiator. So... back to the Solid Waste Committee. Wyoming County was into some heavy negotiations with CID from Chaffee and BFI out of Buffalo to be the hauler of choice for this county wide curb side pick up.

BFI eventually got the contract through the bidding process and the fee was about $180 per house and an additional $1.00 per bag. The idea of charging per bag was to encourage everyone to recycle and thus have less bags that needed to go to our already overcrowded land fills. As I said, Java could not really opt into this program with the Java Lake private roads and many seasonal units. It was simply not feasible.

The Committee looked into the idea of a transfer station. A transfer station provides residents with a place to drop off their recyclables and garbage. The Committee went on a road trip and visited the Bennington and Attica Transfer Stations. We were impressed but we didn't really know if the majority of residents were willing to haul their garbage to a site.

Some things were coming together on this though. In December of 1992 the Town Board agreed to purchase 38.5 acres of land from John Handley. This was a former gravel pit operated by the famous Joe Dupre.

The town had been storing its salt and sand there for a number of years. The property was now for sale. The town needed a site for its salt. Anyone purchasing the Handley property could have a good claim for the town to clean up the area where the salt was stored. Salt is probably the most serious pollutant any town uses. Salt has been know to travel for miles, via the water table. We looked at other properties but finally settled on the Handley property. Now, we had a site for our salt and also for the transfer station and didn't have to worry about pollution claims.

There were meetings, surveys and Department of Environmental Conservation's (DEC) questions. On May 11th, the Town Board voted 3- 2 to open a transfer station. Ron McCormick and Don Roche opposed the action. According to the Arcade Herald of May 20, 1993, " each one stated they had received a number of phone calls in opposition of the plan..." Interesting, huh? I did not nor did the other two councilmen receive these mystery calls. And even if they did really get a number of phone calls, was that number high enough to imply that a majority of residents were opposed or was it received from VIP's? In all the surveys that we received, the majority WANTED the transfer station concept. Finally, in September of 1993, the town opened our transfer station. We would be open on Saturday mornings from 7:00 A.M. until 12 Noon and on Tuesdays during daylight savings time. The DEC Permit prohibited any operation after dark. The charge per bag was $1.00. Not bad, considering the cheapest hauler in town, was Maple City for about $200 per year or CID for over $300. Our family was using about one bag per week, so it was a substantial savings.

The biggest surprise was in the participation. Probably 75% of the Town residents now use it. We were really concerned that it would not be used. Imagine, you had to put a crummy, crappy bag of garbage in your vehicle and haul it to the five corners. People did and loved doing it. It became a community event.

Over the years, it has grown even more. The DEC has inspected it many times and we never had even one violation.

I believe the success can be attributed to Dennis McCutcheon and those that have worked there over the years. Denny would not take any shit from anyone, including myself. He ran it like Stalin ran Russia. He was always there and I never had to worry about a thing.

There were those, like Ron McCormick, Don Roche and Janet Zielinski that bitched every week about it. If it had been up to them, the transfer station would have closed years ago. Thank God, it wasn't up to them. That was another example of their way or no way. They did not use it so they thought no one should. ME, me. More on them later. But this was the start of bad things and bad feelings.

Thanks again to Denny McCutcheon, Deb Zielinski, Ray Wilson, Brenda George and all that worked at the Station and a special thanks to Gary Boorman and the solid waste committee for having the courage to begin the transfer station.

Chapter 15

Chicken Shit Part One

This is a classic and I must serve it to you in all its glory.

Each Town has " Party Representatives " who are appointed by the Party Chairs, as election inspectors. So, we would have a Democrat Rep and a Republican Rep. Their job, is to " INSPECT" the voting machines in each election district. Java happens to have two election districts.

Keep in mind, that each town has a paid custodian of the voting machines who also sets up and inspects the voting machines. Wyoming County has two Election Commissioners that inspect the machines. Wyoming County also has two Election Voting Machine Custodians who inspect the machines. Each candidate has the option to personally inspect each voting machine. It sure doesn't take a genius to figure out that we have one hell of a lot of inspectors for our voting machines. And, guess what? They are all paid. The Election Commissioners even receive health insurance and all benefits. Even the County Custodian of Voting Machines did too, until the Board of Supervisors withdrew it a few years ago. Yeah, we thought it was a little ridiculous to pay an individual full benefits including health insurance when his (her) salary was only $1,000 per year.

Now these two party reps were also being paid in Java. The Town of Java paid each one $5 per general election and/or primary election. Big Deal, Right ? In 1989, our reps requested a raise from $5 to $10 per election district. It was $5 for both election districts. They were asking for $20 instead of the $5 that they were receiving. The Board denied it and we thought that was the end of it.

Our party reps were Paul Keenan for the Democrats and Pete Kline for the Republicans. Well, at the November 7, 1991 Town Board meeting, Paul Keenan gave himself a raise and decided to request retro-active pay back to 1989 at the rate of $10 per election district. It seems as if Paul did not submit bills for 1989 and 1990. He must have forgot the $5 or didn't need it at the time.

Dan McNulty made a motion and Don Roche seconded the motion, to pay $5 per election district for 1991 only. The motion passed 4-1. Guess who voted, no? Ron McCormick. I say that because you will laugh as you read on. And also in 1991, we had a major problem with the voting machine at the Strykersville Fire Hall. A voter could not pull the lever for voting for one Republican and one Democrat. One of the election workers, who will remain anonymous, simply told one voter, " Don't worry about it, vote for the other guy, they're all good guys. " Nice Answer.

We discussed the raise issue at great length that meeting and many others after it. I just could not understand why an individual would embarrass himself in front of the whole Town Board on where they were all Democrats except two. I wondered what happened to community service and public service? Did everyone have to get a dollar for every thing they did? I wondered where was it all going to end? Are these the same political party people that we should honor at the end of their careers? How about the Firemen, Kiwanis, Lions and a host of other community volunteers that do a hell of a lot more than inspect two machines for no money whatsoever. In fact, they probably get more bitching and abuse. To me , the bottom line was if the political party thought this was such a crucial position, then they should pay for it. Or was it simply that the money is more important than the duties. Some of them must have said to hell with civic duty.

To illustrate my point, Thomas Weil from Weil Resources was in attendance. After the meeting, he approached me and said something like, wow , you guys are tough. Couldn't you just give him the damn five dollars, I was about to give it to him just to shut him up. Thanks Paul, one more negative impression of Java. To really make you smile, the next day, I was delivering my monthly newsletter to the Family Mart in North Java. There was Paul Keenan stocking shelves in the store. He had just retired from the State D.O.T. I said, " My God, Paul, had I known it was this bad, we'd pay you retro-active with a raise. " Paul did not see the humor in it. By the way, I NEVER mentioned Paul's demand in my newsletter. I thought that it was a total embarrassment to all. I was wrong thinking that.

Now, we move to 1996. Back in 1995, there were again, two political party representatives. Paul Keenan and Peggy McCormick, Ron's wife. At the January, 1996 Meeting, Peggy presented a bill for $50 for inspecting the machines and Paul's request was for $80. This included retro-active raises. In addition,

Paul actually had an attorney, W. Doug Call write me a letter requesting payment for him. Unbelievable !

Ron McCormick moved and Fran Brunner made a second to pay the bills. Only one negative vote was cast, ME. See what I mean about hypocrisy?

In 1991, the town was not going to pay it. In 1995, with Ron's wife as representative, it is simply, business as usual. They all got their money and I hope they enjoyed it. God Bless the rest of the volunteers all over the United States of America. Submit a bill, next time !

Chapter 16

WCCH

In 1990, The Wyoming County Community Hospital had a deficit and county subsidy of $2.3 million dollars. The entire tax levy was about 7 million. Everyone was deeply concerned.

Java, Sheldon, Bennington, and Arcade tended to utilize the Buffalo area or Springville Hospitals. Attica seemed to lean toward the Batavia hospitals. To expect those residents to throw in another 30% of their property tax was a lot to ask.

Tom Wheatley was the Hospital Administrator, John Wood was the Finance Officer and Carole Butler was the Director of Nursing. The hospital had a horrific reputation and the senior management corps was constantly at the Courthouse asking for more money. There were even instances where they could not meet the payroll let alone pay their bills. The bills were historically over $1.5 million and over 120 days late. These were serious financial problems.

I was the Supervisor representative on the Hospital Board of Managers and I saw it all. The hospital meetings would last for three hours or more. Nothing was getting done. We were being fed bull shit on a monthly basis. I once requested that John Wood attend a Supervisors Meeting and give an update. Mr. Wood attended the next meeting and presented the financial status of the hospital. Someone then asked him to explain the Medicaid reimbursement methodology. The Finance Officer of the County Hospital then told the County Board of Supervisors that they WOULD NOT understand it. How about giving us a chance, John ? John Wood was not going to be the Finance Officer for long.

In fact, in the summer of 1990, Ernst and Young contracted with the Hospital for financial services. A young Ernst & Young employee, Paul Candino was provided to the hospital. Paul was brilliant with finances and had fresh ideas. Tom Wheatley was no match for him and Paul soon replaced Tom as Hospital Administrator.

Paul Candino was exactly what the Hospital needed at that time. He was young,(29 years old) ambitious and was eager to prove himself and begin a stellar career in health care. Paul's financial background produced immediate results.

WCCH was designated as a sole community health provider. That designation was handled by Paul and Congressman Bill Paxon. It really simply stated that WCCH was the only provider within a 25 mile radius. The only exception to that 25 mile was the northeastern part of the County. But the status was given. That brought in an additional $1 million annually from Medicare.

The Hospital was also over staffed and spending at an excessive rate. Revenue was increased by expanding outpatient services. Outpatient services were profitable whereas inpatient (hospital stays) were not. He started an expanded physical therapy department and opened a medical clinic in North Java and Attica. He even began an aggressive fundraising campaign.

The Hospital itself was also given a facelift. New paint and carpeting. New furnishings. Even a mural type painter was brought in to paint soothing pictures on the walls. The results? For the first time in 26 years the Hospital showed a profit of about $335,000 for the first nine months of 1992. The County was still providing a $500,000 subsidy. But that too was soon eliminated.

All were not happy. Many employees and especially, the CSEA (union) were very upset with Candino. But.. what was the alternative? Shut down? A sale?

In 1991, the Board of Supervisors was actually marketing the hospital. We were going to sell it. And if we did? What guarantee for the employees then? In fact, what guarantee for the residents that the hospital would always provide the same level of care. What if the new owner(s) wished to convert it into a profitable outpatient and emergency care facility? Besides being the main health care provider in the community, just think about the economic impact or devastation if WCCH were to close and the county lose some 600 jobs. Believe me, whether you agree with Paul Candino's employee relation policy or not, he WAS THE RIGHT MAN for the job and for Wyoming County.

At that time, the Hospital came under the Finance Committee. Every job change also was required to come to Finance. If the hospital needed to upgrade a temporary telephone operator from part time to full time, the Finance Committee and even the full Board of Supervisors needed to approve it. The hospital was required to come to us for approval to fill a vacancy whether it was for maternity leave, illness, death, termination or any reason.

Purchases had to be approved. If the operating room needed a new delivery table or major purchase, it had to be debated at Finance and if approved there, then on to the full Board of Supervisors. And some of those debates were just awesome. By awesome, I mean laughable.

Picture if you would, myself (railroad background), Barney Erhart (Liquor salesman) or Jim Schlick (corrections officer) debating whether the medical staff at the hospital needed a laser larascopy, immunoassay, colonoscope or even a gastrointestinal fiberscope. I mean, we Supervisors are all-knowing, but don't kid yourself. If I hadn't just looked those up, I would have to guess what they do and where they go. But every month, we'd do it. We'd argue about the medical technician, the admitting clerk and all the others.

Paul, Stu Hemple, the WCCH Board President and I began to inquire about how others handle this technical stuff. Erie County has the Erie County Medical Center (ECMC). How do they do it? Well, lo and behold ! Erie County adopted a local law way back when that gave the Hospital Board the authority to create, abolish and fill positions and purchase equipment if it was in the budget. The budget, salaries and any loans would still have to be approved by the County Legislature. The County Legislature would still appoint and remove members from the Hospital Board of Managers. I presented the Local Law to the Board of Supervisors on July 9, 1991.

The Local Law was adopted. Barney, Ed Hamilton, Rita George, Alex Lane and Jim Schlick voted against it. Life was a little easier.

In fact, in the 1993 November Board of Managers meeting, a resolution was passed to share the profit that the hospital realized of $250,000 with the taxpayers of Wyoming County. The hospital was turning around.

Chapter 17

1991 Elections

Hallelujah, I was unopposed for re-election in 1991. Many Supervisors were not so lucky. Hell, even Sheriff Capwell had token opposition. A gentleman named David Conley ran against Cappy. Even Geraldine Luce tried to make a political comeback and ran for Orangeville Town Board and lost. Barney had competition from Ed Meyer. Ed put on a good race, worked hard, spent a lot of money but he lost. Ron Herman had Arlene Dawson as an opponent.

Larry Nugent challenged Ed Hamilton as the Genesee Falls Town Supervisor and Larry won the seat. Leslie Huber was the victor in a hot contest as the Bennington Town Supervisor. It seems Leslie put out a questionable flyer the week end before Election Day that blind sided Jim and gave Jim no time to respond. Live and learn. The Democrats always pull that crap. Bill Faulkner also was the winner in another hot race. Bill defeated Alex Lane and became the Warsaw Town Supervisor.

Attica was also a real hornets nest. Gus Petri, who had served for eighteen years as Supervisor, was being challenged by three opponents. Gus prevailed and in my opinion that was good news for Attica and all of Wyoming County.

I admired and respected Gus from the very beginning. There was no bull shit with Gus and if he thought someone was spreading a load, he'd tell you and also tell you why. In every decision, Gus had first and foremost the best interests of the people of Wyoming County in mind. He knew the issues inside and out. I spent considerable time with Gus before and after meetings picking his brain for details. He was patient and more than willing to help anyone. Gus truly was one of my most important mentors. His favorite quotes were: " Wait till you get a load of this " or " What a Deal ! ". Thanks Gus.

In the County, Jean Krotz ran unopposed. Gerry Stout was elected to his first term as District Attorney and Mike Griffith was elected as County Judge replacing Charlie Newman, who retired.

So.. we said good bye to some and hello to others.

In Java, Fran Brunner made a comeback after being defeated by Bob Kibler in 1985 and won a seat on the Town Board. Janet Zielinski beat Joanne Kurnik as Town Clerk. Things were still kind of civil in Java.

Chapter 18

Taxes, Taxes, and More Taxes

1992, the County Board of Supervisors began considering hiking the sales tax by an additional 1% to bring the total to 8%. The State already received 4% and the County collected 3%.

There were many reasons for increasing the sales tax. The 1992 Budget called for an increase of about $700,000 in the property tax levy. Many, including myself believed that was excessive and unacceptable. The Pre School Program for handicapped children 3 to 5 years of age was raising its ugly head. The additional 1% would mean an extra $2 million dollars in revenue. That would cover the deficit and also increase the reserves back to where they should be. The alternative would be about a 40% property tax increase.

My belief was and still is, sales tax is the fairest tax of all. Property tax is the most regressive tax that the government can impose. It has no bearing on the ability to pay, wealth, income, personal status or anything else. Property Tax doesn't consider fixed income, lay offs, decrease in income, sickness or anything else. It is simply driven by the assessed value of your property. Sales tax on the other hand is paid by everyone. If you can afford a $30,000 vehicle, then I guess you can afford the sales tax on it. Tourists, visitors and even travelers passing through Wyoming County pay sales tax on their fuel, food or other purchases.

As Chairman of the Finance Committee, it was my responsibility to get the feel of the residents of the County. We went to the Farm Bureau Meetings. The farmers predictably favored sales tax opposed to property tax. Senior Citizens favored sales tax. Even the business community said the additional 1% would have little or no effect on their bottom line. The Wyoming County Business Development Corporation took a survey and the results indicated that their members preferred the sales tax increase to a property tax increase. I did some homework and discovered that in Java, the owner of a $70,000 home (average at that time) would have to pay an additional $200 in property tax without the increase. That same family would have to purchase an additional $20,000 of taxable items to come up with the $200.

There was opposition on the Board of Supervisors to the increase. The Finance Committee wanted to have the sales tax option at budget time for 1993. Now catch this.

The State of New York requires that all sales tax legislation be passed by their great all knowing body to enable passage in any County. In other words, before Wyoming County passed or imposed another 1% on sales tax, it must be voted on by the entire State Assembly, State Senate and signed by the Governor. Wonderful. They can't pass their own budgets on time, but the Counties have to wait for approval from them. Sure... does it make sense for an Assemblyman from Long Island or New York City to vote on Wyoming County's sales tax? Give me a break. But those are the rules and if you don't know it, Albany makes the rules. In fact, they make the rules as they go along. More on the State later, but one comment... If George Washington was resurrected and went to Albany for one day when the Assembly or Senate was in session, he would order the First Continental Army back to active duty and attack the inept, corrupt, ineffective and expensive New York State government.

It was in 1992 that Frank Smith (Yorkshire Supervisor), Howard Payne and myself traveled to Albany for a Town Supervisor's Meeting. Tom Reynolds invited us to see the Assembly in session. I wish he hadn't. The Members of the Assembly sit in a half moon type seating arrangements in rows of about 25 or 30 desks. Tom's desk was in the last row on the left. Let me set the stage for you. The Speaker of the Assembly for the day, because they all take turns (only the party in the majority) was presiding over the meeting. Some Member from downstate was standing and debating the bill that was to be voted on in a few minutes. No one, and I repeat no one, was paying any attention or even listening to this guy. Some were chatting with their buddies, some were actually eating sandwiches but the guy that took the prize was standing with his back to the podium and throwing peanuts to everyone. And we pay these guys $70,000 plus a year? They all vote exactly as they are told by their party leaders. On that trip I first learned that the leaders of each political party disbursed "bonuses" on an annual basis to THEIR members. The bonuses ranged from $5,000 to $20,000 at that time. So... if you were a good boy or girl and voted with your leader, you'd get $20,000 bonus. However; if you were a maverick, you'd only get $5,000. Now don't you think that's against the law? But.. Remember they make the laws, so it's A.O.K. Imagine, a Town Supervisor giving out bonuses to the Town Board Members that voted the way he wanted them to.

In any event on June 26, 1992, the Wyoming County Board of Supervisors requested a one year authority for imposing an additional 1%. It was necessary to pass the resolution by June 27th because the Legislature was adjourning for the year. That's right, they were all done with all their important work for the year. After all, they are part time jobs. Barney, Larry Nugent and Gus voted no.

Chapter 19

Taking a Stand 101

The Town of Java has passed some interesting legislation but in 1992, the Town Board unanimously passed a resolution calling for the State of New York to be divided into two parts.

Actually Assemblyman Donald Davidsen of Steuben County sponsored a bill in the assembly that called for the move. I realize that is an argument that will go on forever and ever. What would the financial condition of the new "Upstate New York " be without New York City. I realize that the higher incomes are in the City. But, let's also face facts that the vast majority of state money goes down to New York City whether it's paying for welfare, roads and bridges or the subway system. Personally, I think it probably would be a wash.

Also that year, I got an idea from the Farm Bureau. They had on one of their lobbying trips to Albany " adopted " a legislator from the New York City area for a day. They explained to him(her) the plight of the farmer in rural New York state. I thought, why not have the Java Board adopt one, too.

I contacted Tom Reynolds. He was very enthused. You know, he really is a great guy and a great representative in the Assembly or Congress. Anyway, I told him that I wanted a liberal Democrat so he could deal with me as a Conservative Republican.

Tom recommended James F. Brennan from Brooklyn. I would send our Town Board minutes along with my newsletter to him on a monthly basis. I also kept him informed on County business. Sometimes a staffer would call me with a question. But... during 1992, when we were considering increasing the sales tax opposed to increasing the property tax, Assemblyman Brennan called me. He wanted to know why I always was crying about property tax. Then the big question, he asked me, " just what percentage of your residents actually own property? " I replied about 80 or 90%. " My God, " he said, " In my district, less than 5% of the residents actually own property. " See what we're up against? Those people don't really care about property tax, it does not affect them. Now for more irony, Assemblyman Brennan was the ranking member of the Real Property Tax

Committee in the Assembly. That's like having Mike Tyson serve on a Woman's Rights Committee. He just doesn't care.

Well, we eventually dumped poor James Brennan and adopted Catherine Nolan from Queens. Another prize. But she just never responded to anything, so we just let the whole thing go quietly. Java wasn't done though.

Just when the county was increasing the sales tax by 1%, the surplus had dwindled by $1.4 million, the pre school handicap was costing an extra million, the jail and Public Safety Building had just been completed for about $8 million, and revenues were short... the State Office of Court Administration (OCA) wanted or demanded that Wyoming County now build a new courthouse.

I treated that as just another unfunded mandate by the State. I have always believed that all mandates should be totally funded by the legislative body that creates them.

The Java Town Board passed a resolution that claimed the State of New York had continued to put an excessive burden on the counties, towns and school districts and their property owners and residents. It went on to include that The State of New York and the OCA were placing unreasonable pressure and demands on Wyoming County and it concluded that the Town Board strongly opposed this mandate and the OCA's general attitude and disregard for the taxpayers of Wyoming County.

Other things were beginning to boil. The state was still forcing the Counties to pay a share of Medicaid. No other state does that. The pre school program was totally out of control. Even the community colleges were mentioned. The aid to the Public Defender for the indigent parolee program was also being reduced. Fortunately, Wyoming County has Norm Effman as its Public Defender and we have historically received the lion's share of state aid in the Public Defender's Budget. More on Norm, later.

As some of you know, the costs of community colleges are shared in thirds. The state pays one third, the student pays one third and the County that the student resides in pays one third. I have no problem with the student that is continuing their education. But.. I do have a problem with the student (loosely) who is attending court ordered Defensive Driving, Bow Hunting or some other class that they just want to take. Why should the taxpayers pay their tuition?

The State was even beginning new programs and also shifting the financial responsibility of some existing programs. In 1992, the State of New York was now mandating that each County appropriate money to fund a Domestic Violence Program in its own County. Now this was before O.J. Simpson put domestic violence in the nation's spotlight.

On December 29, 1992 at the Board of Supervisor's year-end meeting we were being asked to allocate $10,000 in 1992 (2 days) and an additional $25,000 in 1993 for the Wyoming County Domestic Violence Program. We were told that ACCORD, an Allegany County based agency that administers the program would provide part of the balance of the $50,000 annual budget for the program. ACCORD began as a State grant, whose term had expired.

I rose to my feet in opposition. Obviously, not against the program but against the notion that Wyoming County was now going to BEGIN to fund another program mandated by the State of New York. The women from ACCORD were sitting behind me. (By the way, they were all very stern looking and were not real pleased with men, in general.) I said.. " Whatever happened to family, friends and church to help in this type of situation? Why should Wyoming County taxpayers be forced to pay for this program? This 1993 allocation is the same amount that the County allocates to its libraries, Where have our priorities gone? " Well, at that statement, one woman said to the other, " Who the hell is the cold-hearted son of a bitch? " I WAS NOT BEING COLD HEARTED. I was being fiscally conservative.

Granted, I will admit that I was totally ignorant of domestic violence, its causes and effects and everything else. If I were abusing Cindy, I would have to answer to her father, brothers, my kids and everyone else. I never dreamt what happened behind closed doors even in our own town. Fortunately, for women and children most men would never ever even think of physically or mentally abusing their wife or children. Sadly, that feeling is not universal. I now realize that Wyoming County does have a serious problem with domestic violence and it needs to be addressed. Len Opanashuk, Assistant District Attorney, works closely with Victims Services, not only to counsel but also to prosecute. In fact, Len once spoke at an event and mentioned that domestic violence can be traced back to 1849 when a husband(John Shadbolt) was accused of killing his 17 year old wife. The trial also happened to be the first murder trial in Wyoming County. Shadbolt was acquitted based on insufficient evidence. So... I guess things haven't changed so much in 150 years. Shadbolt was acquitted and 150 years later, O.J. was acquitted.

I hope that I have explained myself and made it clear to all that I believe fervently in the war against domestic abuse and will continue to urge the county and state leaders to do the same. Wyoming County, as every other county in the state has got to realize that domestic violence does exist and we have to do everything possible to wipe it out.

Chapter 20

The Times, They are a Changin'

The County had many new and improved proposals on the table for 1993.

The County Administrator position was the number one hot topic. County wide assessment was in the works along with reducing and consolidating the number of Committees on the Board of Supervisors from sixteen to six.

I am going to be brief about the Committee structure. Before 1993, we had sixteen committees. Each Supervisor was a Chair of a Committee. That's a big deal to some. But it was rather awkward and very tedious. Many times, the Committee did not even meet and when they did, it was only for 15 minutes or so. We had a firm do a study on it to tell us exactly what we wanted to hear. You can and should do whatever you want. So, Howard did. He reduced it down to six powerful, meaningful and hardworking committees. A very good decision.

Then there was the hot button issue for 1993. I don't really remember where the idea of county wide assessment originated. Tompkins County (Ithaca) was the only county that had implemented it.

It would eliminate the need for local Town Assessors. It was to make all assessments more equitable and more efficient. It would also provide professional, full time assessors at the County level for concerned residents to confer with. It would also require the issue to be placed on the ballot in 1993 for voter approval.

I introduced the Resolution for the Local Law at the April 13, 1993 meeting. I said that county wide assessment would provide equality, efficiency and stability. With a county wide system, all parcels throughout the county would remain more equal and constant, and updating them at regular intervals would help broaden the tax base. Assessments do not raise taxes, budgets raise taxes. It was also becoming increasingly more difficult to find either appointed or elected assessors. The position involves state certification and training, and that training must be constantly updated. Local governments find it very difficult to pay an assessor what they are really worth. Of course, I also admitted that the county wide assessment would cost more than the Real Property Tax Office and all the towns assessment's budgets put together. Was it worth it?

The proposal called for the establishment of a County Board of Assessment review in addition to each Town's Local Review Board. The residents were actually being given one more step in the grievance process. The Law also provided that all towns must be assessing property at 100% of the market and all towns were going to placed on a mandated update schedule. This actually would take the politics out of it. Just go through an assessment update and you'll understand exactly what I mean.

Public Hearings were held in Bliss, Arcade, Bennington, Perry and naturally Warsaw. They were all well attended by the general public. The business community and the Farm Bureau were supporting the law. At that time we had four appointed assessors doing all Towns except Orangeville, Arcade and Wethersfield. Those towns still had elected assessors. Probably the biggest thing we had going against it was Jim Wheeler, the Director of Real Property Tax.

I was in favor of it for a multitude of reasons besides those mentioned above. I didn't particularly like the idea that some assessors were not current with their certification and they were assessing property. The reason I did not feel comfortable with that, is once you're talking County and/or school property tax, we are all treated "equally" by the equalization rate. In other words, if your town had an equalization rate of 25%, when they compile your county or school tax they will multiply your assessed value by 4 times. That's fairly easy. But, how about a town that is assessed at the rate of 6.7% of the full value. Are you telling me that the local assessor first values the property at 100% (how else could they do it?) And then adjust that to 6.7% of that figure. Yup, sure and monkeys are going to fly out of the assessor's butt, too. At one of the public hearings, the local elected assessor spoke up and said, only he could assess the property in his Town because he knows the individuals. " Excuse me," I said, " what does the individual have to do with the assessed value? " Well, he said if he knew that poor old Henry down the road, couldn't afford his taxes anymore, he wouldn't assess him too much. Great, that should make every one in Town, the County and the School District, rest easy. We now have an assessor that is also the Human Services Commissioner and crusader for the poor and oppressed, in his opinion. Did he review the financial records? How does he determine who can afford their taxes or not? Does he deliberately increase the assessments for the wealthy or the middle class? Oh my God! However, in the interest of good, I am not going to tell you who the assessor was.

Those opposed thought the County was trying to take their Home Rule away from them. The Democrats made it a campaign issue. After all of that the voters in Wyoming County rejected it by a 4,783 to 1,129 margin. Enough said.

Remember Phil Murray, the guy who took the $1.00 annual salary job for his resume? Well. He showed back up in Wyoming County in May, 1993. Lois Bowling, our Social Services Commissioner was retiring. The county advertised for the position and the Human Services Committee interviewed four individuals. Two were from Wyoming County and two were not. Of the two that were out of county residents, one was the famous Phil Murray.

Phil came with the following credentials and background. He was the former Mental Health Director of Wyoming County and then left for Niagara County and the Director of their Mental Health Department. With that type of experience he was not going to come cheap.

Lois did more than an excellent job. She was dedicated and lived for her work. She believed in Social Services with a conservative outlook. The following story has been told to me but I cannot say it is gospel. One of the county migrant workers once injured his back. Due to his injury, he could not ride the bus back to Florida. He and his family were forced to remain in Wyoming County. Upon his arrival at Social Services, Lois interviewed him. She learned that he and his family wanted to return to Florida. They had no desire to remain in Wyoming County. Lois gave the man and his family plane fare to return to Florida. The State of New York , as the story goes, sanctioned her and warned her never to do something like this again. One other story, a young couple with children were sleeping in their van that was out of gas in the Ames parking lot, in Warsaw. Lois gave them emergency funds of $100. Isn't that what Social Services programs are meant to be? Lois Bowling, a great Department Head and a classy lady. All of Wyoming County is, and rightly so, should be proud of her and her career. Thanks, Lois.

Lois was earning a salary of about $43,000 for her life time devotion. The position was advertised for the range of $45,000 to $50,000. The Human Services Committee interviewed the candidates and selected Phil Murray. O.K. But... the range wasn't quite high enough. They had to come back to Finance and County operations. Howard Payne, the Chairman thought the whole Board should be involved. We all went into Room 13, Committee Room which is about 8 feet wide by 20 feet long. It had a huge conference table in the center. Howard opened the discussion with the premise that Phil was the best thing since sliced bread. If he demanded $55,000, then so be it. We decided to listen to Phil. Mr. Murray came in used some Murrayesque on us. He had a loose leaf binder with his achievements and his hopes for the Wyoming County Department of Social Services. Ending his very long and very boring presentation, he pointed out that he was not going to be needing health insurance because for some strange reason Niagara County agreed to pay it and so he wanted an additional $3,600. Well....as soon as he left the room, most were ready to give him the money plus their first born. Howard went around the room, polling all the Supervisors, present. Ron Herman was probably the most supportive. Ron insisted that Phil was going to cut jobs and save all kinds of money. I was the last to be asked. I said loudly, " I just can't believe that this man has got you people totally bullshitted ".

At the full Board Meeting, I went along with the Committee's selection to appoint him but I voted no on the raise. As a side note, by September 14th, 1993, the Board had created five new positions in DSS at an additional cost of over $130,000. In the 1994 Social Service Budget, the increase was only 1.2 million dollars. On May 10, 1994, the Board of Supervisors approved the creation of three more new mid-management level positions at DSS. Their salary range was $25,000 to $30,000. Jim Schlick, Suzanne West, Larry Nugent, Nelson George and myself voted no. I was quoted in the daily News of 5/11/94 as saying, " Mr. Murray was going to save us money. It hasn't happened yet. Thirty thousand dollars is a higher value than some of our department heads. " Rah, Rah, Phil.

On July 13, 1993, Local Law S , was adopted that called for the creation of the position of County Administrator in Wyoming County. A search committee was formed and the advertising began. The salary range was $40,000 to $50,000. We received over 100 applicants. So I guess the range was correct. Wouldn't you know the first candidate said he needed more money.

I'll never forget the day we held interviews. First up, was Bob Bondi, the County Executive from Putnam County, just north of New York City. As County Executive his salary was $65,000 and he thought Wyoming County should pay around $78,000. Hmmm, that's interesting. Bob was elected and was worried about his next contest, thus the interest in our job. He came with his wife and two sons. They had NY Giant jackets on and I told him that he was in Bills territory. Bob was over qualified, over educated and over everything. He and Wyoming County just would never get along. Ernest Zmyslinski of Norwalk Ct. was next. Mr. Zmyslinski was a graduate of the Kennedy School of Government at Harvard University. Ernie hadn't worked since 1992, though. Ernie brought his wife and infant baby girl to the interview. His wife and the baby were in the adjoining room as we interviewed Ernie. Ernie had been acting as Mr. Mom for the last few months and you could tell. The baby started to fuss and cry. Ernie said excuse me, but I have to see if I can do anything. Because of our love of family and motherhood, we offered Ernie the job. He refused. He needed more money. Candidate number three was my good buddy, Eddie Haskell, I mean, Kevin DeFebbo. When Kevin told us he was from the Pittsburgh area, I asked him straight out, Steelers fan? He said "yup". I said well you know you're going to have to become a Bills fan if you get the job. Kevin said, " no problem I can do that". The son 'o bitch. The lyin son of a bitch. Kevin still adores the Steelers, Penguins and even the Pirates. Oh well, Kevin was our choice and a damn good one. More on Kevin later.

I would not be treating you fairly if I failed to mention the nightmare in South Warsaw. The Board of Supervisors had been searching for office space for several years. The County was renting office space, store front and anything else they could find. The Board of Supervisors made a huge mistake in electing to purchase a 10,000 square foot building and six acres of land on Route 19, south of the village of Warsaw off Mungers Mill Road. The price was $125,000. Not bad. However, the building was a structural disaster. The County went out to bids on finishing the interior of the building, a new roof, heating and electrical improvements and of course engineering and architectural services. Guess what ? The bids came in a little over $800,000. Now we had about one million dollars invested. When finished, it did look nice. It was decided to locate the Office of Aging, Youth Bureau and the Job Training Program in the renovated building. Even today, that building still has symptoms of the old " sick building syndrome ". That's why I call it the number one mistake that I ever made and I still call the building a million dollars and a nightmare.

In 1993, there was another questionable " historic moment". Roy Haller, the Supervisor from Orangeville was charged with embezzling or stealing around $90,000 from the Town funds. Remember, Roy succeeded Geraldine Luce, so he had been around a few years. In fact, he was the Chairman of the Taxation Committee.

I don't know the particulars, nor do I really want to know. The State auditors came to do the audit in Orangeville and Roy was done. How or why, I have no knowledge. I must admit that I was shocked, amazed and extremely disappointed. Most of the Board, took it as a personal slap in the face. I mean, all residents would have the idea that all Supervisors were thieves and crooks. Roy was the first Supervisor to spend a night in the new County Jail. There's an honor, Roy. And that was all the jail time that Roy would do. That also upset many of us. There was an interesting story going around. I don't know if it was true or not. Supposedly. Roy was sitting at a coffee counter with a cup of coffee and a donut in front of him. An Orangeville resident sat next to him, reached over and took the donut and began to eat it. The waitress came over and said, excuse me but that's Roy's donut you're eating. The donut robber blurts out, " I don't give a shit, my money paid for it ".

Why people steal from a municipality, I have no idea. You are going to get caught. You simply cannot get away with it. As soon as the Town, Village, County or City is audited, just put your wrists out for the handcuffs.

Is even $90,000 worth it? I don't think so. Roy ruined his life, his wife's life and probably the whole family's life. For what? $90,000 is really not that much money. I don't have $90,000 but then again, I am not about to ruin lives for it either. I guess it's human nature. It goes back to the hypocrites and some small minded people around here.

I can forgive a thief a lot quicker than a hypocrite or a vindictive person. Why do people have to be mean? And... like I said, there they are on Sunday at the altar, nearer to God than me and thee. Don't they think God is watching them? It probably pisses off God more than me. It's a personal insult to God. Oh well, " vengeance is mine ", the Lord said.

The 1993 election came and went. First in the County, we had two comeback kids. Jim Schlick won a rematch against Leslie Huber in Bennington and Alex Lane won her seat back in Warsaw. We also had four new Supervisors. Suzanne West replaced Roy Haller in Orangeville and Paul Agan was the new Supervisor from Attica where Gus had retired. Hank Bush succeeded the retired Barney Erhart from Gainesville. Oh yeah, Nelson George . Ole Nels hornswoggled the Democratic nomination from Irene Glaus. Remember, I said Irene was a really classy lady and a great supervisor. Nelson, in the October 30, 1993 Daily News stated, " They (the county) are just throwing money away over there ". Now there's an intelligent statement. What did I just say about the auditors? Do you really think they would allow the county to throw away money? And, Nels, do you really believe that sixteen supervisors or at least the majority of the Board, were in Warsaw to actually throw away money? BULLSHIT !!!. Then he went on and said, " It just looks like an overall plan to take over highway maintenance and other local functions. " Yup, boy you're right on top of things. The county is always scheming and conspiring and trying ways to screw its residents. That's what we do best. My God, get involved, open your mind, gain some knowledge. Find out what really is going on before you open the spigot. Boy, I was really looking forward to working with this guy. Well, enter Nelson.

I guess it was the year of the rematch, too. Vince George came out of retirement to run against me. You could tell that Vince and Nels were brothers. Vince's campaign theme was anti-county wide assessment and Tom Moran was spending too much money in Warsaw. Vince went door to door. I always went door to door, so I worked just as hard. The voters in Java elected me by a margin of 432 to 232. Another two years.

Looking back, though, it was not a real nasty campaign. Thanks Vince.

Chapter 21

1994

Back in 1986, municipalities were being faced with a real insurance liability crisis. The Town of Java's insurance premium went from $12,000 in 1986 to over $30,000 in 1993. Something had to be done.

The N.Y.S. Association of Towns, the Association of Counties and the Conference of Mayors began years of work by forming an Insurance Reciprocal. The concept was to stabilize the rates and actually offer better coverage and much better risk management.

In 1993, the Town of Java solicited quotes. Even with the supposedly bad insurance market, our premium was reduced from 1992. Again, in 1994, we asked for quotes. The New York Municipal Insurance Reciprocal (NYMIR) was formed and we joined them. Our premium was lowered again and we actually had better coverage.

I was asked to sit on the Board of Governors of the new Municipally owned insurance Company, the New York Municipal Insurance Reciprocal (NYMIR). I was honored and accepted. The Board met on a quarterly basis, usually in Albany. It was a tremendous opportunity for Java and myself and it was a huge learning experience. As part of the Board Meeting, there was always a presentation of some sort on the Insurance business. Whether it was re-insurance, liability, pending cases, it was always an education and I thank NYMIR for it.

Jeff Haber and Kevin Crawford of the Association of Towns were instrumental in the establishment. A firm from Long Island was chosen as the management partner. They would handle all the details, paper work, law suits, reinsurance etc. Bill Fishlinger was the owner. He chose Jerry Elicks to be the President of our division of Wright Risk Management. After Cuomo's defeat, we were able to capture Richard Hsia. I say that because under Governor Cuomo, Richard was the Director of the State Insurance Department. You can imagine the expertise we picked up. Anyway, Bill, Jerry and Richard became my friends and I mean that. They helped me immensely. They were patient and explained the details of the insurance business to the Board, including this poor, uneducated old Railroad man. To handle the marketing end of this huge endeavor, they hired Brian Custer. Brian too, was a natural fit and could get along with anyone. In a short few years, NYMIR went from 25 municipalities to over 250. It was a very rewarding experience. I should mention that I would never have even heard of NYMIR had I not attended a session in New York City at the Association of Towns Meeting.

If anyone ever tells you that all those trips are a big party and a total waste of time, tell them they are full of unadulterated BULLSHIT. That one trip for NYMIR probably has saved the Town of Java over $75,000 in insurance premiums. The County eventually became a subscriber in 1996. All residents should be proud of this accomplishment. Through the three associations they grabbed the bull by the horns and cured the major insurance crisis of the 80's and 90's. And don't think the insurance companies don't realize that. Remember, NYMIR did not have a building named after it, NYMIR did not have thousands of employees, and NYMIR did not have to pay taxes. We did have a huge disadvantage also. NYMIR is regulated by the State Comptroller's office for investing. So, NYMIR only invests in Government backed securities. Instead of the 10% plus from the stock and bond market, NYMIR was relegated to Treasury Bonds of 3 or 4%.

Speaking of the Association of Towns, the President, John Kazanjian appointed me to the Resolution Committee. Again, it was an honor. The Town of Java now had a Supervisor that served on two state wide committees. More on the Association of Towns later.

Wyoming County Community Hospital requested a Bond Anticipated Note of $350,000 to be passed at the July, 1994 Board of Supervisors' Meeting. The Hospital, even though they were governing themselves for the most part, still needed County approval to borrow money. The $350,000 was for renovations for the Emergency Room and Outpatient Clinics, repairs to the parking lot, repairs to the boiler, replacement of the stairs leading to the main entrance and repairs to both the roof over the operating room and the facility's main roof.

Paul Agan and Nelson George actually went on the roof to see first hand, to determine if the roof was in bad shape. Howard Payne was livid. First of all, what the hell would happen if one of them was injured on the roof of the hospital? Secondly, did they think the Maintenance Department at WCCH was snowing us and thirdly, they at least should have received permission from Howard or somebody. You just don't put up a ladder and make inspections.

The resolution was passed by a majority but it did not pass by the required two thirds majority. Paul at least realized that the repairs were necessary. Nelson (Sheldon), Anne Humphrey (Perry) and Alex Lane (Warsaw) all voted "no". Because of the weighted vote, the resolution did not pass. Great ! I stood up and asked the three why they voted no. Anne, said " I would like the hospital management to come up with a long range plan". Now, Anne, does any town, city, village or county have a long range plan for necessary repairs in Wyoming County. Nope, we don't even have an annual inspection of our buildings. We should, but we don't. In fact, Anne and I both tried for just such an inspection when I first became Chairman in 1996 and we were shot down big time. Alex said she voted no because there was a lack of communication between the Hospital Board and the Board of Supervisors. Nelson had no reason, but that didn't surprise me.

O.K. If we couldn't borrow the money, what were we going to do? Wait until some patient or visitor slipped and fell on the stairs or in the parking lot? Wait until the boiler just did not operate and we had to shut down the facility? Or worse... wait until some poor bastard was being opened up on the operating table and six inches of snow and dirt fell into their incision. For Christs's sake, what's the matter with some people?

If the County is going to take responsibility to maintain the Hospital, it certainly requires a boiler, roof and front steps that are safe for its patients, visitors and employees. After all, the hospital had turned the corner. The hospital was running in the black for the first time in years. Under the leadership of Stu Hemple and Lucy Sheedy, the hospital had become an asset rather than a liability. At the August meeting, I re-introduced the resolution to borrow the necessary money. All Supervisors agreed except Nelson George. Boy, I'd like to get into his head once and see the reasoning. On second thought, I don't want to go there.

1994, was election year for Mario Cuomo.

Boy, did I ever have a problem with Mario. He was arrogant and seemed to deliberately put burdens on counties and towns. He had just raided the State Retirement System the year before. The bottom line was that all towns, counties, villages and cities had to pay more. Many of them actually had to borrow the money. The State was going to allow them to "repay" the owed money but it was something like ten percent interest. Far more than they could actually borrow it for. Java and Wyoming County were fortunate. We were able to pay it off with our reserves. Now, you might ask why did we owe the money? Well, Mario restructured it so that you paid the retirement bill up-front. In other words, in December you will pay for next year's share. We had always paid it when the State calculated the bill and submitted it. It was usually 12 to 18 months behind. Therefore; in his mind, we all owed the 12 to 18 months bill plus next year's. Cuomo was always thinking. He loved creative financing. Remember when he changed motor vehicle registration to every two years? It was the same fee, but the State was getting double for one year. It closed some revenue loss. Sure, but what happened in year two. Maybe that was when he sold the prisons. The State had such a bad credit rating that the N.Y.S. Thruway Authority had to borrow the money that was due the Counties and Towns for their Highway Improvement Programs (CHIPS). Sad to say, but that practice is still going on today. Imagine, borrowing the money for a bill that you knew was there when you budgeted. That would be like you or me charging our electric bill every month to Master Card. Sure we could do it, but sooner or later, you HAVE TO PAY THE BILL. Yet, he would not acknowledge the problems that he was creating. George Pataki, a Republican State Senator, from Peekskill was the candidate for Governor.

Tom Reynolds was very active in Pataki's campaign here in western New York. Congressman Bill Paxon had scheduled a Town Meeting for Saturday, July 23, 1994 at the Java Town Building. On Thursday night, Tom Reynolds called me and wanted to know if I could provide a good crowd for Saturday, if he brought George Pataki. " You bet I can, Tom, " I said. I called some good Republican friends and we had the building packed. In fact, people were standing in the parking lot. My kids, Mike (6) and Bridie (8) gave George a Good Luck card and made a banner welcoming him to Java. He autographed the banner which I still have and a picture was in the Daily News of Mike giving him the card.

Pataki's campaign focused on New York's high taxes, unemployment, jobs leaving and the refusal of Mario to sign the

death penalty bill. He had vetoed it every year for all twelve
years that he was in office.

On election night, 1994, Cindy, Carl and Debi Heterbring and
myself all went into downtown Buffalo at Jim Kelly's old bar for
the Erie County Republican Election Party. Dennis Vacco, Tom
Reynolds, Dale Volker and a host of other Republican officials
were there. As the night wore on, it looked like Pataki had a
chance. A buzz went around the room, if Pataki could carry Erie
County, he would win. The excitement was totally awesome. A
band was playing all good rock and roll music.

Then the word came out. George Pataki had defeated Mario
Cuomo and was going to be the first Republican Governor in
years. Hallelujah!!!!!!

Tom Reynolds was like a little kid. He was so happy. He
was like all children are on the last day of school. And us too.
We were going nuts.

I'll tell you more about the Inauguration later.

Chapter 22

Irish Diplomacy

The Office of Court Administration is a very powerful branch of New York State Government. It is considered the Judicial branch, therefore, neither the Executive or Legislative branches have much control with the exception of the budget.

Back in 1987, the NYS Legislature passed a Court Facilities Act. This act provided that the Office of Court Administration would assume the financial responsibility for security and most maintenance of all court facilities. The counties in return would have to provide " adequate " court facilities. So...as usual, the counties were screwed again, by their friendly partner, the State of New York.

It took the OCA three years to find Wyoming County. In 1990, the OCA reared its ugly head and appeared before the then Judges and County Clerk Committee of the Board of Supervisors. Alex Lane was the Chair, with Rita George, Urlin Broughton and Bob Bowles as the other members. Harry Brand was the Executive Assistant of the Unified Court Systems, 8th Judicial District. That means he was our main contact. Mr Brand's offices were located in Buffalo. Keep in mind that in 1990 we were right in the midst of building the new jail. Why hadn't OCA called on Wyoming County before we had designed the new jail? Maybe then a Jail/Courthouse Complex would have had support. Not now.

Let me describe the Courthouse and what occurred on certain days. The Courthouse was originally constructed in 1842. The plans were approved in 1841 by the Board of Supervisors, when they voted to have the treasurer secure a loan of $2,000 to begin work on the Jail AND the Courthouse. In October the Board contracted with Josiah Hovey to erect a Courthouse and County Clerk's office underneath, the same to be completed by November of 1842 for the sum of $2,650 . One month later, the Board changed their mind and decided to build a separate building for the clerk. The new total was now $2,828.68.

Here's a little story that will give you a background of the Board of Supervisors even back then. According to an issue of Historical Wyoming written apparently by Anita Ripstein in 1986 when she was the Deputy County Historian, Josiah Hovey may have even designed the building. Regardless, Josiah was a resident of Warsaw and a builder by trade.

Josiah Hovey, his two sons, daughters and wife all played a part in the Courthouse. He actually rented a boarding house nearby for the laborers to stay. His wife and daughters prepared all the meals and rooms for those workers. The wood for the stove too, was from the Hovey's farm. In fact, even the wood and timbers for the Courthouse came from their farm. It wasn't too long into the project that Josiah realized his bid was too low. He went back to the Board of Supervisors and requested an additional $1,397.66. His argument was that materials were higher than anticipated and there were change orders even back then. Well, I can imagine what the Board told him. He was one of thirteen bidders. They probably told him to go pound rock salt. Josiah though, being a righteous man, completed the project. According to the Board of Supervisor's Proceedings, Josiah Hovey returned numerous times to their meetings requesting the additional money. He was in his own words being, " pinched by the hand of poverty ". I have to sympathize with him and say that Wyoming County may not have had a legal obligation but certainly they had a moral obligation. Ten years after the completion of the Courthouse, Josiah and the Board agreed to a settlement of $100 to close the books on the claim. Nowhere is it recorded how the $100 figure was reached. Josiah allegedly stormed out of the meeting and was never seen or heard from again. Some even say that he went home and hung himself. I suppose one could find his grave if you were really interested. But... Josiah's craftsmanship and artistic work still remains. Strange things happened in the Courthouse sometimes too. Doors would open or shut by themselves. Noises could be heard. I always thought it was a ghost of an old former Supervisor until I read the Josiah Hovey story. I am convinced it is poor Josiah looking for his just payment.

Between 1877 and 1878, the County Clerk's Office Building was completely demolished and rebuilt for $7,780. According to Historical Wyoming, the Clerk, Charles J. Gardner wrote a letter to the Board of Supervisors that basically said the building's exterior was in very good condition and the interior was in fair condition. But as I say, the Board of Supervisors always knows best and they decided to demolish and rebuild. In 1892, improvements and repairs were made to the Courthouse along with an addition for Surrogate Court records. The total cost of these improvements were $6,468. In 1910, another addition was made to the back of the Courthouse and again it was for Court records. In 1927, the Sheriff's Committee recommended new construction of a Courthouse to include the Clerk's Office. But then the great depression hit and all plans were shelved. After the depression, in 1935 plans were again brought out for the building project. The Board agreed that an addition would be constructed to actually join the Clerk's Office and the Courthouse that would provide additional space for everyone. The only other major construction was the elevator in the rear of the Courthouse in 1985.

So we had a Courthouse that had been renovated many times yet was truly a historical building. Just think of the craftsmanship that was put into it. Now back to 1990. We all know that the Courtroom is on the second floor. There is a hallway that is about 4 foot wide and maybe 20 feet long. There is one public restroom at the opposite end of the hallway from the Courtroom. That restroom is used by the public, court attendees, prisoners and the staff of the Board of Supervisors. The hallway has chairs along one side that could seat maybe 15 or 20 people. On Family Court days, it was not unusual to see a wife and her children sitting on chairs opposite her estranged husband. Not a good environment or situation. Then the kids would play on the floor in between. On some occasions the contents of their diapers would fall or leak out. Just about that time, some Correction Officers from Attica would escort an inmate who is completely shackled past the kids.

Some of these inmates were nasty. In fact, I would say that there are not too many nice guys in Attica. Think about it. With the judicial system today, it's probably their 6th or 7th conviction that lands them in Attica unless they are sentenced to life or something. Because there was only one public restroom it was a generic one. Both men and women used it. These same inmates would use the same restroom that the County's female staff would use. It even made the Supervisor's and myself uncomfortable to walk by an inmate who's eyes are focused on you and looked like they would wipe you out for any reason. I can clearly remember one such day. This inmate who was serving a life sentence was on trial for murdering another inmate. Yeah, I know, who cares? This guy was the meanest, coldest person that I had ever seen. I was coming into a meeting and walked by him. JESUS, he scared the shit out of me and he was shackled and being guarded. It had such an affect on me that I went into the meeting and said you people have got to see this man. He was the epitome of a cold blooded murderer. So you can see, the OCA did have some reasons to expect new and improved facilities.

I must inform you that in August of 1989, Alex Lane presented a case to build a Jail/Courthouse complex. She was very convincing. Alex made several points in a prepared statement at the 8/8/89 Board meeting. They were:

1)Renovation and expansion is required. The present facilities are overtaxed.

2) If we were to build both, we may even keep costs down

3)The Court System is far more complex than the Supervisors realize.

4)The County may even be able to save the old Sheriff's House.

She made one mistake. The mistake was that she presented these facts by herself. Alex is Alex. Alex was also confrontational, cantankerous, defiant, rude and sometimes nasty. However, Alex was also intelligent, articulate and always well informed. She would spend many hours researching issues. She also had a friendly and warm side to her. I remember when my Grandmother died, she was about the only Supervisor that sent me a sympathy card. I know she always did what she thought was best. I can honestly say that I not only admired and respected Alex, but I really liked her. I also loved to go at it with her. During one meeting, she decided that another meeting was required and she wanted to have it on November 15th or 16th, something like that. I said, No, ma'am that's opening day of deer season.

Alex said, " Doesn't that start at 7:00 A.M., you can hunt for an hour or so and come down here by 9:00 A.M. ".

Instead of going ballistic, I shut up and stewed. Later in the day, at another meeting, it was decided to reconvene at a later date. I blurted out " December 25th, 9:00 A.M. "

Alex says, " NO, No, that's Christmas ".

I replied, " Listen, get up at 7AM, open your gifts for an hour or so and come down here for the 9:00 A.M. meeting ".

" O.K. Mr. Moran, I get the picture, " Alex replied. She almost always called me Mr. Moran. It could have been worse. She always called Jim Schlick, " Schlick " . I also remember in the 1994 election, Dennis Vacco was running against a militant lesbian for Attorney General of New York State. I walked into the coffee room, where Alex, Jim and Ken Lowe were all sitting before a meeting.

" How ya doing, Tom," Ken asks.

I said " pretty bad, this country is going to hell in a basket, the next Mayor of Washington D.C. our nation's capital, is going to be an ex-convict, drug user, and user of prostitution services.(Mayor Barry) and here in New York, I just heard on the radio that the militant lesbian is ahead in the polls to be the next Attorney General of New York."

Alex was shocked and screams, "You gotta problem with that?".

"Yes, I do, Alex, I don't have a real problem with a lesbian but I don't think it's quite right to have a militant lesbian writing and interpreting the Laws of New York State." I said.

WELL, SHE ACCEPTED THAT ARGUMENT. Alex would always bring her own coffee to meetings. She had her own thermos. I don't know if she thought our coffee was tainted or she thought maybe we got it for free. Alex would never accept anything. She didn't even eat at the Hospital Board or Health Board Meetings. Anyway, Paul Agan was new on the Board and we were in a committee meeting. Paul had brought a cup of coffee in and was now in need of a refill. He looked at me, then looked at Alex's thermos.

I said "go ahead, help yourself." HOLY SHIT.

Alex almost broke Paul's arm. " What in the world do you think you're doing? That's my own coffee", she barked. Alex was also the only Supervisor to ever, ever give me a kiss. Yup, the morning after one of my elections, as soon as I walked into the Committee Room, she came over and gave me a kiss on the cheek. I smiled and said, I knew you'd rather have me down here than Charlie McCormick. She smiled, sat down and began to snarl at me again. I love ya, Alex.

Her proposal was totally rejected and Urlin even made a motion to table the entire Courthouse issue. Then in June 1990, Alex announced that her Committee had met again with Harry Brown and the Committee would request proposals from architects for designs. The Board did just about nothing until 1991.

At the April 9, 1991 Board of Supervisors meeting, Rita George introduced a resolution that authorized the Chairman to sign a contract with MRB Architects of Rochester for design development of the proposed Courthouse. This was for $142,800 plus an additional $4,000 for soil borings. I again voted no but the resolution did pass.

Howard Payne was the Chairman. Howard knew the votes were simply not there. Because of the need to borrow the money, it would require approval by two thirds of the Board. No Way ! Every once in awhile, Howard mentioned that the OCA called him. Yeah, who cares. Then in July of 1992, the OCA wrote a threatening letter to Howard. It stated that failure to comply could expose Wyoming County to section 39 of the Judiciary Law. Section 39 authorized the withholding of state aid from any County that fails to meet its obligation under the Court Facilities Act. How about that? Could or would the State actually withhold our money? They were talking Medicaid, welfare or any source that we receive state money from. It was my bet that they didn't have those kind of guts. I was furious. Howard sent it back to committee. Now Bill Faulkner was the Chairman of the Committee.

On September 18, 1992 Howard called a meeting that was to include myself as Chairman of Finance, Mark Dadd and Mike Griffith, County Judges, Nick Capra and Harry Brand of the OCA. It was held in Room 13 and Mike and Mr. Capra were not able to attend. Howard opened the meeting and turned it over to Mark. Mark explained the need for improved conditions and additional space. Harry Brand then explained that if the County failed to act, he was going to more or less call in the dogs. I stated that the taxpayers could simply not afford the increase. I said we needed more time. I had the financial figures and budgets to prove my case. Property taxes would have to be increased by at least $1.00 per thousand. Our residents could not tolerate it, nor should they. Harry then looked across the table and asked me very calmly when I thought the county would be able to build it. I replied in ten or twenty years.

Then he shouted, " I find that totally unacceptable".

"Excuse me. Excuse me Mr. Brand ". I too now was shouting. I said," who the hell do you think you are to come to Wyoming County and demand that we increase property tax by $1.00? Who the hell are you to find my suggestion totally unacceptable? You are not my boss. I answer to the residents of Java and Wyoming County." At that point, Mark Dadd and Howard got in the middle and asked us to calm down. I did. I left the room. The S.O.B.

Then came the Faulkner Resolution on November 10, 1992. This one was in more detail. It even had dates. It stated that Wyoming County would approve plans in 1994, begin construction in 1995 and completion in 1996. Guess what? Without even knowing the costs and results of those costs, the Board approved it with Java, Bennington, Orangeville and Castile voting no. You bet we're going to meet that deadline.

The Java Town Board immediately passed another resolution attacking the State and its mandates. We did get good press but no satisfaction. We owed it to the taxpayers.

At least the OCA left us alone for a couple of years. We did plenty of studies. The studies cost close to $200,000. I was livid. Why are we doing all this stuff, knowing full well that we did NOT intend to build a new Courthouse?

August 11, 1994, Nick Capra wrote Howard Payne another threatening letter. In this one, he stated that not only would he impose financial sanctions on Wyoming County by withholding revenues but it will also begin a lawsuit. The OCA is also prepared to begin construction and Wyoming County would pay for it. Now, doesn't that sound like a true partnership? But back then, we never heard the word collaboration. Howard was genuinely concerned so he called a special session of the Board of Supervisors for August 23, 1994.

The only item on the agenda was a presentation from Mr. Nicholas Capra, Director of Court Facilities Management and Mr. Harold Brand, Executive Assistant, OCA.

Howard opened up the meeting and turned the show over to Nick and Harry. As I said, Nick was from Albany and Harry was from Buffalo. Mario Cuomo was the Governor. New York State was financially assisting cities and counties to build baseball, football and hockey stadiums, also.

Mr. Brand and Mr. Capra started off by saying that we were going to have a discussion and come up with solutions. Mr. Capra mentioned the 1987 Act, adding that N.Y. State assumed the costs and responsibilities for the Courts by being a " good neighbor ". However, Wyoming County does not have a choice. He gave us a deadline of December 1st. Remember now how slowly things move.

He also said, " The Office of Court Administration will not be made a fool of by Wyoming County. You will build it or we will. " He added that he did not have a gun, he had the atomic bomb. Nice, huh?

Ron Herman rose and stated that his family farm paid $28,000 in taxes but only saw a return of $20,000. He then threw about ten feet of tax bills across the floor. Where he got them from, I don't know. But it sure did provide special effects. Ron also said that the taxpayers, especially the farmers could not afford anymore taxes. I rose and gave my most emphatic speech at that time. It went like this according to the proceedings of the Board:

" This all began in 1991 and in June 1992, things began to develop quickly. Mr. Brand came down and met with some of us. The meeting was not productive or congenial. He was demanding, arrogant and pompous. The Town of Java passed a resolution in July opposing this mandate and OCA's general attitude and disregard for the taxpayers of Wyoming County. I forwarded copies to the Board of Supervisors, Assemblyman Reynolds, Senator Volker, Governor Cuomo and Mr. Brand. I received replies from everybody except Mr. Brand and Governor Cuomo.

As Chairman of the Finance Committee, let me provide some facts and figures. Since the summer of 1992, the County has increased the sales tax to 8%, the property tax levy still went up even last year by $677,061. That was because of the $1.5 million increase in Medicaid, snow removal, Pre-school Handicap Program, Human Services etc. The total indebtness of the county is $14,660,000 or $366.50 for every man, woman and child in Wyoming County.

In August, 1991, the Courthouse was estimated at $6.3 million. It would be at least $8 million today. In 1994 tax dollars, it takes 10 cents per thousand to raise $80,000. The debt principal and interest based on 6% would be about $800,000 annually for thirty years. That means an increase of .80 per thousand. That does not take into consideration any normal or abnormal growth in DSS, Public Health, Highway, Human Services etc. It does not consider the fact that in 1995, we will have to begin paying back the retirement system that Governor Cuomo raided a few years ago. It also does not consider that we have not had a county subsidy for WCCH the last couple of years. We really don't know what the impact of health care reform is going to be. It does not include employee raises that are called for by the CSEA and other union contracts, Health Insurance increases. It will also increase our indebtness to $22,660,000 or $566.50 for every man, woman and child in Wyoming County.

In conclusion, I personally take exception and in fact I am offended that two bureaucrats from Albany and Buffalo have the audacity to come to Wyoming County and demand that we increase property tax for a new courthouse that most of our taxpayers will never utilize. We are a small, modest and neglected county. We're not in the process of building a hockey arena with a little help from Cuomo or remodeling a football stadium with a little help from Cuomo. We are a very proud County that asks little of the State and gets little in return. But I will and am taking a stand on this issue. Enough is enough and I for one am not going to take this any longer. My state taxes and fees go to paying the salaries of everyone in the OCA and Albany including Cuomo. Simply put, go take care of some other county that the Governor actually visits. Leave us alone in Wyoming County ".

Pretty powerful, huh? Well it's not over.

First Nick came over to my desk and I quote from the Daily News of 8/24/94, and said, " I resent the fact that I'm referred to as a bureaucrat from Albany. I usually don't invite someone to my house and insult them ". I replied that I did not invite him to Wyoming County and I sure as hell did not ask him to come over to my desk. I walked away.

The Daily News followed up with an editorial opinion of their own. " Wyoming County or any county should be able to disagree with any state agency..... If the state insists on total control of the project, it ought to provide total funding for it. Otherwise, it ought to do more listening and less demanding. " (9/2/94)

The day after the meeting, Sue Aldinger, who was then the Deputy Clerk to the Board of Supervisors, presented me with a plaque. Sue had made it herself and inscribed the following:

IRISH DIPLOMACY
The ability to tell a man to go to hell
So that he'll look forward to making the trip

Things simmered for a few months. Howard figured he should give it to another committee. One that I was not on. Anne Humphrey was Chair of the Planning Committee and that's where the Courthouse project landed. My relationship with Howard was never quite the same after I spoke up against the OCA. In fact, Howard had already decided not to run for re-election in 1995. Now you would think that he would leave things as they were but he didn't. He shuffled the committees around and removed Jim and Ken from Finance. I still don't know why. Maybe before the end of this book, we will all know.

Immediately in January of 1995, Anne introduced Resolution 16 that called for the Board of Supervisors to " commit and implement and *provide for the appropriate and necessary financing* of the court facilities plan as approved and submitted by the Wyoming County Board of Supervisors *through* its Chairperson and the Court Facilities Capital Review Board ." Again, Java, Warsaw, Bennington and Wethersfield were the No votes.

The Planning Committee then tried to figure out how to get anything done. About all they really did was start the process of selecting an architect.

Because George Pataki was our new Governor, I had high hopes that we could squash the whole thing. I worked through Reynolds and Volker, playing all of my cards. The OCA was still a powerful agency . But now we were beginning to gain support from the Association of Counties. We also were going to have a new Chairman in 1996.

The general feeling was drag it out as long as we could and see what 1996 brings.

Chapter 23

The Java Town Park Saga

It's truly amazing to me that you can raise taxes in order to provide Highway improvements, purchase equipment, raise the salaries of elected and appointed officials, BUT... Don't you ever spend one penny on a Town Park. Believe it or not, that was and still is the philosophy of some of the residents of Java.

In 1992, the Town purchased some 38.5 acres of land mainly for the purpose of storing the rock salt. The Town Board looked at several suitable parcels but an agreement could not be reached. We agreed to buy the Handley property that was the former Centerline Gravel Pit on Route 78. John Handley was an avid supporter of Kiwanis Little League Baseball and was even a former Commissioner of the Little League program. There was money already in reserve or put aside so no borrowing was necessary. It was agreed unanimously.

So, a sand/salt storage building was constructed in 1993 on the site where the Town had been storing it for years. The Department of Environmental Conservation (DEC) was encouraging all municipalities to enclose their salt piles to prevent run-off into wells etc. As a further enticement, through the County Highway Department, the town would receive reimbursement for the next 30 years at 50%. It wasn't a major factor, but it was nice. The main reason we built it so far back from the highway, was that Don Roche convinced us that sooner or later a new Town Building would be necessary and that building should be up front. Good planning, Don !

As you already know, the transfer station was opened up at another building on the site and the sheriff's sub-station was also moved to the site.

Some of us considered the decision to purchase the property as a blessing. After all, God is not making any more land and the site was perfect for a town park. At about that time, I was directed by the Board to apply for various grants to develop the park. Grants are typically awarded to communities with large numbers of voters. Java did not qualify.

However, through the contacts of Bob Kibler, a town councilman and Army Reserve Officer, the town applied for help from the Army National Guard. At first, they too, turned us down. Bob is fairly stubborn and he kept on them.

In September, 1994, Bob provided me with another contact within the Guard. They were ready and willing to assist the town in anyway. At the Board Meeting, the Board authorized me to sign the agreement whereby the town agreed to provide fuel, meals and lodging for the soldiers and the Guard would level off the park. Because this was the site of a former gravel pit, very little of the terrain was level. In fact, it was really nothing but steep slopes and cliffs.

The Department of Environmental Conservation (DEC), the Environmental Protection Agency (EPA), and County Soil and Water were all involved. We had to get excavating permits to do the work.

The 152nd Engineering Battalion of the N.Y. Army National Guard arrived in Town on February 24, 1995. It was a nasty, snowy cold day in Java. The group was under the command of Major Charles McNeil in Buffalo and on site under the command of Lieutenant Timothy J. Strunk. Sergeant Charlie Whyte was the number two man. Others included Frank Pagels, Tom Koza, Joe Schultz, Mike Malinowski, Don Howard, Norman T. Kob, Paul Bieron, Russ Lons, Mark Gaesser, Jerome Kester, Tom Carmichael, Terry Graham, Robie Skrabacz. These men were great. They took pride in their work and I think they really enjoyed themselves while here in Java.

As I said, the agreement called for the Town to provide fuel, meals and lodging. Conroy Motors donated the fuel tank and the first 500 gallons of fuel. Almost every business in Town followed suit: Hogans , Strykersville Plumbing and Heating, Fisher Brothers, Strykersville Hardware, Sad Dog Saloon, Kevin Zielinski and the North Java Fire Company all contributed materials and/or services. Paul Freyburger was another huge contributor of his time, contributing his employees' time, equipment and materials. It could not have been fine graded without Paul. Cliff Stephan, a leader in the Park development, would deliver the Sunday newspaper and donuts to the men every Sunday that they were in town. The Unit also gave an open invitation to visit them either while they were working or just to stop by and say hello. Remember, the Guard on other exercises would have to move piles of dirt from one spot to another. This gave them the sense of accomplishing something - something good for the community. I think they actually felt like part of the community. Almost every Saturday, Cindy and a group of our friends would get together with the Guard either at the Park or Sad Dog's. They even came to our house once or twice. It was truly a rewarding experience.

They stayed in the little white building that is now the Sheriff's sub-station. The soldiers brought their own cots and sleeping bags. The building was spotless every Sunday evening when they would depart. We provided them with vouchers for the North Java Inn, the Shamrock, Sad Dog's and the Village Pub. The Guard was here for over a year and the total meal bill was $1,707. So you can see everybody did very well. The entire cost to the Town of Java for a year's worth of work by twenty or so men and equipment was $5,559.

I was donating my salary of $5,000 each year to the Park Fund. So that more than paid for the expenses. But people still bitched.

The Park Committee which was appointed by the Town Board and consisted of Keith Kersch, Bob Daley, Bob Kibler, Ed Freyburger, Janet Beechler, Cliff Stephan, John Meyer, Ron McCormick and myself. Kathy Wilson of North Java headed up a separate fund raising committee. Her purpose was to purchase playground equipment for the smaller children. She did a great job and today you see the results of her hard work. Kathy did it just about single handed. She ran raffles, Monte Carlo night and several other events. She did it ! Today, there are picnic tables, sandbox, swings and other playground equipment that was NOT purchased by the Town or tax dollars. In fact, Ray and his kids assembled the equipment on site on an extremely cold and rainy week-end. I didn't see anybody helping except Mike Zielinski. Thank you, Kathy and Ray. It was gratifying to see the unselfishness of some people.

It was decided that the Town should show its appreciation to the Guard. On May 13th, 1996, an Appreciation Dinner was held at the North Java Fire Hall. Mark George of Java A's fame, was our guest speaker. Cliff and Keith recognized each and every member of the Guard for their contribution. But... to say the least it was not attended well. The cost was $5 per person or $15 for the entire family. We were able to keep it that low through donations again. Of course some people said the Town was paying for it. Petty Bullshit ! The National Guard's work was estimated by local contractors to be in the $200,000 to $250,000 range.

The Park issue got so damn picky that some were even arguing about what should come first, baseball diamonds, swings or a hockey rink. Joanne Almeter was dead against it and she convinced Ron McCormick, Don Roche and others to stand by her. There was even an adult fitness trail planned so some could lose weight if they leaned that way.

The Park Committee in a committee progress report of 4/26/95 stated that the Committee stood behind its original decision that the ball diamonds must come first. There were many reasons but it was thought that Little League involved many more people than other sports do. There were no diamonds on Town property in Java. There were no regulation size diamonds. In addition, ball fields would provide the ability for running, kite flying, flag football, soccer and many other activities. The Kiwanis committed itself to building a pavilion, which stands today.

The Varysburg Lions Club donated and erected a beautiful sign for the entrance to Veteran's Park. Oh yeah, that was another bitch. Ron McCormick did not like the name of the Park, " Veteran's Park ". Who the hell came up with that? The Committee came up with it! Jesus, Ron ! If it hadn't been for the National Guard, we wouldn't have any park. If it hadn't been for all veterans, we wouldn't be free to even consider a Park and maybe we wouldn't even be here in the good old U.S. of A. We owe our freedom to the veteran's of this country. Every one of them, thank you! You know, it's people like that who just cannot understand the sacrifice that ALL servicemen and service women take on. It doesn't really matter if it is wartime or in peace. If any reader doubts there is true loyalty and honor in America, read John McCain's book on his experiences as a POW in Hanoi, Viet Nam.

In the spring of 1997, through the efforts of Tom Reynolds and Dale Volker, I was able to secure a grant from the State for $7,500 for baseball backstops, benches, and safety fencing. On Sunday, July 26, 1998, we held our Park and Flagpole dedication.

Tom Reynolds was the guest speaker. As always, he did a great job. Bob Grover, Commander of the Strykersville American Legion, provided the color guard and a bugler. It was a moving ceremony. It was held in conjunction with the Java Strykersville Kiwanis Little League All Star Game. Alex Dominick and Jim Keenan, two great baseball fans, threw out the first pitches. Alex and Jim are also true gentlemen, in every respect. God Bless you guys. There was at least 300 people in attendance. Kathy Wilson's Committee provided Java Town Park water bottles as a memento of the occasion. It was one of my proudest moments. Fran Brunner and Don Roche, Councilmen, for their own reasons avoided the ceremony.

Mike Becker and Bill Thomson, both coaches of the little league team spent days and I mean days, on the ball diamonds. They even had the kids working on the fields' preparations before and after practices. Mike rustled up some of Bill Becker's equipment to help. Bud Youngers from Varysburg, spent a couple of days spreading more topsoil and grass seed. The kids sold raffle tickets and ordered a sign for center field. " Home of the Java A's "! Finally after a year or more of hard work, the diamond was ready for league play.

On June 3,1999, the "new" Java A's opened their home season. Mike and Bill honored me by allowing me to throw out the first pitch. The entire team autographed the baseball which I will cherish forever.

You see, Java and Wyoming County really do have some great people. I could not list everyone and all the businesses that contributed in some way. God will give you your reward. In the meantime, God Bless You and thank you!!!!!!

Chapter 24

Inner Workings of the Board of Supervisors

1994 brought the arrival of Kevin DeFebbo as County Administrator. Now that was good news or at least I thought it was. Some didn't quite see it that way.

Michelle Millen was the Clerk to the Board of Supervisors. Michelle was able, competent, knowledgeable and definitely experienced. Michelle, however, was not a poster child for " Customer Service". After Kevin's arrival, there was a definite feeling of tension and noticeable friction in the Board of Supervisors Office. I really don't know if Michelle viewed the change as a threat or what.

Believe it or not, the Chairman of the Board opened up all mail addressed to him. Junk mail, free credit cards, Publisher's Clearing House etc. Whenever, Howard was on vacation, I would have to trek to Warsaw if for no other reason, than to open the U.S. Mail. One such day, I opened an envelope containing grant papers that should have been sent to Marty Mucher at the Office of the Aging. I went into Michelle's office with the documents and asked her to mail them to Marty. She IMMEDIATELY gave them back and told me to mail them. I said, " You're the goddamn clerk, you mail them " and threw them on her desk. Michelle and I never had a cordial relationship after that incident.

In early 1994 we had Michelle appear at the finance committee and directed her to cooperate 100% with the new county administrator. On April 12, the Finance Committee issued a letter to Michelle indicating that her attitude must change immediately. For the next several months we waited for the attitude adjustment that never occurred.

Around November, Michelle went on medical leave and we appointed Sue Aldinger as Acting Clerk to the Board of Supervisors. It was a wise decision and beneficial for the County. Sue was then appointed permanent in January, 1996. Sue's abilities were only exceeded by her desire to do the job right.

Sue picked up the ball and ran with it like she had been born as the clerk to the Board of Supervisors.

In addition to Kevin's arrival, 1994, the County began to study our Worker's Compensation Insurance Plan. All sixteen towns, villages and all schools except one were in the county plan. Volunteer Firefighters were also covered by the County. Ray Luce was the Administrator of the program.

The premiums were based on the assessment values for each town, village, and school. It was not based on experience, loss or risk. One of my serious concerns was that if the Workers Comp Fund needed an appropriation at the end of the year, the county would simply take the money from the general fund. We never knew where it should have come from. In essence we were paying as we went. The county had no written plan or agreement between municipalities. The county also had no injury management policy and the county did not even track injuries. We did not set any money aside for any injuries. For example, if someone was going to be off work next year due to an unexpected injury, we did not budget that. We just picked a number from the sky. And we usually got away with it. Marsh, McClennan (a large insurance actuarial) was contracted to do an actuarial study. That study told us who should be paying what and what the rate should be. This study took a very long time.

Through the efforts of Bob Bowles and Kevin the county now is operating a Workers Compensation Pool that includes all the above and the rates are now equitable. The County has contracted with a private firm to act as the third party administrator. We now have injury prevention programs and a light duty policy. Without a light duty policy, any injured employee was considered a 'lost time' injury case. The employee was off from duty and the county paid a percentage of the salary along with all benefits. Many times, the employee really wanted to work but because of their injury, they could not perform the duties of their job. For example, a nurse at the hospital sprained their ankle. Obviously the nurse could no longer complete their rounds on the floor, using crutches. However; that same nurse could assist in the nursing office and perform other duties. The employee received their full pay and benefits and the county received some service from the employee. Win, win.

The reform of the Workers Comp Program was no easy chore. It was reported very casually in the local papers. Good news is not treated as news. Newspaper articles about elected officials doing good things, simply do not sell papers. The Board never received the credit that it should have. This was major reform. There are insurance and workers comp experts throughout the State that applauded Wyoming County. Hundreds of thousands of dollars were saved and we believe we have also eliminated the potential for fraud and abuse. There, now it is said.

On March 11, 1997, I gave each town board member a copy of the new plan. Java's rate for workers compensation in 1996 was $9,768 and for 1997, it was going to be $4,943. A REDUCTION of about 50%. Wyoming County gave each municipality the option of joining the new Workers Compensation Pool. The deadline was May 1st. After reviewing the plan for a month, the town board on April 8th voted unanimously to enter into an agreement signed by me as Town Supervisor for Java. I had checked on other premiums. Java could have gone on its own and paid a premium to New York State of $22,070 and Java would also be responsible for the volunteer firemen at another $15,000 premium. Because of the 5-0 vote that directed me to sign the agreement, I thought it was done and over with. How stupid of me! Ray Luce wrote me a letter reminding me that Java was still not in the plan and asked if we were going elsewhere for our Workers Compensation Insurance coverage. I telephoned Janet Zielinski, the town clerk, to see what the hell had happened to the documents. Ms. Zielinski informed me that Ron McCormick, councilman had a 'problem' with it and she would not send it in.

EXCUSE ME !!! Keep in mind, this plan and the documents were presented, in the proper procedural manner, to the Board in March. I think if anyone had a 'problem' with it, they should have brought it to someone's attention before the deadline. By the way, every town, village, school and county attorney had already reviewed the agreement and did not have any problems with the document. Ron McCormick and Janet Zielinski stepped way out of bounds on this one. In addition to a lackadaisical attitude towards the residents, town employees and the volunteers of the Fire and Emergency services, McCormick and Zielinski completely ignored the town board that voted unanimously for the motion. The unanimous vote also included Ron McCormick. No one, not the Supervisor, Councilmen, Town Clerk or anyone else has the authority to arbitrarily decide to table action that was agreed on at a regular Town Board meeting. This unethical and illegal little show could have cost the taxpayers of Java over $40,000. And... guess what, nothing was ever mentioned again. No apology or even regrets were ever expressed.

Also worthy of mention was in December of 1994, the Java town board created the temporary position of town prosecutor. Java was the first town in Wyoming County to do so. This was actually at the request of both of our Justices, William Horton and Michael Skrzypek. " This will be a ground breaking for Wyoming County," Justice Skrzypek told the Arcade Herald in the 12/22/94 issue, " It's time to get into the modern age, even though we are a small town". Reasons for the decision were: 1) it removes the Judges from awkward or potential conflict of interest, 2) it expedites court cases. Previously, the district attorney is in each town four times a year. Traffic cases can now be heard monthly. 3) By plea bargaining, a 'second' chance is given to first time traffic offenders and 4) it brings in additional revenue. The decision was adopted unanimously. Later in 1996, it would become personal. It continued on a temporary basis until 1996.

In October, I presented the 1997 town budget to the public and Board. I had included $3,600 in funding for the position but had also increased anticipated revenues by the same. There was to be no cost to the taxpayers. I was also quoted in the Arcade Herald of 10/22/97 as saying, " It takes the judges out of any conflict of interest situations where they have to act as judge and prosecutor. "McCormick was quoted in the same article as " I found out that it wasn't beneficial to the people of the town of Java. I couldn't justify the added cost." What was with that? There was no added cost and I don't have the foggiest notion what the first sentence meant. Three councilmen, Fran Brunner, Don Roche and Ron McCormick voted to eliminate the position of prosecutor from the budget.

In December, these same three voted to actually abolish the position of Town Prosecutor! Even though the prosecutor doubled the revenue. Yes, that's right. The revenues doubled from the previous year as a direct result of the plea bargaining down to parking fines wherein the town receives all of the money. Now instead of being neutral or saving money, these three were forcing the board to raise taxes in order to express their personal feelings of animosity toward me.

The District Attorney, Sheriff's Department and State Police were all supporting the prosecutor position. Justices Skrzypek and Horton were also endorsing it. Again, in addition to increasing revenue it was 'user-friendly' to our residents and removed the justices from possible conflict.

Two hundred years ago, the authors of the U.S. Constitution provided for the separation of powers between the legislative and judicial branches of government. It's interesting, that in 1996, those three town board members believed they knew what was better for the town court system than our own elected justices.

With those three votes, the board actually abolished the position and finally with the arrival of common sense and Ron Falconer, the position was re-instated in 1998. In 1998, the position brought in over $8,000 in additional revenue to the town.

Chapter 25

Inauguration - 1995

New Year's Eve, 1995 was not our usual welcoming in the New Year party. Cindy, Bridie, Mike and I all traveled to Albany for the inauguration of Governor George Pataki.

Tom Reynolds provided us with tickets. We left Saturday morning 12/31/94 and arrived in Albany early that afternoon. If memory serves me right, we stayed at the Day's Inn on Wolf Road. Most rooms were already booked, but we got lucky.

I thought it best to scout the downtown area before Sunday's big event. I wanted to know where we should park, the entrance to the then Knickerbocker Arena or elsewhere. While we were downtown, we also were looking for a Catholic Church to attend. We found the Cathedral of the Immaculate Conception, downtown. The Mass was at four o-clock. Perfect.

When we returned to the church, there were State Police all over the place. The Mass was the Inaugural Mass for Governor-Elect George Pataki. It was a closed ceremony for about 300 except for parishioners. As we approached the doors, a state policeman just nodded and said, " Parishioners, right?" Cindy nodded and in we went.

The Albany Symphony and the University Choir were both performing. It was a Mass of the likes of which I had never attended before. All the Pataki children participated as readers. There were security officers at the end of every pew. A special program was distributed which of course, I still have. It truly was the most moving Mass that I have ever been to. What a way to start the week-end off.

It was suggested that we be at the Knickerbocker Arena by 11:00 A.M. on Sunday, New Year's Day. We were. While we were in line waiting for the doors to open, I saw Jess Fitzpatrick from Cattaraugus County and also Warren Schmidt, everyone's favorite.

Bridie was nine and Mike was seven years old. But... remember they had actually met George Pataki in Java. Anyway, our seats were at the other end of the arena. It was like sitting in the middle of the end zone and looking straight ahead to the opposite end zone where all the action was.

Again, New York State Police and West Point Cadets provided the security that you could recognize. The seats were bench like bleachers. As soon as we located them, we sat down and Bridie took off her shoes. One of her shoes then fell down off the footrests. First Cindy got a Trooper and a Cadet to look. Nope, they couldn't find it. Then I tried. They would not let Cindy or me under the bleachers for security reasons. We could not convince them the shoe MUST be under there. " Look at Bridie, " I said. She only had one shoe on. " Sorry, sir, you will have to wait till the ceremony is over and the arena has vacated. Then you can look for yourself ", they said.

The ceremony was awesome. I probably will never witness any thing like it. I felt like I was a part of it or at least a part of the cause for celebration. I had great faith and great hopes in this new Governor that George Pataki would turn this state around.

After the ceremony, the four of us went down to the floor to find Bridie's shoe. As soon as I ducked under the bleachers, I found it. Now we could go to the receptions.

The receptions were all being held in the Empire Plaza. The Empire Plaza is all underground. It is a total maze of wide hallways and little shops, cafeterias and small offices. It is the hub of the Legislative Office Building and Capital Building. They had beer, wine and every kind of food that you could imagine. Chicken wings, shrimp, beef on weck, hot dogs. Everything. The kids got balloons and some other trinkets that I don't remember. They were just as much in awe as I was.

After we had our fill, we decided to leave. We went up a stairway. I was packing up the stuff, because we still had to walk back to the car and it was snowing and colder than hell. All of a sudden, we heard a lot of commotion.

There came Governor Pataki and his whole family with about 20 state troopers. He stopped and said hello to us and thanked us for coming. What a great trip!!!!!! Oh and by the way, this trip was paid for by the Moran family. I thought that I should make that perfectly clear.

Chapter 26

A Federal Conspiracy

Here's another scenario for you. The Town of Java has three post offices. There is a post office in Java Center, North Java and Java Village. The rural delivery is hubbed in the North Java Post Office. I have no idea why there are three post offices. No other town has that many. Even Warsaw, Perry, Arcade and Attica have only one each.

Anyway, the post office in Java Center was in front of the home of Margaret Fisher. Margaret was the post mistress for many years and it was very convenient to have the post office in her home while she was raising Dick and her daughter Donna. But then Margaret retired. She still allowed the post office to rent the space even though she was not making any real money. I really believe she allowed it to continue because she thought if she didn't , the post office would close.

Mr. Harold C. Wood , a real estate specialist for the United States Postal Service contacted me in 1994. The Post Office wanted out of Margaret's house and needed a new location. They preferred to keep it in Java Center. The Town did have the corner lot where the Hart House once sat, at the intersection of Routes 78,98 and 77.

The Post Office at that time anyway, preferred to have the building constructed according to their specifications and then they would lease the building from the developer. The developer for the Post Office was Mr. J. Peter Willard from Rochester. The local contractor was Steve Beechler. Peter Willard was to lease the one acre lot from the Town of Java for $1,200 per year for twenty years and then the lot and building would belong to the Town of Java unless other arrangements were to be made.

At no time, was there any so called conspiracy to close any other Post Office in Town. If someone wanted to read something into it that just wasn't there, O.K. The Java Center Post Office was built and it is a welcome addition to Java and Java Center. In spite of everything being above the board and out in the open, Joanne Almeter insisted that they were closing the North Java Post Office and it was my fault because a deal had been cut.

Others in Java Village mistakenly thought their Post Office was closing.

Java Village did have some legitimate fears. In 1995, Steve Niedziela, manager of Post Office Operations in Buffalo conducted several public hearings to consider the closing of the Java Village Post Office. I immediately contacted Congressman Bill Paxon who was on our side from the beginning. Even though, we had three Post Offices, the savings were not going to put a dent in the national debt.

It became an election issue in 1995, when it should not have. Some residents tried to politicize it in Java Village and were blaming me for the closing.

I drafted a resolution opposing the closing that was then passed by the Town Board. I forwarded that resolution to Congressman Paxon, Senator D'Amato and Senator Moynihan. I also forwarded a copy to the Post Office review Board in Washington.

The Postal Service's contention was that " three Post Offices in five or six miles doesn't make a whole lot of sense". Kenneth Thompson, a member of the review team also said, the fifty customers , estimated in Java Village by the postal service, would require about one hour and ten minutes of service, daily.

In any event, we were successful and the Java Village Post Office remains open to this day. And, from those who were so vocal in their condemnation of the closing and my handling of it, I NEVER received an apology or a thank you. I did from many others though. Thanks, see you in church.

Chapter 27

The Year of Turmoil (1995)

1995 brought more concerns and worries at both the county and town level. These concerns were political in nature and then there was the 1996 county budget which I'll talk about later.

Howard Payne announced in June, that he would not seek re-election as Town Supervisor for Arcade. Oh, Oh, now what? Ken Lowe, Ron Herman and Jim Schlick all approached me and said that I should be the next Chairman of the Wyoming County Board of Supervisors. Hang on fellas, we have five months to go even before the election. And.. what an election it was going to be.

Now, why did I say 1995 was a tumultuous year? Let me count the ways. First the county, was facing a very difficult budget negotiations. Finances were beginning to get tight. There was uncertainty as to who was going to be the next Chair. The Planning Committee was having a hard time wrestling with the courthouse issue. Kevin was just getting his feet wet, and he was being faced with obstacles everywhere he turned. Sue was new as the Clerk to the Board. That meant Janet Coveny, her Deputy was also a rookie. Supervisors were actually fighting with each other over trivial issues, for the most part. Howard was not real pleased with some Supervisors, myself included. Phil Murray was still creating jobs, needing more money and still making promises. Marty Mucher was creating his own Community Action Department divorced from the County. The Work-Fare Program, (part of our Job Training Department) was a total disaster. The old jail and sheriff's house was still an eyesore on Main Street in Warsaw. It was fenced in by beautiful orange plastic fencing. The additional 1% sales tax was being fought by Alex Lane and Nelson George, for whatever reason.

The contest for the Chair was developing into a competition between Bob Bowles and myself. Everyone was talking about it and asking about it and even giving their opinions on it. The competition was spreading to committee meetings and the full board meetings. At some meetings, you could just about cut the tension with a knife. Bob was always a gentleman. I guess the two of us were being put into that position by our friends and

Thomas R. Moran

supporters. We were two trains bearing down on each other from opposite directions but on the same track. Bob and I also knew we had to win the town elections first. But it was difficult not to be campaigning at meetings, lunches or both. Looking back, it was fun.

In the town, things were really beginning to heat up. The "Java Six"Joanne Almeter, Don Roche, Charlie McCormick, Janet Zielinski, Ron McCormick and whoever was the special guest of the week, were attempting to create dissention everywhere. They complained about their assessments and the assessor. They whined about the Park, even though we were developing it basically for free. They cried about cable TV. They bitched about the need for improvements to the water district. They riled people up about the post office in Java Village, weight limits on roads and even supported a golf course that was designed on the back of a pizza box.

Nick Grover was our sole appointed assessor. Remember, when Java decided to eliminate its elected assessors, the town had to appoint one assessor for a six year term. Nick was one of three sole appointed assessors in the County. He was doing six Towns. You would have to rate him as AAA+. Nick was experienced, certified and a true professional.

Gerry Crabb had just built a house in Town and was extremely upset over his assessment, which was calculated by Nick. The real property tax law calls for a grievance process. First, the property owner confronts the assessor. If still not happy, the property owner appears before the Board of Assessment Review, which is appointed by the Town Board. Both parties then present their cases. The Board then rules on the case based on facts. If the property owner is still unhappy then he can file a small claims case in County Court. If still unhappy, the property owner can sue the Town for unfair and inequitable assessment. Gerry went the full course on his. That is his right. I had no problem with that.

However, he convinced Don Roche and Ron McCormick that he had a good case against the Town. Gerry would attend the Town Board meeting every month. The case was in litigation and by law the issue simply could not be discussed. Even if the Town Board agreed with Gerry Crabb, we could not change the assessment. It had to be a court ordered change or court settlement. There are obvious reasons why the State does not allow the Town Board to over-rule the assessor. First and

124

foremost, the Town board is not qualified to assess property, even though some think they are. Can you imagine if politics became part of the assessment process?   Look Out !! In addition, the Town Board has no legal authority or ability to assess or change assessments on properties.

In the September 28, 1995 issue of the Arcade Herald, " Both Crabb and Arcade builder Bob Salzler criticized Grover's method of assessing , and agreed he was not doing a sufficient job for the Town." They also convinced McCormick and Roche. In October, we went through it all over again. Nick's appointment was up October 1st. A motion was passed to reappoint Nick Grover as the Assessor. Don Roche and Ron McCormick voted no on his appointment. Nick was doing six towns at the time and was considered one of the very best. To put it bluntly, Nick Grover did not put up with any bullshit from the Town of Java. Within three months, Nick was gone from Java and became the Assessor for Orangeville.

Now, we needed to find another assessor. I put the responsibility squarely on the shoulders of Roche and McCormick. Hey, if Nick wasn't doing a good job, they could find someone who could. They were sweating bullets for awhile. Laura Eddy saved their ass and became the assessor. But guess what? Last year (1999) there were many critics of her performance. Let me try and explain why assessments are so damn sensitive.

In a perfect world, all property would be assessed equitably and at 100% of its value. Then everything would be great.

But... It doesn't work that way. For instance, let's say that the assessor is doing an excellent job and all residents are happy with their assessments (hahahaha). That would be great for town taxes. But in order to compute the county and/or school taxes, all parcels in the county or school have to be at 100%. Now, how do they know what your town is assessing property at? The State provides an " Equalization Rate " for each municipality. The state calculates the equalization rate based on comparable values and recent sales of comparable homes. The simplest example would be ten houses sold in a town for $100,000 and the town had each one assessed at $50,000. The state would calculate that town's equalization rate at 50%. In other words, the town is only assessing their property at 50% of the full value. The equalization rate usually is right on. So now your Town's equalization rate is 50%. That means when the county compiles their tax rate, they are going to double your assessment to bring it up to 100%. Now if the county had elected to go with county wide assessment, we would not have had a problem. There would have been at least four professional assessors in the county to turn to for a solution.

Remember assessments do not raise taxes, budgets do!!!

Speaking of budgets, I provided some entertainment for working on the County budget. I was a huge fan of Rush Limbaugh. Notice, I said that I was. Not anymore. This past primary campaign between John McCain and George W. Bush turned me away from Rush. Limbaugh insisted the whole primary was a Democratic conspiracy. So, no more Rush. But I used one of his quotes when I provided the Supervisors and Department heads with quotes of the day to help prepare a budget. Some of them were really good. Here are some examples:

Thomas Paine, " Society in every state is a blessing, but government, even in its best state is but a necessary evil".

William Ellery Channing, " The Office of Government is not to confer happiness but to give men the opportunity to work out happiness for themselves."

Rush Limbaugh, " Too many people are waiting for government to solve their problems instead of taking the initiative themselves."

According to the Institute for Policy Innovation, " There are more people in America working in government (19.2 million) than in U.S. Manufacturing (18.1 million)."

By the time, we adopted the 1996 Budget, I think everyone was sick of me and my quotes. It was a tough year. I did manage to piss some people off.

Phil Murray, the Commissioner of Social Services, appeared before the Finance Committee. Phil brought his three ring binder full of treats, graphs and what I believed were inappropriate pictures. Social Services felt they needed more help in the child welfare and abuse section. Phil brought in pictures of abused children. I did not appreciate it. First of all, it was a cheap trick. These kids did not have to be put on display to show the need for more jobs and/or money. If a department head cannot justify his needs without exploitative pictures, I have a serious problem with that. But.. He got the jobs and the money and the taxpayers paid for it.

The Business Education Council (BEC) re-appeared before the Finance Committee. This time, Richard Tindell lead the charge. The BEC provides education and assistance to high schoolers in applying for jobs, being interviewed, work ethic, job shadowing and a host of other things. Many of us, felt that the BEC was a duplication of services. If this type if service was warranted for our youth, shouldn't they be receiving this in high school? We did not think the county had any business in the education system or deciding its curriculum. The County had always given them $10,000. In 1995 we cut it to $7,500 and told them that they would have to find alternate financing. We were not going to fund them any longer. Well, that didn't deter them Richard brought Howard Payne in with him. Bob Bowles was also on the BEC's side.

We squeezed them till they really had enough. In fact, Howard left the room in disgust. My good friend, Anne Humphrey said and I quote, " This year's the last. You had better get control. If I'm still here next year, it's going to be zero." Alex Lane agreed. They got their money, but boy you better not come back. Guess what? They're still getting their money.

Chapter 28

1995 Elections

The 1995 election was by far the dirtiest election Java had seen up to that point. More was to come. The Democrats throughout the County were after us. John Hickey of Bennington fame, became the new Chairman for the Democratic Party in Wyoming County, replacing Barney Erhart who passed away. John moved to Java Lake in 1989. John and I had many private talks. He was a good man. He certainly did have faith in his party. Sometime in October, I ran into him at the North Java Post Office. John told me that Alex Lane would be the next Chairperson of the Board of Supervisors. As a true wise ass, I said I didn't think so. Then, who will it be, he asked. "You're looking at him", I said. I saw him walking into the same Post Office the day after election, I couldn't resist the opportunity to pour a little salt in the wound. He took it like the trooper he was.

Charlie McCormick came out for a return match as my opponent. Word had it that the Democrats poured $2,000 into his race against me. He had ads, pens, and those signs all over the place. His pen was a classic, " Charlie's the Won"? We could never figure out what the hell it meant.

Charlie was blaming everything from the weather to the national debt on me. He even was blaming the weighted vote issue in the County on me. As a result of law suits in the 1970's against counties that had Boards of Supervisors, Wyoming County elected to stay with a Board of Supervisors and initiate a weighted vote system. The system is based on population and obviously, Towns with more population have more votes. I was NOT in office in the 1970's. The ad from the Pennysaver was the epitome of nastiness, including his picture. It was the issue the day before the election. It stated that under the supervision of Howard Payne and Tom Moran, Wyoming County was now $15 million in debt. Before the ink was dry, Howard called me. He was furious. Why should he be mentioned in an ad when he wasn't even running for re-election.

On the surface Charlie McCormick was accusing me of being a free spender. HaHa. In one of his print ads he stated, " We need to address and rectify the serious property tax

129

inequalities our newly reappointed assessor has ignored." The Town was in good financial condition because the councilmen were doing their job, he claimed. That was BULL SHIT , Charlie !!!

However, going door to door was a different matter. There were all sorts of allegations that I don't really want to get into at this point. Charlie, Charlie, Charlie. Shame on you, Charlie.

Charlie and the rest of the Java Six thought they had me. When the votes were counted on Election night, I trounced him again, this time 476 to 218. Poor Charlie was sitting with Don Roche at the Fire Hall in total disbelief. I only wish that I could have run against Charlie McCormick every time.

The race for Howard's replacement in Arcade was the race of races. Doug Berwanger versus Fred Warner. Election night it was 465 for Doug and 463 for Fred. WOW !! Fred had the backing of Howard and the Republican Party. Doug was endorsed by the Democrats but remained a Republican. He held on to win the election with the absentee count.

I know both Fred and Doug and either one would have been a good Supervisor. But... in my fourteen years, I have never seen a Supervisor sit down and take charge in such a short time, like Doug did. He was a player from January 1, 1996.

Doug has the unique talent of distinguishing bullshit from fact, immediately. That comes in very handy in politics. You deal with more bull shit in politics than a Texas cattleman. As Kevin DeFebbo said, Doug was a breath of fresh air. I don't really think Howard believed he would be as good as he is. I know that Howard respects and believes in Doug now. Doug was a gracious winner and immediately began to attend the Board of Supervisors Committee meetings and full board meetings.

From now to the close of the book, you'll come to recognize the impact Doug Berwanger has had on Wyoming County. God bless ya, Doug.

Chapter 29

The Power Struggle

The day after election, the real race began. Who was going to be the next Chairman of the Wyoming County Board of Supervisors? Department heads, judges, town board members, and the average citizen all wanted to know.

Frankly, I wanted it. I telephoned and contacted each Republican Supervisor asking for their support and also telling them why I thought that I earned the Chairmanship. Bob Bowles wanted it too. Bob was doing the same thing that I was.

In my corner, I had Ken Lowe, Jim Schlick and Ron Herman as active supporters. Bob had Anne Humphrey and Howard for sure. The rest of the Republicans did not indicate their preference with the exception of Arnold Cox. I think Arnold wanted Bob.

Maggie Dadd was the Chair of the Wyoming County Republican Committee. Maggie wanted it settled before it became a floor vote, but she also stayed out of the mix. Maggie was a tremendous Chair. She is very much like Ross Roberts, she's a perfect lady, intelligent, informed and someone who all of Wyoming County can be proud of. I have seen many chairs of the Party, Charlotte Smallwood-Cook, Bill Bruyere, Terry Murphy and Carole Butler. Terry was involved in the Ross versus Urlin fight, which he handled very well. Charlotte and Bill were very strong Chairs and either one of them could have handled it. Carole Butler, the current chair, would not have been able to handle this situation. But Maggie rose to the occasion.

As I mentioned earlier, the Chair is usually the choice of the Party in power. The Republican Supervisors held their first caucus on November 27th at the Port of Ale in Warsaw. It was scheduled just prior to the budget hearing that evening. There were eleven (11) supervisors present and of course Howard Payne was the 12th. At that time, Howard did not feel sure enough of Doug's Republican loyalty, to invite him. All Republican Supervisors were there except Dwight Gillette from Pike. I thought that I had him on my side, too.

Maggie opened up the meeting and thought the two candidates should each speak, followed by questions and answers. I was chosen at random to speak first. I outlined my experience as Vice Chairman and Chairman of the Finance Committee for six years, Member of the Hospital Board, on the Executive Committee of the Association of Towns, on the Board of Governors of NYMIR, Treasurer of the County Republican Committee etc.etc.etc. I then stated that I thought we should follow the direction that Howard had taken. Workers Compensation had to be reformed and we must stand up to the State concerning the Courthouse, Pre K Programs and other unfunded mandates. I was told that it was a pretty decent speech. When I concluded, I asked if there was any questions. Anne Humphrey had one. Anne asked, " Tom, what are you going to do for the women of Wyoming County ? " Well, it was as if someone had hit me in the stomach with a sledge hammer. I was speechless for a couple of seconds. Then I said, " Nothing different than what I intend to do for the men of Wyoming County ". Looking back on it, I still am surprised by the question. I have always insisted that I am not a sexist by any means. And.. I was probably the most progressive on the Board regarding women. My God, I remember in Committee one time when Anne Herod, the Director of Probation said that we would all miss her if she quit and that we would have to pay a lot more in salary to replace her. Howard Payne said, that depends if we hire a man or a woman. I think he was kidding. I hope so.

Bob was next. His speech highlighted his experience in the GLOW solid waste area and his active participation in Western New York inter-county. There were no questions for Bob. I think all supervisors present would have been happy with either one of us. Bob and I were both qualified, experienced and capable of getting the job done.

It was time for a vote. Remember, 11 republican supervisors for the year 1996, were present. The vote was counted by secret paper ballot and guess what. Six votes for Bob and six votes for me! It was a tie!! Howard voted and I am not sure who he voted for. Deadlock.

Maggie scheduled another caucus to be held at the Attica Hotel on December 6, 1995. As luck would have it, Bob and I were both in Warsaw for a Finance Committee meeting that morning. After the meeting, Howard Payne called me into the office. Bob was already sitting down. I sat down and Howard opened up the discussion. Maggie had called him and asked him to intercede and have an agreement reached as soon as possible.

Much was at stake. Neither one of us, wanted this to go to the floor. If we allowed the Democrats to make the choice, the winner would owe the Democrats big time. Keep in mind that I was confident of Doug's support and probably the Democrats with of course the exception of Nelson George. But I still didn't want to owe Alex and the rest of them. It was our dirty laundry and we were not about to hang it in public.

So... Howard looked at me and immediately asked, " Tom, what will it take for you to get out of this race ". I just as quick replied, " Nothing, I am in it until the very end, I believe that I have earned a shot at the Chair and will accept nothing less." Howard then asked Bob the same question. Bob said he would be happy with the Vice Chair and Chairman of Finance Committee. " Fine with me, " I said, " but I do have to call Jim, Ken and Ron for their blessing. "

I called each one and they said, do whatever it takes. Now, that says a lot for Jim Schlick, Ken Lowe and Ron Herman. We had all thought that Jim was going to be the Vice Chairman and the Chairman of Finance. Jim Schlick accepted this for me and for the good of the Republican Party. So, now it was agreed. Tom Moran was going to be Chairman and Bob Bowles was going to be Vice Chairman and I promised that I would appoint him as Chairman of Finance.

We went to lunch with Howard and Anne Humphrey. Bob broke the news to her and she seemed satisfied. To get even with her, Jim Schlick, at the 1999 caucus when Anne was running for Chair, asked her what she was going to do for the men of Wyoming County. We all had a good sense of humor and hold no grudges, with a few exceptions.

I was on cloud nine at the Attica Hotel caucus. I believe the Board was genuinely content with the choice. Some of them saw me as strident, abrasive and loud. Whereas, Bob was a kinder, gentler soft spoken man. But, we sure as hell made the best team that Wyoming County had seen in awhile. We didn't know then that we would actually complement each other. I owe a tremendous thank you to Bob. Without his loyalty and dedication to Wyoming County we could have never accomplished what we did.

To demonstrate my desire to operate as a team, I appointed Ken, Jim, Anne and Bob as an almost quasi-executive committee. I asked them for their advice and input for the Committee structure and appointments. I continued to do so, every year.

The newspapers were bugging everybody. Who was the choice? Wait til 1/2/96 and you'll see. The Batavia Daily came out with an article in the December 23rd issue that said that I was the choice. Howard was quoted, " I think it would be a great choice. I've worked with him very closely for the last six years and I think he'd do a great job if elected". Thanks Howard.

A few words about Howard Payne. I think in many ways, Howard was more than my mentor and colleague. He was always concerned about my health(shoulder) and my family. I remember when he first put me on Finance and County Operations. He asked if I could handle that plus work full-time on the Railroad. I said I'd give it a try. Howard was like that. He may not want to hear it, but he really was a warm and fuzzy guy. He usually had the full cooperation of the full Board. The Board respected him and the position. Everyone liked Howard. His shoes were going to be big to fill. I would give it my best shot.

The Batavia Daily in the 1/9/96 issue wrote,

" In Wyoming County, the County Board of Supervisors elected Thomas R. Moran of Java as Chairman on a 13-3 vote. He replaces Howard Payne who retired. Moran has big shoes to fill. Payne was a strong leader, who led the County through many changes. Moran, who fortunately has the benefit of experience - ten years as Java's representative and six years as Vice Chairman of the Board under Payne. His selection to the chairmanship was not unanimous, apparently falling under party lines. The Republican will need to forge a new working relationship with his Democratic colleagues. Moran believes he is up to the challenge. That attitude and his experience will serve him well"

Chapter 30

The Changing of the Guard

The Holiday season was spent preparing for the Chairmanship and the Committee restructuring. I met with Bob, Anne, Jim and Ken several times. It was agreed to increase the number of Committees to allow for more Supervisors to become active participants.

The organizational meeting of the Wyoming County Board of Supervisors was to be held on January 2nd, 1996. Even though I had commitments from all the Republican supervisors, I was still nervous. I decided that I was not going to the Courthouse until after lunch. The meeting was to start at 2 PM.

To make it easier for me, Jim and Helene Schlick and Ken and Fran Lowe agreed to meet at the Heidelberg Restaurant in Warsaw for lunch. Cindy, Mike, Bridie, Deb Zielinski and Cindy's Uncle Leonard all joined us. I don't know if any of us even knew what we were eating. I know my thoughts were just spinning about everything.

It's very hard to describe in words what it's like. We had the Republican caucus. Everyone knew who was to nominate the Chair, Vice Chair and the Clerk to the Board. We knew we had the votes. So what was the problem?

As an example, I received many Christmas gifts that were designed and planned for my " new office ". I was not going to be the Chair until the full Board of Supervisors elected me. It would have been presumptuous of me to move into the office.

When our entourage arrived at the Courthouse, most of the other supervisors were already there. This was my big day. Because it was also Doug's first meeting, there were even more people. Department heads such as Sheriff Al Capwell, Ron Ely, Lucy Sheedy, Ray Barber, Anne Herod, Marty Mucher and many others were also on hand.

At about 1:50 P.M., Alex Lane called for a Democratic Caucus to be held in Room 13. They were going to plan their course of action. The three Democrats, Alex, Hank Bush and Nelson George also invited Doug Berwanger to attend. Doug told them that he was a Republican. It didn't matter, they said. During the caucus, Doug told me that Alex and Nelson asked him to please vote no on my election. Doug made a statement that he was a loyal Republican, that his family and friends were there to witness this, that he was a friend of mine for years and our kids even go to school together. He also mentioned that there were many people from the Java/Strykersville area present and there was no way that he was not going to vote for me. He said, " No, I am going to vote for Tommy Moran." According to Doug, Alex then slapped her hand on the table, pointed to Doug and shouted, " He's no Democrat "!

2:00 P.M. HERE WE GO , I thought!!!

I sat outside the circle to await the decision. Suzie Aldinger called the organizational meeting to order. Sue then requested that Ron Herman and Paul Agan escort Doug to his seat as the new Supervisor for Arcade. Then she asked for nominations for temporary chairman. Out of respect and honor, Ken Lowe, the senior member, was elected as temporary chairman.

Ken asked for nominations for chairman. Paul Agan and Arnold Cox nominated Thomas R. Moran, from Java as the Chairman of the Wyoming County Board of Supervisors. There were no other nominations. A ROLL CALL vote was taken. All Republicans voted AYE for 1,203 votes. All Democrats voted NO, for 415 votes. I should mention that Alex and Hank's vocal " No " vote was very subdued and polite. Not Nelson. He couldn't wait. There he was in all his glory. Nels was leaning back in his chair which caused his pants to raise high enough that we could view his gorgeous white athletic socks. Ken did the roll call, " Sheldon ", Ken intoned. Nels screams out as if in pain, " NO " . Bob Bowles was elected as Vice Chair by the identical number of votes. Sue was elected unanimously. Way to go, Suzie !

Then it was time for my acceptance speech. It went like this:

" Ten years ago today, I was escorted to my seat by Norm Smith and Barney Erhart, as the newly elected Supervisor of Java. That day, I was so overwhelmed that I never even thought that I would be on this Board for ten years, let alone be your Chairman. I am extremely honored and proud to serve as your Chairman for 1996.

I had a speech completed last week, but I ripped it up yesterday morning. It focused on the general theme of goals and objectives and all the mini-crisis that we will face next year.

We all know that 1996 will be a year of challenge and change being forced upon us by the State and Federal governments. There will be unprecedented cuts in all areas. Health care, as we know it will be completely revamped. The County must also step forward and will with the Cooperative Extension and Farm Bureau to assist the agricultural community anyway we can. Wyoming County will be entering the computer age in 1996. We will actually become a part of the information super highway. Property Tax will be the top priority. The state has to recognize that an unfair taxation system that was created 200 years ago has simply outlived itself.

New Year's Eve, I watched one of my favorite movies, "Rudy", based on a true story. It was about a young man with little athletic ability and below average intelligence, but a whole lot of heart and motivation. His dream was not only to go to the University of Notre Dame, but to actually make the football team as a walk on and play in a game. The theme throughout the movie was, HAVE I DONE EVERYTHING I POSSIBLY COULD? This Board of Supervisors has the same attitude. I can honestly say that every Supervisor in this room puts the people of his or her Town first. This Board does not take any issue lightly, whether it's a three dollar ($3.00) mileage bill or a three million dollar ($3,000,000) courthouse project. Wyoming County is the least taxed county in New York State. I believe that's because of our form of government. As Howard said at last month's meeting, ' There are many counties in the state that envy us'. All of Wyoming County should be proud and I am prouder to serve as your Chairman in 1996. Thank You. "

It's Over !!!!

It's was official. I was the new Chair. The first Chairman from the Town of Java since Frank Cooper in 1912. There's some trivia for you.

Outside it was snowing like hell. Cindy and I had invited everyone to join us at the Port of Ale for an informal reception. We provided cheese, crackers, pepperoni etc. They provided their own drinks. My two buddies, Dave " Sad Dog " Hackett, his wife Dorothy and Bill Becker and his wife Alice also came. So did Mike Zielinski after he got off work. So did Pat and Dave Herrington. I think all Department Heads except Phil Murray were there. Hank was the only Democrat to visit. But.. that's because Hank has class. Hank came up to me at the Port of Ale, and said he was sorry but he had to vote "No" on my election or the rest of the Democrats including this guy, Bob Kersch, the Democratic Chairman would never speak to him. Hank probably wishes he had now. HaHa.

After most people left, Mike and Deb took the kids home. Dave, Dorothy, Bill, Alice, Cindy and myself went over to Smitty's Amber Lantern. Just what we needed, a nightcap for a snowstorm. But, I felt that Smitty's was going to be my satellite office and in many ways, it was.

I couldn't wait for the next day. I moved in and I mean I moved in.

Chapter 31

The Association of Towns

The chairman needs considerable assistance in dealing with Albany and other lobbying efforts. I already had a good rapport with the Association of Towns and now was going to utilize their services even more. The Chairman of the Board must represent not only his (her) fellow Supervisors but all citizens of Wyoming County. I took that responsibility seriously. I made a commitment that the voice of Wyoming County would be heard throughout the State of New York.

I had always been active in the Association of Towns. In fact, I was now serving on the Executive Committee of the New York State Association of Towns. Java, as one of the smallest towns in the state had a representative on the Executive Committee! In 1996, I was also asked to monitor some sessions at the Annual Meeting in New York City. I'll explain.

Back in 1986, when Bob Kibler, Mike Witkowski and myself went to New York City for the Annual Training Session of the Towns, we had no idea what we were doing and we did not know a soul.

The Annual Training Session is always held in New York City. It is expensive to attend. But the results far outweigh the cost. The sessions deal with every aspect of town government; zoning, planning, solid waste, personnel, highway, DEC, Town Board, accounting, comptroller's office, insurance etc. There is also an exhibit area that has just about every state agency located in it. They are manned and available to answer all questions and provide assistance. The sessions are free to walk in and out of. In other words, if a particular session on zoning is concentrating on high rises, you can leave and walk into another class. Jeff Haber, the executive director, once put it best. The people elect the town officials and usually they have no experience or training for those town offices. The Town of Java has over a $600,000 budget. I don't think anyone in Java, wants the Supervisor to be un-informed or ignorant of his (her) responsibility or duties. In the case of Java, we actually saved thousands of dollars by our decision to go with NYMIR for our insurance needs. We would not have known about NYMIR had it not been for a trip to the annual training session. The "networking" is what I always enjoyed best. I don't care if it was at breakfast, break or in a bar, if you talk to the person next to you, you'll find they have the same problems that you have or maybe did have. You can benefit a great deal by listening to their solutions. Of course, in addition to all of the above you will also form friendships that will last for years. Those same acquaintances many times, have the ability or talent to help you or your town in the future. As you can see, I believe fervently in the Association of Towns.

In 1997 at the Annual Training Session, several of us went out to dinner. After dinner, we stopped in at Rosie O'Grady's across from the hotel. We walked into the bar area for a drink when someone shouted, " Tommy, Tommy Moran." I couldn't see where it was coming from or didn't recognize who was yelling. " Tommy Moran, you asshole, you don't even know me." Then I saw who was doing all the hollering. It was Gerry Curre. I hadn't seen Gerry probably in twenty years. Maybe more. We were buddies back in High School at McQuaid. Imagine that!! Go to New York City and you run into Gerry Curre. How the hell did he know it was me? He did have an advantage. Gerry was the President of Rochester Real Estate and was a presenter at one of the sessions on Assessment and Appraisals. He saw my name as one of the moderators and inquired if it was the same Tom Moran he knew. We spent the whole night reminiscing and updating each other. We had lunch together the next day but I haven't seen him since.

I met lots of fantastic people. I still see many of them. One of the greatest people that I met was George Canon from the Town of Newcomb in Essex County. George and I hit it off right from the start. He doesn't take any bullshit and neither do I. John LaPointe and John Kelly come to mind quickly. So does Larry Scott from Farmington, Jeff Hack from Holland. I can't mention them all here. One of the kindest and nicest people was Jack Gilfeather, the Supervisor from the Town of Red Hook. Jack was a Democrat and was even in the minority in his own town. Jack is a gentlemen in every sense and I am proud to have known him. Cindy and I had a few dinners with Jack and his lovely wife, Anne. Great dinners, great conversation and great friendship. In 1999, I had the pleasure of meeting Congressman Rick Lazio from Long Island. I was a moderator at one of the afternoon sessions. The audience was drifting off until Rick filled the room with electricity. As a result of that acquaintance, I was able to schedule Rick as the guest speaker at the 1999 fall fundraiser for the Wyoming County Republican Committee. I hope the future holds great things for Rick.

Essex County is without a doubt, my favorite County next to Wyoming. Not only is it in the Adirondack Park but it also has the greatest people in the State. I once told Cindy that I would love to retire to the Adirondacks. That got a great response. George Canon, Jean Raymond, Dale French also had the best hospitality suite that you would ever want to see. They always invited me and I always went. By 1999, Ron Falconer, John Meyer, Bill Horton and myself had spent considerable time in their suite. We felt that we should help out in some way. I asked George what they needed for supplies. Well, George said they were low on Vodka. Bill Horton, during one of his breaks, bought a bottle at a liquor store.

That evening before dinner, we were going to run it up . Their room was on the 34th floor of the Hotel. John Meyer and Ron Falconer were going to meet me at the bar. I said I'd be right down. I went to the bank of elevators. It was unusually crowded. A large group piled in and we went nowhere. Finally the doors opened and we all got off. I should have known better. I get right back on another elevator. There were probably six or eight people on it. When the doors closed, the elevator shot up like lightning and then down like a rock. Up and down we went, along with our stomachs too. Some of the women were screaming. I don't think I was. Maybe I was, I don't know. I was scared shitless. Jesus ! Then a woman grabbed the phone inside and yelled to someone to have the elevator stopped. Finally, it stopped, the doors opened and we were about 2 feet from the floor of what looked like the basement. I dove through the crowd and jumped out. No, I don't think I knocked anyone over. I looked behind and yelled, " Get off, what're you crazy?" One guy followed me off. The doors immediately slammed shut and the elevator went nuts again. We were in the bowels of the Sheridan Hotel in New York City. There were catwalks all over. Big boiler pipes and stuff like that. The guy behind me asked, "do you know where you are going?" I replied that I knew I wasn't about to go back on that goddamn elevator. After a maze that seemed like a mile long, I opened this huge steel door and there we were. Right at the bank of elevators where we started the trip from hell. I went to the bell desk and told the bell boy that he was going to have to deliver this bottle. I wrote a note where it should go and who it was from. He looked at me as if he was waiting for a tip. Yeah, right, your elevator ride just about killed me and I'm going to give you a tip. I went into the bar to meet Ron and John. Ron told me that he had never seen anyone look like that before. They asked what the hell happened. I told them the story. They laughed and laughed. Ron said it was a good thing that I wasn't on the Titanic. The hell with the women and the children, save your own ass. After dinner, we went back to the bar and saw Dale French from Essex County. I asked him if the vodka was ever delivered. He said No. That son of a bitchin bell boy. I knew he wouldn't deliver it because I refused to give him a tip. I stormed out of the bar and headed for the Manager's desk. I repeated the story. He apologized and gave me a voucher for free drinks at the bar. OK. I guess that made us even. Fire that son-of-a-bitchin' bell boy, though! The next morning I saw George Canon and told him that I really did try to deliver the bottle. George says," Oh yeah, we got that. A bell boy delivered it, thanks." Oh shit. Well, I'm sure the bell boy got another job.

There was also the year when I was a huge fan of Rush Limbaugh. Rush was doing a daily television show from New York City. I wrote them and called them every week for months asking for tickets. No Luck. Finally, I contacted the right person. I explained what a fan I was and that I only visited New York once a year. He asked how many tickets I needed. I told him that I needed ten tickets. I took Ron McCormick, Peggy McCormick, Mary Weinman from Wales, Anne Humphrey, Jeff Hack from Holland and some others. Rush autographed his book that Jeff and I brought to New York. It was great. Rush taped two shows that evening. All of us were on both shows, even though it was for only a brief moment. Afterwards, we all went out for a few drinks promising that we would never forget the evening. Rush, before one of the shows did say that he knew there was a liberal in the audience and if that liberal did not stand up now, he was going to have to embarrass him on national television. The liberal was some guy who had an earring in his ear. You the man, Rush !!! Now leave John McCain out of your wild insults. I still have no idea why Rush believed there was a conspiracy between McCain and the Democrats in the 2000 New York State Republican primary for president. But, he did.

Bill Horton, my good buddy and the Java town justice went every year. Bill is not only a great guy, but he's really a pleasure to be with. Bill had it rougher than most of us. He not only had to attend full day sessions (classes) but he also had to pass a test at the end. That's how he got the certification. The rest of us did not need testing, thank God.

Bill and I would always manage to secure tickets to either a New York Knick's game or a college basketball game at Madison Square Garden. One particular year, we sat in the same section with Woody Allen, Spike Lee and Michael Jackson. We weren't really impressed, we thought we were just as good as they were. Some years we would fly and some years, we took the train.

Just to illustrate what nice guys we were. Janet Zielinski went to New York one year, it was her birthday. John Meyer, Bill and myself treated her to drinks all night. In fact, at one bar, Bill even asked the waitress to bring out a piece of cake for Janet. The entire bar then sang Happy Birthday !!! Of course that was the same year, we had a bad experience at St. Patrick's Cathedral. I almost always attended the Cardinal's Mass on Sunday, while I was there. It was really beautiful, full of pomp and circumstance. This time, I was examining the 'lady' sitting in front of me. Oh My God!! That's no lady, it was a transvestite. Not only did she (he) have hair on his/her arms but he (she) had apparently not shaved that morning. When it came time to shake everybody's hand during the ' peace be with you' routine, I turned around to avoid this person. Janet shook hands with him (her) though.

While in New York City, I always made my annual trek to Mickey Mantle's Restaurant across from Central Park. I would usually have at least one or two lunches there. Mickey Mantle, now, the Mick was my hero. I had the thrill of meeting Mickey twice. Once as a young boy about nine or ten years old. My father and sometimes my mother, would take my brother and myself to see the Cleveland Indians play the Yankees in Cleveland. We would have General Admission for the bleachers. My father always made sure that we got there early enough to sit in the front row in the left field bleachers. The rules were simple. Watch the game, enjoy it, be thankful and don't ask for anything. We always behaved and never asked for a drink, hot dog or anything. But my father would always buy us a drink or something. Now that was about 1958 or 1959. The Yankees team was made up of Yogi Berra, Whitey Ford, Hank Bauer, Elston Howard, Enos Slaughter, Bobby Shantz, Don Larsen etc. Well, this one Sunday, between games of a double header, Bobby

Shantz on his way to the bullpen, throws a baseball up to us. My brother caught the ball. No problem, it's his ball. We are all excited. My father decided that we should hang around after the game to see if we can get any autographs for the ball. The only one we really wanted was Mickey Mantle. I couldn't tell you how long we waited, but sure enough, out of the stadium, came the New York Yankees. There was Yogi, Elston Howard, Bobby Richardson and we were walking along the street with all of them. They were patting us on the head, we were in heaven. Then...... We found Mickey. My brother walked up to him and gave him the ball to sign. Just about then they arrived at the hotel and Mickey was going through the door with OUR baseball. The doorman would not let my brother in. I ran around or under him and yelled to Mickey going through the lobby, " Hey, Mick, give us back the ball." Mickey threw it back and I caught the baseball. Now, I thought it was my baseball. My father decided to have my mother make a ruling on it. She ruled it belonged to my brother. I still dispute the decision. Even today, if I want to start a family fight, all I have to mention is the Mickey Mantle baseball.

In the early 1980's, Cindy called me and said that Mickey Mantle was at the Thruway Plaza in J.C. Penney's promoting Lazy Boy Chairs. I was working 3PM to 11PM in Buffalo and decided that I should stop on my way to work. There was a small line for autographs. I went to Walden Books so that the Mick would have something to sign. I couldn't find a Mickey Mantle Book, but I did find a Yankee paperback book. The title was " Inside the Yankees " by Ed Linn. The cover had a picture of Billy Martin and Reggie Jackson arm in arm. If you are a baseball fan, you will know that Billy Martin never had any love for Reggie Jackson and the feeling was mutual. So what. I flipped the cover open so Mick could sign it quicker. I got up to number one in line, said that I had seen him play as a boy and he was always my hero. He asked me my name and he signed the book, " To Tom, Best Wishes, Mickey Mantle ". Then he flipped the cover closed, saw the picture and asked me where the hell did I buy this? I told him at the bookstore. He was sort of curiously staring at the picture of Martin and Jackson, when I asked him, " are you saying that picture is bullshit "? Mickey replied " you're absolutely correct, it's bullshit ". Nice story, huh? Then a couple of years back, Cindy was having a garage sale and had the book for sale with a price of fifteen cents. Thank God, I found it before anyone else did. From now on, I watch what Cindy is selling very, very closely.

Now back, to New York City. There were some traditions or rituals that we did every year. St. Patrick's, Mickey Mantle's, Fifth Avenue, F.A.O. Schwartz and Central Park. The theme of it all, was that we met some great people, bartenders, cab drivers, waitresses, town officials, state officials, vendors and many others that all had a part in improving and educating our fertile minds.

The last few years, it seemed as if I knew everyone there, other town officials, vendors and the people from the state agencies. It gave us even more influence around the state. They all knew where Java and Wyoming County was. In 1999, I was given the ultimate honor. I was elected as a Vice President of the Association of Towns. Had I stuck around for about three more years, I probably would have become the President of the Association. The first in Wyoming County since Woody Kelly from Perry. I have no regrets about going and would urge all town officials and residents to urge their officials to attend the training session and become involved in the Association. They are there for your needs. In fact, Jim Schlick and myself used their services rather than pay a Town Attorney for his opinion. It saved a lot of money in our towns. They could provide the town with a sample Local Law or Ordinance for just about anything imaginable. I hope that I have made the case for the Association of Towns.

Hats off and special thanks to Jeff, Kevin, Murray, Marie and many others at the Association of Towns. You made my job a lot easier. You were always there with one thing in mind, how can we all improve town government for the benefit of the people.

Chapter 32

Change is in the Air

One of the first changes that I made, after taking over, was in the handling of the mail. I called Sue, Janet Coveny, the Deputy Clerk, Kathy Schwab and Cheryl Mayer all in for a staff meeting. Kevin DeFebbo was also there. This is what I told them.

I was not going to open the mail for various reasons. If I opened it, I would have to forward or distribute it to the necessary parties. I did not know everything about everything. I am not a very good filer, to put it mildly. The extent of my files are simply, correspondence to and from and meetings. I was elected as the Chair, not clerk or secretary. Also, I asked them to please give me only copies and to always keep one for the Official Board files. Simple enough.

My door was always open. I believed that the employees were the people that made the County. The employees in the county also made the department heads and Supervisors look good. We always had a theory on the railroad that if you really wanted to know what was going on anywhere, all you had to do was ask the janitor. I still think that's true in any organization. I managed through empowerment. I empowered the employees to make the correct decision. Usually they would too. I hate and I mean I hate, micro-management. That is where all the fighting begins.

The classic example of micro management is the practice of the Supervisors reviewing and approving every bill that is submitted to the County. Wyoming County has had it both ways and many times in the last 14 years. When I was newly elected, I was on the audit committee, chaired by Barney Erhart. The committee would meet in the evenings. Sometimes, the meeting would last for hours. The meeting wasn't about the bills though. It was down right nit picking with a general theme of nailing someone.

It can be a potentially dangerous activity. It allows the Supervisors to target certain departments or individuals that they have a problem with. It can become highly personal. I know, I've been there. Take the youth department for instance.

One year, Patti Hughes decided that she and the Youth Committee were going to assess fines on three towns, including Java. Well, one of the other towns was Eagle and Supervisor Rita George (Democrat) and myself were on the audit committee for bills. We focused on every bill for the Youth Board. It was personal and I admit, we were trying to get even by trying to force Patti to change her mind. The other problem that I had with the bills was that we hopefully hired the best people available as our Department Heads. They were experienced and educated in their fields. Who were we to tell a highway superintendent that we thought they could find a wacthemcallit at a better price at the local hardware store. Who are we to tell that same highway superintendent that we didn't believe he needed that certain item for his operation. If that was true, then we didn't need him. We should be the highway superintendent. For those that believe we should scrutinize each bill for math and policy, we do. There is staff in every department that checks the math, the department head then signs it and then the Audit Clerk in the Board of Supervisors rechecks and verifies that it is a legitimate and legal expense to the County.

We worked at stopping or reducing micro management at the county level and I know we did make some great progress.

All travel requests previously had to be signed by the Chairman. Even if the department head or employee was only going to Batavia or Buffalo for a one day training session, or a deputy had to transport a prisoner, the Chairman had to sign the form. I eliminated the need for the form altogether if it was only a day trip out of the County. Overnight travel still needed committee approval but not the Chairman's signature. Then we modified that too, and gave the county administrator the authority to approve travel. While I was Vice Chairman, sometimes I would come and have to sign a stack of travel forms that meant absolutely nothing. If this travel is in the budget, it apparently was necessary. If there was abuse, we could fire the abuser. We did not want to punish all others including ourselves for no reason.

I also gave all grievance procedures and union matters to the county administrator. I did not think it was proper or ethical to have an elected individual rule either against or in favor of one of their constituents. It also takes the lobbying from the union out of the equation. Anyway that's what we pay Kevin the big bucks for.

I also wanted the Board of Supervisors to focus on setting policy and direction for Wyoming County. In an ongoing battle, Kevin and I urged all department heads to go through the county administrator's office for requests. We did not want a department to go to their committee chair or the Chairman of the Board on any issue. Of course, if the department head disagreed with the county administrator, they could take whatever action they felt proper.

I think the most revolutionary change was the atmosphere that we were creating. At the committee meetings, we no longer wanted to hear how great the department heads were. We wanted to know what the real problems were, what we would be faced with down the road. Kevin and the Board of Supervisors wanted to make it perfectly clear that no idea was out of bounds. We were a board that would consider any change for the good of the county and its residents. We all wanted to make a difference.

The Board, Kevin, Sue and myself had high expectations.

Chapter 33

Nasty, Nasty, Nasty

Let me preface this chapter by informing you that the following chapter alludes to some devout Catholics or at least they perceive themselves that way. In fact, one or two of them are Eucharistic Ministers in the Church. All of them attend church on a regular basis. Therefore; if you believe the catholic religion to be the only true religion, please do not read any further. I hate to piss in your Cheerios but I am going to show you that a great many Catholics, in Java at least, are true hypocrites. Anyway, here goes.

1996 started off nasty. It only got worse. Remember, I had defeated Charlie McCormick when many thought that I was going to lose the election. In January, Ron McCormick suggested that Charlie attend the Association of Towns Meetings in New York City. The motion passed and Charlie was on his way. This was the same Ron and the same Town Board who did not think it proper that Justice Horton attend. The same Ron and the same Town Board who did not think the Court Clerk should attend at 50% cost sharing between Java and Holland. The same Ron and the same Town Board who wanted to limit the number of town officials from attending. Charlie was attending as the Zoning Board Chairman. Imagine ! The little Town of Java was now going to spend $700 + to send Charlie to the Big Apple.

I saw Charlie three times while I was in New York. Sunday night, while Bill and I were talking to about a half dozen people from around the state, Charlie poked his head into the Lounge and pulled his head out just as fast. The next morning at breakfast, I sat behind him. He didn't know that I was within ear shot. Charlie was bitching to the guy next to him about me. The third time was later in the day, he was standing at the top of the escalator at the Hilton Hotel, in New York City in all his glory. Get the picture ? At March's meeting, he said and I quote, " I got a lot out of New York." Well... OK Charlie.

Ron and Don nit picked everything. They even refused to reimburse Darlene Hackett, the Court Clerk for $22 for the purchase of some office supplies. They had serious problems with Town Attorney Jim Maloney because of his friendship with me. Ron thought I spent too much time in Warsaw. They were both opposed to the transfer station, town park and the prosecutor position.

Now I'm no genius, but why would they expect me to appoint somebody that was a real thorn in my side to be my deputy supervisor? Anyway.. I abolished the position of deputy that Ron had held. It made sense to me. Well, he went bonkers. In the minutes of the Town Board meeting, he demanded that we go into executive session to discuss it. I said, sure we can go into executive session, but I am not going to change my mind. " You are done ", I told him.

Now add Joanne Almeter, MY BOOKKEEPER and MY APPOINTEE and Janet Zielinski into the stew. Now, Ron, Joanne, Don and Janet were establishing a "secret society". Joanne kept the books from me. I even had to request them at Town Board Meetings. Janet was not notifying me of zoning and planning meetings. "Keep the Supervisor" in the dark was the general theme.

Some bills and reimbursement payments were not being paid. Either because Joanne did not want to or she thought she could hurt me personally. The books were never at the town building. There was a question at the March Board meeting on a bill so I went to the file and the books were not there. This was verified in Janet's minutes. The Town Board could not get explanations and answers. In July, 1996, I could not produce my Supervisor's Report because Joanne had not given me her revenue figures. In September, I had to formally request that Joanne provide me with the books so that I could complete the town budget. Again, this was documented in Janet's minutes. The Wyoming County Bank was calling me more often because we were overdrawn on the checking account. The reason for that was that Joanne was intentionally not informing me when a transfer was needed!!!

I talked to other Supervisors about how they handled the bookkeeper duties. Some, contrary to recommendations of the State Comptroller, did their own. Most contracted with someone else. Warsaw contracted with an accounting firm in Nunda. Towns in other counties, used accounting firms, other people and some towns in Monroe County used Paychex. I had a representative from Paychex attend two meetings. The poor guy was treated rudely, discourteously and nastily. Ron, Don and Joanne all stated in the board minutes that the state comptroller did " not like the idea " or " something is wrong there ". When I contacted the comptroller's office, I was told otherwise. Ron erroneously said that the comptroller's office did not like electronic transfers. Now I know that to be not true. The state utilizes electronic transfer whenever they possibly can. Don said on July 9, 1996, " I don't like computers." Maybe we should have brought Bill Gates in for lunch with Don. I had contacted another firm in Arcade, who also gave us a proposal. The savings to the taxpayers was over $2,500, annually. No go, though, because of Ron, Joanne and Don..

In addition to being the new Chairman of the Board, I had also been appointed to the Executive Committee of the Association of Towns, and appointed to various other boards including the Advisory Committee of the Wyoming County Bank. I think all that recognition and responsibility was pissing them off. Ron and Joanne in the Town Board minutes claimed that the Bank Advisory Committee was a direct conflict of interest. I asked the Association of Towns to research past opinions from the Comptroller. The decision was that it was NOT a conflict nor did it even appear to be a question of unethical action.

The last moment for Joanne as bookkeeper came in November. The board had unanimously approved a resolution to borrow $42,000 from the Wyoming County Bank at 4.15% interest. The $42,000 was for the balance due for a new loader. A couple of weeks after the borrowing, Joanne asked me where the $42,000 was. I told her that the bank had automatically deposited the money into the highway account. This conversation was on a week-end. She then told me that the money was NOT in the bank and she had notified the comptroller's office. I did not sleep well that week-end. My mind was racing. Was it one of those terrible electronic transfers? Did some bank employee make an error or worse? Did some employee somehow embezzle this money? I could not imagine. As soon as the bank opened the next Monday morning, I called Donna Powers who verified that the money surely was there and had been in the highway checking account. "Could you fax that to me, Donna? ", I asked. She did. The day that I told Joanne that I was not going to reappoint her in January, I asked her why she would make a false statement like that. She did not respond. Some of this is discussed in the " Meeting from Hell " which follows.

The Town Board usually conducted a year end meeting to pay any bills that were received between the board meeting and the day of the year end meeting. It is not a requirement. In fact, for many years, there was a party atmosphere at year end. Everyone would bring a dish to pass etc. Some towns would even go out to dinner. I scheduled our 1996 year end meeting for December 26th at 10:00 A.M. If anyone takes the initiative to check the minutes, they read mistakenly 12/28/96 at 8:00 P.M. The meeting was Saturday morning at ten. It was my worst meeting ever. It was the worst day of my life. It was by far my worst day as Supervisor. It was, for sure, the worst that I ever felt. These people were friends whom I had done favors for over the years. It hurt and I mean it really hurt. It went something like this.

I had given Joanne the news that she was not going to be reappointed. The following people were, for some reason, roped or urged to show up at the year end meeting to watch the town board only pay the bills. There was nothing else on the agenda. According to the minutes: " also present, Joanne Almeter, Ron George, Shawn and Pat Almeter, Gert Hamm, Jeff Hamm, Paul Keenan, Mark Powers, Ken Unger, Ron Bishoff, Dick and Pat Anger, Dan McNulty, Nelson George, Town of Sheldon's Supervisor, Charlie McCormick, Jerry Crabb, Henry Rose, Herman and Esther Miller, Tracey George."

That meeting was simply to beat up Moran. And they did. I got blasted from most of them for everything from the Town Attorney, Town Prosecutor, Bill Horton's telephone bill, why Bill was going to New York and who the hell did I think I was to fire Joanne?

First, I TRIED to explain that she was not fired, she was simply not being reappointed. I also tried to explain over their shouting, that the bookkeeper position was the appointment of the Supervisor. I had checked it out with an attorney, the comptroller's office and civil service. I think everyone knows now that I was correct. Otherwise, my decision would have been overruled. The mob, and that's really what they were, did not want to hear it. They had already made up their minds. I was wrong and Joanne and the rest of them were the only ones capable of telling the absolute truth or so they thought.

Most of those in attendance had a ball. They were smiling, joking and laughing at my expense. One even inferred that perhaps I was guilty of something if I could not sleep the night

Joanne said the $42,000 was missing or not in the bank. How dare they! I hope that each of them has spent some time considering that awful morning. I am quite sure that they have seen the light now. I also really hope that no other elected official ever has to experience that.

As soon as we were adjourned, I left the building to laughter and sneers kind of like a bunch of hyenas going in for the kill. I went home immediately. Cindy looked at me and asked " what the hell happened? " I told her and she said, " Quit, let those assholes run the Town if they think they can do a better job." I said " you know you're probably right ". I was the Supervisor because I loved the town, the people and the job. If it was coming to this, what's the point. I mean it was public ridicule. They were mean. They were vicious, malicious, hateful and definitely not Christian. Again, I don't want to sound like a woose but JESUS CHRIST. I hope none of the readers have to ever experience an attack like I did that morning. It was not deserved nor was it justified.

To put it bluntly, I could not get along with Joanne. Joanne was MY employee and I had to let her go. Period. Had personalities not come into it, the town would have contracted with the firm from Nunda and we would have realized $10,000 in savings with no problems regarding the books. But... I was not allowed to exercise my right as Supervisor. Even in January of 1997, when I appointed Debi Heterbring as the bookkeeper, I recommended a salary of $2400 and a contract with CPS of Arcade to do the payroll for $1680. No Go. I was overruled. The Town Councilmen wanted the salary to be $5,000. Sure, let's pay an additional $1,000 !! It's only going to be paid by the taxpayers.

Afterward, I went to the Sad Dog Saloon. I told Dave Hackett what had happened. " Those dirty son of a bitches, " I said. He said that he understood how I felt and would not blame me for quitting. He did say that I should stick it out. Dave was apparently so concerned about my well being, that he went over and shut the lights off and locked the doors, in the Saloon. He did not want any of the attendees to come in from the meeting. Thanks, Dave. One other mention, John Meyer actually came down in the afternoon to see how I was doing. Thanks, John. No one else did.

Still, it got much worse than that. More accusations and lies were about to surface.

Of those twenty eight in attendance, I probably am one of the worst for attending church on a regular basis. But, I can say that I could not do what they did. Nor could I ever tell a lie or start a rumor about someone that I knew was going to hurt them and their family. I've often wondered why anyone would start a rumor. Do they get up in the morning and say, well I think I am going to hurt someone today? Maybe they actually dream these rumors up in church. They're obviously not listening to the priest or the prayers. I really do believe that a rumor spreader is morally right behind the assailant. <u>The assailant inflicts bodily injury and the rumor spreader inflicts emotional injury on the target and his family.</u>

I would consider that this book was a success and well worth the effort if I could just convince one person out there not to spread or even listen to a rumor. After all, in the Holy Bible, Book of Exodus, Chapter 20, verse 16 when God gave Moses the Ten Commandments, He instructed us not to bear false witness. Do the rumor mongers just forget that or do they only have nine commandments?

Chapter 34

The Removal of the Old Jail

Well, I survived that mean spirited ordeal and was now ready to move onto more important issues, like the old jail.

On Friday, July 5, 1901 the building committee of the Board of Supervisors designated the exact location of the new jail and sheriff's residence. The low bid went to VanDorn Iron Works, a very reputable jail construction firm out of Cleveland, Ohio. On Friday March 14, 1902, Sheriff W.S. Sanford, accepted the keys to the jail and his new residence. The total cost of both buildings was $24,987.42. There was a brick addition built on in 1948. It remained as a jail and sheriff's residence until Allen L. Capwell was elected in 1973. Sheriff Capwell and his family decided that they would remain in their own home. The sheriff's residence was then converted to office space for the department.

After the new jail was built in 1991, the Sheriff's Department relocated from the old one to the new one in January of 1992. The jail and the sheriff's residence now stood exactly as they had when they were vacated. Utilities were shut off and the buildings deteriorated. When I say, they were allowed to become run down, I mean everyone was responsible. The Public, the Board of Supervisors, the Historical Society, and even the residents. It did not take long before it became necessary to fence the area in. It was now not only an eyesore but also a serious threat to safety and health. After one ice storm, the tree in front came crashing down on the residence. More damage was done. It was a disgrace and an embarrassment to the Historical Monument District and to the Courthouse.

After becoming the Chairman, Jim Schlick, Ken Lowe, Doug Berwanger and myself walked through both buildings. The buildings had to be removed. There was no other alternative. We had no other option. They were both disasters. They had to be removed and the quicker the better. Besides the safety issue, it was assumed that the site was eventually going to become the site of the new Courthouse, if we decided to build it.

The demolition was one of my top priorities. Not all felt the same way that I did. There were many preservationists that wanted to save the buildings at all costs. Some even wanted to convert it into office space. The cost estimates for that type of renovation were astronomical.

On February 15, 1996 the Board voted 12 - 4 to spend $7,000 for the Sear Brown Group to develop specifications to proceed with the removal of asbestos and lead based paint and demolition of the structures. Alex Lane, Anne Humphrey, Nelson George and Suzanne West voted no on the resolution. In March, the Board agreed to actually solicit bids for the demolition.

I began corresponding with the N.Y.S. Office of Parks, Recreation and Historic Preservation (SHPO) about our intentions. I was dealing with Richard Lord who was the Historic Sites Restoration Coordinator. I also was in contact with Ray Barber, the county historian, the Wyoming County Historians and, of course, David Lane of the Warsaw Historical Society.

All of the above had legitimate concerns. If we had all the resources and more land, we could have attempted to restore the buildings. The Jail portion was out of the question. The bars of the cells were separated from the floors and walls. The structure was actually coming down on its own. The bars were covered with lead based paint. There was simply nothing to save in the jail. The house was just about as bad. In fact, after the demolition bids were accepted, it was discovered by the contractor that the roof was not safe enough to put men on it to remove the asbestos. The contractor was required to secure a variance from the State DEC to allow the asbestos removal of the roof to take place after the building was down.

I wanted to satisfy those concerned with historic preservation wherever we could. It was agreed to save as many bricks and window sills as possible. Today, the sign in front of the new courthouse includes bricks and the portals from the old sheriff's house and jail. There also is a bronze plaque that notes the site of the original sheriff's residence.

Finally, on June 11, 1996, the Board voted to contract with Integrated Waste Special Services of Rochester for the demolition for $57,895. Bob Bowles joined Alex, Suzanne West, Nelson George and Anne Humphrey voting no on the resolution. So, there we have it, they built it for $24,987 and we demolished it for $57,895. Justice?

Anne Humphrey is a real preservationist and this action truly disturbed her. Anne felt and still does feel strongly that it is our responsibility to maintain and preserve what we can. Jim Schlick does not quite have the same feelings and opinions. In one of our tense meetings over this issue, Jim spoke faster than he was thinking. Jim said to Anne, " Don't worry about it Annie, we'll build you another historic building. " Believe it or not, it did ease a great deal of stress in the room and I think everyone smiled, except of course Nelson. Anne still reminds Jim of his promise that day.

I did have several conversations with Mr. Lord from the State Historic Office. They were not all good ones. Mr. Lord had a job to do and I can understand that. However; Mr. Lord had never visited Warsaw to see the conditions of the buildings. He simply wrote three page letters with technicalities as to why the County could not demolish this complex. I invited him to Warsaw to have a personal inspection, first hand. On July 28th, he called again and said that he would appreciate a little more time. "A little more time, Rick, where have you been for the past seven months". I snapped back at him and then told him that " he better think fast because the building is coming down tomorrow. "

On July 29, the work crew began their task and by the end of the day, all that was left was a pile of rubble. It took months to remove all of it but it was done. David Lane in the Daily News of 8/17/96 said it was worth fighting for and , " We did what good citizens should do, which was bring it up to the supervisors. They chose to go their own route." Lane said he was concerned about the courthouse. David was right to be concerned and the Board is still addressing that issue as I write this book. The original courthouse will be renovated, brought up to standards and will remain a part of a beautiful Monument Historic District.

Looking back on the demolition, I still don't think we had a choice and if we did not take that action my question would be,

" WHERE IS THE NEW COURTHOUSE GOING TO BE ?"

Chapter 35

The Mouse that Roared

In the 1980's a tax-rich and liberal Federal Government passed legislation that would provide services for children with disabilities. The States were given great flexibility to comply with this federal mandate. New York State not only complied but surpassed the mandates. In New York State, the counties have been mandated to fund this program since 1989. We were the Cadillac of a service provider. New York State also passed the enormous cost of this worthwhile program on to the counties.

As is the case with all laws, it had good intentions. The Early Intervention (EI) Program and the Pre-Kindergarten Program would allow most of these children to be mainstreamed in the school system when they were five years of age. Their disabilities ranged from simple speech and motor delay to more severely handicapped conditions such as cerebral palsy and autism.

I will attempt to give you a theoretical example of the governmental process:

- *First, Parents notice that little Tommy age 4 does not speak or speaks very little. Then*
- *Tommy is referred to the local Committee for Preschool Special Education (CPSE).*
- *CPSE then sends the parents a list of evaluators.*
- *The evaluation is completed and results sent back to CPSE.*
- *An evaluator determines the services Tommy needs and*
- *Tommy's parents are given a list of providers.*
- *Tommy's parents choose the provider they prefer.*
- *Tommy is then provided with transportation, unless the parents are able to provide it and then*
- *the county begins to pay up-front for the tuition and transportation costs*

Obviously, I have deliberately made this example very simple and basic. Sometimes, the child needs year-round services. Sometimes, the child needs an attendant in the bus or vehicle. The state's fiscal year runs from April 1, till March 31. The State Education Department (SED) will not even entertain a reimbursement form until the completion of the school year.

Now, you can see that the county is beginning to pay Tommy's tuition and transportation costs in September with no money coming back until June of the following year. The State is required to reimburse the county at 59.5%, when it gets around to it.

In 1989, the entire budget for the Pre School Program was $660,000

In 1996, the budget was $1,362,270!!!

That's double in my math. In 1996 the county served **62** children

In April of 1996, the State Education Department owed Wyoming County $661,000. That was not acceptable. That figure translated into almost 10% of the entire real property tax. It seemed we were becoming a loan bank for the State of New York. One month earlier the SED had asked the counties to please hold all reimbursement vouchers because they were out of money. Imagine, the State Education Department was out of money. SO? What were we supposed to do?

Wyoming County took the lead in rectifying this problem. Bob Bowles, Chairman of Finance Committee and Madonna Barber, Chair of the Public Health Committee took charge. On April 9, 1996, Madonna Barber introduced a resolution that stated that Wyoming County would no longer fund the state's share of the Pre-K program. John Zagame was the Executive Director of the New York State Association of Counties in 1996. John knew what we were doing and was fully supportive. In fact, in an unprecedented move, Zagame telephoned my Office while we were in session. Kathy Schwab interrupted the meeting and I called for a recess to talk with John Zagame.

Zagame informed me that NYSAC (New York State Association of Counties) was willing and able to provide the legal backing for Wyoming County. He also told the entire Board over a conference call that he had written to Governor Pataki and asked for his intercession. Zagame called it a courageous action and one that should have state wide support.

Now it was time for me to call the roll. Alex Lane was absent. The vote was 14-1. Nelson George voted no, as usual.

The Board's intention was not to hurt or halt the programs. We wanted to send a message to Albany that we were mad as hell and we were not going to take it anymore.

There were many other reasons why the state could not pay its bill to the counties. The pre school program was historically under funded. As an example, in 1996, the state budgeted

$464,100,000 and actually spent $813,216,851. This was a program, or I should say an unfunded mandate, that was totally out of control.

Almost at once, I was asked to attend a meeting between the County Board Chairs and the Governor, in Albany. I traveled to Albany for about the fourth time in three months. I was beginning to know the city, in more ways than I wanted to. I saw the REAL grid lock, the games and the pettiness that are part of day to day activities in Albany.

The day before the meeting, I was traveling on the Thruway, when Mary Hanak of the County Legislators and Supervisors Organization called me on my cell phone. Mary asked me if I knew that I was going to speak at the meeting on the Pre-K Program and what it was doing to the counties throughout the state. Nope, I did not know that. Great!!!

I arrived at the Omni Hotel in Albany and ran into my old friend and fellow board chair, John Walchli from Allegany County. In the bar, I met many of the board chairs from around the state including Bob Gaffney, George Canon, Ray Meier and others. John Zagame, Ken and others from the staff were also there. We decided to have a few beers and decide what I was going to tell Governor Pataki, the next morning.

That morning, I decided to pay a visit to the State Education Department. It was similar to the trip to see the Governor, but I had another purpose this time. I approached the first receptionist and introduced myself. " And what can we do for you? ", she asked. " I just came here to see if the check is ready to be picked up for Wyoming County ", I explained. I was directed to the proper department and I asked them the same question. I did get a lot of smiles as I hoped I would. However, I'm also sure that those in power heard about my request.

It was the hottest day in April in Albany history. People were lying out on the grass rather than in their offices. It was like a hot and humid August afternoon. We were to meet in the Governor's Chambers at 1:00 P.M. I did not know for sure what I was going to say.

There were probably about thirty of us, including staff from NYSAC. Gay Petri, was one of the experts on the staff that did a great job in briefing me. We waited and waited for the Governor. Sweet Jesus, it was hot. The windows were still shut for the winter and the air conditioning was not ready to be turned on yet. Finally, this huge oak door opened and in walked Governor

George Pataki. The Governor sat down at a table in the front of the room. We were all seated in rows of chairs in front of him, and of course I was in the front row. There was a microphone in the center. As soon as the governor sat down, one of his aides brought in a pitcher of ice water. I think the pitcher had more ice cubes in it than it did water. But my God, it looked good. I was dying of thirst. Pataki poured himself a glass, slowly sloshed it around and even more slowly sipped from the cold glass. It was as if I had been on the desert for days without water and here comes this guy who was unknowingly torturing the shit out of me with a glass of ice water.

John Zagame opened the meeting and introduced Bob Gaffney, the President and county executive from Nassau County. Bob Gaffney was a terrific speaker and thanked the Governor for taking the time to meet with the Board Chairs.

" Now, I'd like to introduce Tom Moran, the Chairman of the Wyoming County Board of Supervisors", Bob Gaffney announced.

I thanked the Governor for his time and proceeded to tell him how bad things were out in the field.

"Governor, do you realize that the State owes little Wyoming County nearly $700,000? We would have to raise property tax by ten percent if this continues. Wyoming cannot afford to lend the State money. We are a small rural county. Let me tell you how small we are. If every man, woman, child and inmate in Wyoming County attends a Buffalo Bill football game in Rich Stadium, the stadium would only be half full. We don't ask a lot of the state. Simply, pay the bills please."

The Governor sympathized with us, but..... it was out of his hands, he said. The State Education Department is free to do what they want. Zagame then mentioned yes the SED is an independent agency, but the Governor and legislature control its budget.

On Memorial Day, May 26, 1996, Bob Bowles and myself traveled to Albany again. This time, we were there to file a lawsuit on behalf of the Association of Counties against the State for late payment and money owed for the Pre-K Program. The lawsuit papers were being filed at the Albany County Courthouse and John Zagame asked if we would please attend.

Tuesday morning, Bob and I went to the NYSAC Offices to meet with Zagame. John was also going to have Mike Breslin, the Albany County Executive there. We all walked from the

NYSAC Office to the Courthouse. I asked John Zagame if I was going to have to speak. John immediately said, " No, I'll do the talking." Great ! Phew!

At the Courthouse, there had to be twenty or thirty reporters from newspapers, magazines, tv and radio stations. John Zagame did an excellent job of giving the explanation for the lawsuit. Without missing a beat, he then said, " And now I'd like to introduce the Chairman of the Wyoming County Board of Supervisors." Gulp and double gulp. Zagame and Bob said that I did alright, but I was not prepared at all. That's the way John Zagame was. I had and still have the utmost respect for that man. John Zagame really cared for the counties of New York and always had their best interest at heart. He also had guts.

It did not take long for action. By the time Bob Bowles and I returned to Wyoming County, the State Education Department had called Patti Hughes, the Coordinator and Director of Wyoming County's program. The SED said they did not owe us that much and our figures were wrong.

Patti and her Fiscal Manager, Keri Belden worked the next couple of nights. Kevin DeFebbo and I also had our auditors check and double check the figures. Sorry, the state does owe Wyoming County over $660,000. I received a call from the state education department, they were ready to settle this mess. They would immediately cut a check for $11,000 and we were even. Excuse Me?

I telephoned Mike Brady from Assemblyman Tom Reynold's Office. Mike had some influence in Albany and used the Budget Office to verify our figures. We were right!! Patti and Keri Belden did a nice job!

Do you see what I mean, you just can't trust somebody from Albany? Remember what I said about governments working slowly. Well, at least the Governor did appropriate more money so Wyoming County could get our money. The County was sued by the providers of the services, so we had to relent. NYSAC held their lawsuit in abeyance as a weapon for future state refusal to accept their responsibilities. Unfortunately even as late as 1998, we were still finding it necessary to travel to Albany to present our case. The last time though was the best. Madonna Barber, Patti Hughes, Kevin DeFebbo and myself all went.

We had made arrangements to meet with the budget department people, the State Education Department people and Tom Reynolds' staff. Tom sent Steve Guerin who was simply fabulous. Steve probably knew more about Albany and its workings than Nelson Rockefeller. We had boxes of documents that substantiated all of our figures. Patti was more than prepared.

Everyone walked in. I opened the meeting and turned it over to Kevin. Kevin basically said, that we were sick and tired of making this trip. We want our money and we want it now. Kevin also told the budget people that they did not know what the hell was going on and that State Education Department simply wanted to make it difficult and at times impossible to receive any reimbursement. Finally the SED representative said he needed proof. We said that it was fine and to take these boxes back, review them and send us a check. They did on all counts. Wyoming County was the first county in the state to receive all the dollars owed to us.

What were the results of this? As I said, the Governor began to budget more money for the program. The State Education with the advice of NYSAC began to make some reforms to the program. Wyoming County was known in Albany. Whenever and wherever I traveled, I was treated with respect because I was representing Wyoming County.

To this day, there are counties in New York state that do not have the foggiest idea of how much if any the State owes them for the pre-K Program. Wyoming County does. It was because of Bob Bowles, Madonna Barber, Patti Hughes, Keri Belden and of course Kevin DeFebbo. I am confident that with the addition of Paula Parker, Wyoming County will never be in that position again.

Before I close this chapter, let me summarize:

- *The Federal and State Government created a very worthy program but -*
- *It really was a Federal and State Program and -*
- *The State did not fulfill its responsibility to the counties and did not pay its fair share of the costs*

Chapter 36

The New Courthouse

Since late 1995, when Howard Payne gave the Planning Committee the responsibility of handling the new Courthouse, no real action was really taken. In 1996, when I became Chairman, I left Anne Humphrey as chair of the Planning Committee and requested that she and the committee continue to do what they were doing which was nothing. The committee was meeting, and discussing the issue but deliberately was taking no action. Then in the second week of 1996, I received a nasty letter from the Office of Court Administration inquiring as to what exactly Wyoming County's intentions were.

On Tuesday, March 12, 1996, the New York State Association of Counties through the efforts of John Zagame and President Bob Gaffney, scheduled a meeting with the remaining fourteen (14) Counties that had not satisfied the requirements of the Office of Court Administration (OCA). The meeting was held in the office of Judge Jonathan Lippman who was the Deputy Chief Administrator of the State Court System. Judge Lippman's office was located in the Empire State Plaza in Albany.

That meeting happened to be the second Tuesday of the month which was also the full Board of Supervisor's Meeting and also the Java Town Board Meeting. Therefore; Bob Bowles had to conduct the County Board Meeting as it was necessary for me to fly to Albany because of the contentious situation in Java.

Things were so bad in Java, that I must tell you what the rumor was regarding my flying to Albany. In March, the Catholic Diocese, annually conducts the fund raiser for Catholic Charities. Don Roche was one of those volunteers that went door to door collecting for the good cause. Don told two of my friends that I was drunk at the Town Board Meeting on March 12th.

My good old friend, Don. Apparently he too forgot Moses and the Ten Commandments.

Java is a small Town, so I learned of this " rumor " almost immediately. I telephoned Don Roche and confronted him about the rumor. At first, Roche denied ever saying anything like that. I was relentless and insisted on knowing why he would say anything like that. " Don, you know full well, that I have never even had a drink or a beer, the day of a Board Meeting or any other meeting." There are plenty of witnesses to that also. I also told him the names of the individuals whom he did tell.

Finally, Don Roche admitted he did say that I had been drinking before the Board Meeting. Why, Don, would you say something like that? Roche assumed that because I had flown to Albany that day and everybody drinks on airplanes, I was drunk. Yup. Because I flew to Albany on a plane, I must have had been drinking because that's what everybody does on a plane.

Imagine !!! Don was collecting for Catholic Charities and then spreading a malicious, totally fabricated rumor. Was it political desperation at its worse or was it personal animosity?

Back to the Albany meeting, John Walchli, Chair of Allegany County, Jim Keane and Steve Casey from Erie County were also present from Western New York. I should mention that Scott Schrader, the Deputy County Administrator from Jefferson County was also there. Scott is a native of Strykersville and a very good friend of mine.

John Zagame and Bob Gaffney opened the meeting up with their own remarks. The general theme was that fourteen counties simply could not afford new courthouses at this time. These counties needed cooperation, a little patience from the state and would appreciate a five year moratorium on the OCA mandates. NYSAC also wanted to see some of the standards relaxed in the event that a county could build a scaled down version of a courthouse, that would ultimately be less expensive.

Erie County was by far the biggest county that had still refused to comply. Jim Keane who is also a dear friend of mine was representing Erie County. Jimmy said that Erie County had not even chosen a site yet. They wanted some breathing room not deadlines. Erie County also had a public hospital that was facing huge cuts. In fact, all of the counties were also being faced with deficits from their county nursing homes. Onondaga County (Syracuse) indicated that they were faced with a $300 million dollar clean up of the lake in addition to being required to build a new $15 million jail. John Walchli said that Allegany had reached its constitutional debt limit. John also had letters from the county judges, district attorney, public defender and the county attorney stating that they did not think there was a need for a new courthouse.

I restated my position that we only have 40,000 residents. Wyoming County simply did not have the tax base to spread such cost around. If built, it would increase the property tax between $.75 cents and $1.00 per thousand of assessed value. That did not take into consideration the union contract with our employees, cuts to the hospital, probation, district attorney, public defender and all the other threatened cuts from the state. Wyoming County always tried to do more with less.

Judge Lippman responded to us all, in general. He was very eloquent. The Judge would not agree to any five year moratorium because in his view, nothing would get done including planning and design etc. He stated that he did sympathize with us and would work in full cooperation to come up with an agreed solution. Judge Lippman promised that communication would improve and continue to improve. Nick Capra was also present from the OCA. Remember, Mr. Capra was the official that got in my face at our meeting in Warsaw. Nick never said a word. Thank God.

All of the counties then went back to the NYSAC offices for a debriefing. It was the general feeling that the counties could not publicly say NO, but the OCA was not about to impose any sanctions on the counties either.

I reported back to the Planning Committee and the full Board what had transpired. We were going to continue what we were doing. Nothing. But we were not going to publicly refuse to build the courthouse. Another thing to keep in mind, was that prior to this " Communication and Cooperation " era, the OCA was actually dictating the size of the facility and the design.

We realized that we were now being given more time and much more flexibility. The Office of Court Administration did not like the idea that the county representatives were actually scrutinizing and criticizing their actions but they were also aware that the general public had disdain for mandates. We were truly in nowhere land.

About three months of silence went by. Mr. Nick Capra then requested an informational meeting to be held in Warsaw on May 7th, 1996 at the Courthouse. I issued an invitation to all supervisors and urged them to attend. The OCA wanted the meeting to determine the status of the old projected timetable that had been passed back in 1995. That timetable was due on June 1, 1996. Yeah, right.

Nick Capra, Harold Brand and Jeanette Helms were representing the OCA. Judge Mark Dadd and William Beyer were representing the Wyoming County Judicial System. Kevin DeFebbo and almost all the Supervisors except Nelson George were present.

I opened up the meeting. I stated that Wyoming County was in the process of removing an old fuel tank from the premises of the old jail/sheriff's residence. We had just installed a fence around the buildings to prevent anyone from being hurt by falling bricks etc. I also mentioned that the demolition of those buildings were being worked on for the last several months. The county was also being faced with problems from the State Historic and Preservation Office. Ron Herman mentioned that the new jail was built with provisions for three (3) holding cells, conference rooms and a storm sewer system that was to be tied into a new courthouse. Anne Humphrey said that her committee had been working very hard on this project but it was her opinion that we did not have the necessary 2/3 vote to carry the project.

Mr. Brand stated that he was in Wyoming County in 1989 and both he and Mr. Capra were back two years ago and they had seen no action from the County. Mr. Brand even stated how many wedding anniversaries he had since and also bought two new vehicles since 1989. Mr. Capra then requested that on or before September 15, 1996, Wyoming County submit an implementation plan to provide suitable and sufficient court facilities for the residents of Wyoming County. The plan must also include an implementation schedule.

My take on the meeting was that yes, we must continue to proceed. However, we were also beginning to see an offer by OCA providing greater flexibility and a more reasonable position. Mr. Capra and Mr. Brand were by all means very cordial and polite this time.

We were by no means in the clear with the OCA on what had been a decidedly dictatorial relationship on their part. Still, we did want and expected some considerations regarding Wyoming County's fiscal and logistical constraints in the future.

After consulting with Kevin, Jim Schlick, Ken Lowe and Doug Berwanger, I established the Courthouse Committee. I made this the committee of the whole. In other words, all sixteen supervisors were named to it. I knew that it was definitely going to be more cumbersome by having sixteen members, but I also knew that we were going to have an informed Board. I named

Doug Berwanger as the Chairman of the Courthouse Committee. I realized that Doug was only on the Board for about five months at that time. I also thought that it was an advantage for him, Doug had not really taken sides on this issue.

On June 6th, 1996, the new Courthouse Committee had its very first meeting. Most of us really intended to drag our feet as long as possible. Wyoming County needed the time to put money aside so that when we did have to build, it would not have a huge impact on property taxes.

All hell broke loose on the 4th of July week end. The OCA was in the process of initiating sanctions on Erie County. During the week end, Erie County Executive Dennis Gorski held a press conference and surrendered to the State. Erie County would build a new courthouse. Now keep in mind, Erie County had not done anything. However, more importantly, Erie County was the largest of the counties that were still not in compliance with the State OCA. When I heard Dennis Gorski put up the white flag, I knew, we, in Wyoming County had absolutely no choice. We were going to build the courthouse. If Erie County did not want to take a chance on fighting the OCA, with all their resources, what chance would we have?

We immediately met and decided that it would be in the best interest of Wyoming County to agree to build a new courthouse but on our own terms. We did feel that we would have the cooperation and understanding of Mr. Capra, Mr. Brand and the OCA.

Wyoming County was not in quite the dire straits as we purposely made it out to be. The Finance Committee, after closing the books on 1995, had set aside $1.5 million for the project. The Finance Committee also agreed to set aside an additional $500,000 per year to put towards the construction project. We really wanted to build this courthouse on our terms. We did not want a Taj Mahal, we wanted a scaled down version that would meet our needs and still be a facility that all of Wyoming County could be proud of.

Remember what I said about Doug Berwanger. He had not been involved in the fighting and nastiness with the OCA. Doug took this assignment with all of his heart. I doubt if any other supervisor could have accomplished what he did. The Board of Supervisors was truly torn apart on this volatile issue. Some with good reason, some with not so good reason. In any event, through Doug's leadership, a vote was taken on August 20, 1996 to start the process of planning for the construction of a new courthouse, hopefully not to exceed $3.5 million dollars. The vote was 8 for and 0 against. Unbelievable.

On September 10, 1996, Doug Berwanger introduced the resolution that called for completing plans, hiring an architect and constructing a new courthouse. The plans called for the new building to contain courtrooms, jury rooms, offices for the Judges, District Attorney, a court library and the Probation Department. It also called for construction on the vacant property between the existing courthouse and the New Jail. In the Buffalo News, I was quoted as saying, " We held off the State Office of Court Administration as long as we could. The Committee believes that by 1998, the county will be able to afford the court building without much of a tax increase." I declared, *"Call the roll "*. The roll was taken and again, 16 - 0 , all in favor. At the October 8th meeting, Doug introduced a Resolution that called for a contract with SWBR Architects of Rochester to design the building. 16 - 0 again.

The Courthouse Committee began meeting on a regular basis. The Committee then charged SWBR Architects with the task of determining the space needs within the parameters of a $3.5 to $4.5 million bottom line. SWBR gave us three options.

1) Plan A - provide 35,000 square feet of space and accommodate Courts, District Attorney and Probation, with a link for prisoner movement to and from the new Jail. Early on, the County Clerk's office was eliminated from the new Courthouse due to funding.

2) Plan B - provide 29,500 square feet and accommodate Courts, and District Attorney with a link for prisoner movement to and from the new Jail.

3) Plan C - provide 23,500 square feet and accommodate scaled down court space and the district attorney's office with a link for prisoner movement. This option required a variance and/or approval from the OCA. It called for shared office space and Courtroom space.

The Committee unanimously endorsed the compromise option of Plan B. The Architects and others advised us that we would have had a hell of a battle with Plan C with the OCA, because of the limited and shared office space. So... Plan B was passed unanimously again. Frank Greene of Ricci Associates from New York City was chosen to actually design the new building.

As you can see now from the completed building, Frank is a very talented and gifted architect.

Many members of the committee and the board assumed that the design of the building would be similar to the old courthouse and the new Public Safety/Jail Building.

I can remember one particular meeting when Frank Greene became a little animated over the issue. Greene said if everyone would design all their new construction based on old design (1930's etc), the 1990's would have no architectural legacy of its own. No one ever put it quite that way before. That's because Frank's got a creative mind and architecture is a creative process.

Now, how were we going to connect the New Courthouse with the Old Courthouse? Just because of the county clerk's office still being in the old building, it was really necessary for some type of connection. The Court system and the county clerk's office are constantly running back and forth with records and documents.

The building could be connected by a "breeze way" type connection. Nice, huh ? Build a $4 million courthouse and connect it with a vinyl roof and texture 111 imitation plywood. Well, what else were we going to do?

Alex Lane, Supervisor of Warsaw (D), had a vision. Alex suggested that the two buildings be connected via a ' rotunda' type structure. Frank Greene thought it was great. He was going to blend it with a general theme of Wyoming County being made up of sixteen towns. It was not an easy sell. I loved the idea at once. Doug Berwanger fully supported the concept. It was our job to convince the other supervisors that it was worth the extra money to go with a rotunda connection. We did it!

The existing rotunda has eight pillars that have two Towns listed on them. All sixteen Towns are represented. We even debated the format for placing the Towns on the pillars. I suggested that we start alphabetically on top and alphabetically with the last eight Towns for the bottom position. Great idea, everyone thought. In other words, Arcade is on top with Java on the bottom. Attica on top with Middlebury on the bottom. And so on. It was also decided that we would rely on the construction workers as to what pillar would be the first. You see, everything was at random. That made for no fighting.

Frank Greene even incorporated the Town concept to the front of the Courthouse. If you look, you will again see eight pillars that represent the Towns. The huge amount of glass and windows in the front is to give off a ' front porch ' effect. Frank noticed that almost every house on Main Street in Warsaw had a front porch. He thought the new courthouse should too.

Now that we knew basically what we wanted, we needed to move on. Next on the agenda was the selection of the construction manager. The committee interviewed six different firms. It was an extremely difficult task. The construction manager is probably the most important player in a building project.

Bovis Construction of Ithaca was selected again unanimously. Kyle Tuttle, Vice President was going to be our major contact and Mark Balling of Strykersville was the local on site manager. The Construction Manager typically supervises the construction site for safety, materials, workmanship and in general, is the County's representative. They would make sure that our interests were heeded. However, Bovis was also actively involved in the planning decisions and provided their own estimates of costs.

In fact, Bovis conducted a detailed planning session where Kyle Tuttle acted as a facilitator between the judges, architects and the Board of Supervisors. In late summer of 1997, all the estimates were coming in higher than we had anticipated. Bovis led a "Value Engineering Session". At this session, we discussed every item and its costs. As a result of the session, we were able to bring the Courthouse project back within budget. Due to the efforts of Bovis and Doug Berwanger, the Committee stayed focused.

One other major player that must be mentioned is the Honorable Judge, Michael Griffith. Judge Griffith picked up the ball and ran for the game winning touchdown. One thing that I have learned through construction projects such as the new jail, skilled nursing home addition and others, is that a committee or a board can almost bring a project to its knees. The committee in charge cannot be required or allowed to drown in minute details. The committee normally does not inhabit a building upon completion. Therefore; the committee cannot foresee how some things must be included while others are not absolutely necessary.

Wyoming County was very fortunate to have Judge Griffith. First of all, Mike agreed to take on the additional work and gave of his time. A County Judge is extremely busy just doing their own job. Mike spent hours, days and weeks with the committee, the OCA, the construction manager and of course the architect. The Judge decided that we should use most of the existing furniture from the court rooms including, jury chairs, tables, even the Judge's bench. The furniture was sent out for refinishing and the County was able to save money and at the same time have some truly beautiful furnishings.

The Courthouse Committee brought everyone involved to the table. Gerry Stout, the district attorney was asked for his views. We invited Mayor Dan Moran of Warsaw so that he too, would know what our intentions were. By the way, Dan Moran is no relation to me but I can tell you that he is one hell of a man and a great mayor for Warsaw.

The Committee wrestled with the decision of whether to have a basement or not. They knew that the results of the soil bores were leaning towards needing no basement. The cost of a basement was close to $1 million. However, if there was no basement, we still needed space for mechanicals and storage. When the Committee took all that into consideration, the cost difference was about $300,000. When they included the water table issue, it was agreed that there was not going to be a basement. The mechanicals were going on the roof. The water table on that site was simply too shallow. The soil borings indicated water within a few feet from the surface. It was going to be very expensive to dig and pour a basement and then guarantee that it was going to remain predominantly dry throughout the year.

The Committee directed Frank Greene of Ricci Associates and SWBR to prepare a model for presentation to the Board of Supervisors and the general public. I wanted it to be available for our annual meeting at the Wyoming County Fair on August 12th, 1997. I proposed having the regular Board of Supervisors meeting at the Fair Grounds during fair week. I thought that having a meeting on the grounds, would give more people an opportunity to attend a meeting. Some supervisors were not thrilled. Some were. I think it was a bigger hassle for the staff because they had to bring everything from Warsaw. I also requested that all Departments Heads be available. Often, Tom Reynolds, Bill Paxon or Dale Volker would also show up at those meetings.

Anyway, on August 12th, Jack Fisher delivered the model to the fairgrounds. We had it covered with a sheet and when the time was right, we unveiled the model of the new Courthouse to the public of Wyoming County. The feedback was great. Most everyone loved it and thought it would truly be an asset to the County of Wyoming and the Village of Warsaw.

In September of 1997, the Committee directed SWBR to develop the construction documents for review by Bovis and hopefully approval from our Judges Mike Griffith and Judge Mark Dadd.

For the next four or five months, construction design documents including floor plans went back and forth between all parties. Always, considering the views of our judges and of course the costs. This is where Mike Griffith shone. Mike actually worked hand in hand with Randy Sickler from SWBR. Mike wanted to make sure that this building was going to be adequate and yet still within the County's budget.

When these documents were finally submitted to New York State Office of Court Administration it was a no brainer. The OCA blessed our plans like the Lord blessed all those attending the Sermon on the Mount. Hallelujah!!!

We were now ready to go to bid. In February of 1998, we went to bid on the Courthouse Project that was talked about for years. I believe we did it the right way and at the right time. Again, I also truly believe that it would not have happened without the leadership of Doug Berwanger.

On April 2, 1998, Doug Berwanger and myself teamed up to turn over the first bits of dirt for the new Courthouse. Those attending the ceremony included of course, the Board of Supervisors, Judge Mark Dadd, Judge Michael Griffith, Judge Vincent Doyle from Buffalo, Harry Brand, Frank Greene, Randy Sickler, from SWBR, Kyle Tuttle and Mark Balling from Bovis, many Department Heads and County Employees.

I was quoted in the Batavia Daily News of saying, " Rome wasn't built in a day. Now in Wyoming County, we're building a beautiful court facility that Wyoming County needs and deserves. " Doug Berwanger said, " We've put in a ton of time. In the last eighteen months, all of the supervisors' resolutions relating to the courthouse project were approved unanimously. Without Mike Griffith's astute planning we wouldn't be here today." Judge Mark Dadd noted the new county facility will be the first of its kind in 72 years. " I think that we have planned a project ... that will be appropriate. Appealing but not grandiose", Dadd said.

In addition, the county was not only building a new courthouse, but the N.Y.S. Department of Transportation was also planning to tear up Route 19 throughout the entire village of Warsaw. Suzanne Coogan of the Warsaw Chamber of Commerce and Mayor Dan Moran invited me to several meetings to discuss the parking and traffic in the Village. With Kevin DeFebbo's assistance we were prepared for the worst. If need be, we would provide shuttle bus service for employees and visitors to the Courthouse. The Chamber planned for everything. They had sidewalk sales, " dusty dollar" and other promotions. I cannot say enough good about Suzanne Coogan and the Chamber. Looking back, all went smooth because of the extreme patience of the Village of Warsaw residents. God Bless you all.

The Courthouse Committee was meeting on a weekly basis. Mark Balling and Randy Sickler were giving weekly updates and Kevin DeFebbo was handling the daily routines. I am not going into much detail of the construction itself, but it should be pointed out that the change orders were almost non existent. There are three main reasons for change orders. First, the contractor has run into an unexpected problem during the construction, Secondly, the owner decides during construction to add, modify or remove some item or lastly it is simply an oversight on the architect and/or construction manager.

There was one article in the Buffalo News during the construction that stated the county was going to be over budget. After one meeting, Nelson George asked aloud, "who the idiot was that said that." Doug Berwanger standing about ten foot tall and bullet proof shouted, " I'd be that goddam idiot ." The whole room emptied as if there were a fire drill. Doug went over to Nels and I have no idea what transpired.

The actual construction period went rather smoothly. Mark Balling of Bovis and Kevin DeFebbo were working together constantly. The courthouse committee continued to meet on a weekly basis. We were all given budget updates and progress reports on a regular basis.

The construction workers seemed to enjoy their project and it was obvious that they were working with a great deal of pride. As the summer months came, it also seemed as if some of the female county employees were enjoying the construction, if you get my drift.

The completion date was originally scheduled for August of 1999. Then it was June. In early 1999, Bovis predicted that we would be cutting the ribbon by May 1st. Enter Mike Griffith again. Judge Griffith decided to include a time capsule as the corner stone of the new building. Mike contacted every school district in the County for entries and ideas on what should be included. It was a great idea and I know that the time capsule area is jammed packed with material from all over the county.

Because this was only the second courthouse constructed, the Committee decided to make the event a real big deal. The "Ribbon Cutting" was scheduled for 11:00 A.M. on April 30th, 1999.

Officials from other counties were invited, as was Tom Reynolds, Dale Volker, Dan Burling and even a Representative from Governor Pataki's office. Nick Capra, Harry Brand and Jeanette Helms from the OCA were present. Judge Vincent Doyle and other visiting judges were on hand.

The invitations and programs were designed and created by Sue Aldinger and Melane Spink. They did a great, professional job. Sue and Melane also handled all the arrangements. The Wyoming County Bar Association sponsored a luncheon immediately following at the Moose Lodge in Warsaw. Marge and Cliff Cleveland at the Moose and all the others did a great job. The Lord provided us with a beautiful, sunny and warm day.

We had public tours from 10 A.M. to 11:00 A.M. The ceremony began at 11:00 A.M. in front of the rotunda. Jim Kemp, county highway, secured a much needed platform for the speakers. Jim Reger from emergency services provided the speaker system. In the rotunda, there was a sign book for all guests to register which became part of the time capsule. Doug Berwanger arranged for Pat Burns, photographer from Arcade to take some great candid shots of the big day.

I welcomed everyone and immediately turned it over to Frank Hollister, County Director of Veteran's Service, for the flag raising dedication. As the flag was being raised by the Honor Guard, Dave Hurlburt sang a moving rendition of the Star Spangled Banner. In all the County events and ceremonies, I had never seen a priest or a minister from Java. I thought it was appropriate that being from Java, I should invite Father Edward Muerder from North Java to give the invocation and Father Bart from Warsaw for the Benediction. It was then my honor to introduce all the distinguished guests. I did and I don't think that I missed anyone.

I then thanked Nick Capra and Harry Brand for their patience. I also acknowledged and thanked the Courthouse Committee, Doug Berwanger, Chairman, Jim Schlick, Bob Bowles, Paul Agan, Ron Herman, Howard Miller and of course, recently departed Dwight Gillette. I told the story about poor Josiah Hovey, which is in Chapter 21. I said that I was sure that Josiah Hovey was looking down on Wyoming County that day. I then turned the program over to Doug Berwanger.

Doug then proceeded to give not only the speech of his life but I can honestly say the best speech that I had heard in fourteen years from any government official. He did it with style, humor and above all a tremendous amount of class. Doug thanked everyone including the workers, architects, construction manager, judges etc. Doug was quoted in the Batavia Daily News saying, " With this courthouse the county begins a new era in the history of this area. From the start we were told by the engineers that this project would succeed if we worked together as a team. As it progressed it became apparent it was going to happen. Every vote on the courthouse was 16 - 0. We felt it was the voice of the people of Wyoming County speaking to us."

Kyle Tuttle, Vice President of Bovis Construction presented the Board of Supervisors with a clock in memory of Dwight Gillette who had passed away earlier in 1999. It was a beautiful clock that hung in the Chambers until we moved and I am sure it will be hung in the newly renovated Chambers of the Board.

Judge Griffith handled the time capsule ceremony and Judge Dadd introduced all the guests of the Court System.

Participating in the ribbon cutting besides myself, were Doug Berwanger, Judge Mark Dadd, Judge Michael Griffith, District Attorney Gerald Stout, and Judge Vincent Doyle. There are some great pictures of the occasion. It was truly a great and proud day for Wyoming County. I know that I will never, ever forget the ceremony and the dignitaries that were in attendance.

Since that day, the building was the recipient of the Award for Design Excellence by the Design and Build Rochester Group. This is a group of architects, builders, historic preservationists and other professionals. It is a very prestigious award. In fact, Judge Griffith and Doug Berwanger were guests of the group on November 6, 1999 to receive the award.

I have never heard a nasty comment on the Courthouse. In fact, all I have ever heard are compliments and great remarks. The best one was when I overheard a potential jury member remark to another person, " We used to have to travel to Rochester or Buffalo to see a beautiful building like this ".

I now repeat myself and thank everyone involved but especially the Board of Supervisors who put the whole package together and made it all possible. Great Job !!!

Chapter 37

Let Them Drink Swampwater

This by far, is the chapter of the book that I was not looking forward to writing. I had even thought of just ignoring the whole North Java Water District controversy. But... for the sake of history, I am compelled to relay it to you. For the weak of heart, please skip to the next chapter. For those that cannot understand or tolerate ignorance and/or hypocrisy, please skip to the next chapter. For those that revel in the mud and dirt, here goes nothing.

The North Java Water District consists of about 88 hook ups and physically is Route 98, Wethersfield Road, Perry Road and East Avenue, in downtown North Java. The District was established in 1931 when the water lines and reservoir were installed. That to me is still amazing. Imagine, back in 1931, with NO HELP from the Town, County or State, a group of progressive residents had the foresight to form a water district. They knew that the close proximity of the homes along with septic tanks and well, could easily pose a health problem or worse. It was not until the late 1960's that the Town of Java became involved in the Water District. In order to borrow money, the District needed the Town's administration. Improvements were made to the reservoir, springs and the installation of a chlorinator. Everything else was basically intact from the 1930's. Since 1931, there were obvious connections made. Some were documented and mapped. Others were not. This created quite a problem when the State or any utility began digging around North Java. The contractor would notify Underground Utilities who in turn would contact the Town and ask for the water lines to be flagged. How could we flag them when we did not know exactly where they were. Some houses were connected to each other, so they did not even have a shut off, in the event of a leak. Some were actually connected and serviced by plastic garden hose!

In 1986, when I took office, the water rates were $70 for an home owner. Cliff Sheer was the Water Superintendent then. After the completion of the Perry Road project, the water rates were doubled to $140 for residents. They remained at that rate until this printing. That is a pretty damn good buy for water. I can say that the average electric cost for a pump is higher than that. And pumps have to be replaced.

The Water District ate up considerable time simply with its leaks, complaints, and numerous water emergencies. It seemed as if I was always doing something for the Water District.

Gordon Hildebrant was the replacement for Cliff Sheer. Gordon did an excellent job as Water Superintendent. Gordon was always around and really dedicated himself to the position. As I said in an earlier chapter, I was asking all our representatives and all government agencies for grants for water. Every seminar, trip or visit to any government official, I would mention our problems.

On October 23, 1992, the Wyoming County Health Department issued a report on the findings of their inspection of the North Java Water District. I will summarize the report:

- Since the primary source of water to the hamlet is from springs, it should be known that the system may fall under the realm of the Surface Water Treatment Act. This meant that if it was considered surface water, we were really in deep doo doo. Fortunately, all parties have concluded that the water is not surface water.

- The reservoir needed to be cleaned on a regular basis. Locks should be installed to prevent public access. Some minor repairs and changes were mandated such as brush removal, roof repairs etc.

- It was recommended to completely replace the old chlorination system. The chlorine was injected at the reservoir with no analytical reasoning or prescription. The Health Department wanted a system that was based on demand and needs.

- There was concern that due to the lack of mapping, North Java could be left in a precarious position with supplying water should failures begin to occur regularly.

- It was disclosed that there were service connections made to neighbors' line instead of the main water line. The Health Department wanted these violations rectified as soon as possible.

This inspection was actually the result of a resident's complaint of a failing private sewage system adjacent to the water main lines. Water is serious business and should not be taken lightly. Imagine, if sewage was to leak into a main line that had deteriorated badly enough. To simply state that " If it ain't broke, don't fix it" is a dereliction of one's duties and responsibilities. As a note, there was actually a hand painted sign that read like the above during one of the District's votes. Smart, huh?

On January 11, 1993, a meeting was held at the North Java Fire Hall. We discussed the Health Department concerns and the possibility of improving and replacing the lines on Route 98 from the intersection of Perry Road north to the Family Mart. Herm Miller made a motion to proceed but not to borrow the money yet. Chatfield Engineers were going to be used to provide an estimate of the costs. The estimate came in at $30,000. Then all hell broke loose. Some thought we should do the whole district because of the possibility of major leaks somewhere else etc. The Commissioners (Chuck Kmicinski, Don Almeter, Carl Hanley) directed me to inquire about grants.

On February 7, 1994, Gordon and myself went to Salamanca to meet with Tom Mazerbo from the USDA, Rural Economic Community Development. At that time, it was part of the FHMA. Then it became Rural Development. The office was located in the then almost deserted Salamanca Mall. It was after that visit that I completed a preliminary application for a grant to install new lines, a chlorinator and distribution system.

It was at about the same time, that I was meeting with Chris Nill from Rural Community Assistant Program (RCAP) of the federal government. RCAP was a branch of the federal Housing and Urban Development. Chris assisted me in filing grant applications for HUD Grants. One of the requirements at that time, was the community needed to fall under low income ranges for its residents. In order to be eligible 51% of the community must fall under the low to moderate income bracket. A financial survey was mailed out to all North Java residents. The results were that North Java did not meet the low income standards.

Every summer, the District was experiencing leaks somewhere. The leaks would be repaired and then another would pop up somewhere else. During this time, it was also necessary to issue water ban notices. These notices would ban all but essential water usage. In other words, no garden watering, lawn sprinkling, car washing etc. These water bans really began to occur from 1993 thru 1998. One time, it was so bad, that Jack Fisher, the Emergency Services Director for the County had contacted the State Emergency Management Office and had them on stand by in case North Java needed truck loads of water delivered. In addition to the leaks, in June of 1995, the chlorinator failed which was very serious. It meant that the water to the homes was not being treated at all. It was then necessary to issue a " Water Advisory" that urged all residents to boil water until the chlorinator could be fixed. I am not going to dwell on the bans and leaks. They occurred constantly and were costing the District thousands of dollars. The average common sense resident knew that something had to be done.

In addition to the problems with the system, we were experiencing problems with people. The District was changing Commissioners and Water Superintendents more frequently than some people change their underwear. The Water Superintendent position went from Gordon Hildebrant to John McCormick in 1994 and then to Pat Harrington in 1996. For the last interview, we did not even receive any applications from anyone inside the District. Once selected by the Commissioners and the Town Board, the candidate then had to successfully complete a home correspondence course and put in an apprenticeship with the Superintendent. It was also an ongoing credit type of relationship. The Superintendent was required to complete training. I worked very well with each of those gentlemen and I thank each of them now for their dedication and cooperation. They put up with a lot of bullshit for little money. They were criticized for everything. Because of all of the leaks and repairs, it was necessary for the Superintendent to work over and above a part time basis. It was agreed by the Water Commissioners and the Town Board that anything above twenty hours per month would be paid at the rate of $10 per hour. There were several residents that had a problem with that.

We were also going through Commissioners like there was no tomorrow. Pat Anger, Neil Miller, Chuck Kmicinski, Ray Wilson, Tony Romesser, Don Almeter, Henry Rose, Doc Eddy, Carl Hanley, Ray Wilson, Chuck Eley, Ray Eley and I probably missed a few. But, you get the picture. There was, a silent, sneaky movement underway that was actually sabotaging our every move.

On March 2, 1996, I issued a letter to all residents of the Water District that we had been awarded a loan/grant from the USDA Rural Development. In the letter, I pointed out that it was THEIR decision and only the discussion as to whether to accept or decline the grant. I then scheduled three Public Information Meetings to be held at the North Java Fire Hall on Monday, March 18th at 7:00 P.M., Saturday, March 23rd at 1:00 P.M. and on Thursday March 28th at 7:00 P.M. In the last paragraph, I stated that the Town Board will comply with the wishes of the majority of the residents of the Water District.

Between all three meetings, there were over 70 people in attendance. Paul Chatfield from Chatfield Engineers was also on hand to answer technical questions. I had prepared an amortization table with estimates of the pay back schedule. I stated back then that the absolute worse case scenario would double the existing water rates. It was also agreed that the meeting of March 28th would be considered a voting meeting. I sent out another letter urging all residents to either attend or telephone me with their vote. I also indicated that the Town would hold a public meeting on April 9th to consider approving or declining the grant/loan.

On March 28th, a vote was taken and recorded by Janet Zielinski, Town Clerk. The vote was 29 in favor of accepting the grant/loan and 16 opposed. At the April 9th, Town Board Public Meeting, Ron McCormick moved and Don Roche second a motion to accept the USDA/RD grant/loan for the North Java Water District. It was passed unanimously. Also, a bond resolution was passed. Neil Miller and Carl Hanley were present from the Water District.

To this day, I don't believe that most residents realize just how fortunate North Java was to be awarded this grant/loan. Competition is fierce. In addition to the income requirements, the USDA had other criteria to contend with. As an example, the benchmark for water rates was $695 per year, per water hook up. That meant before a grant was even considered, the rates must be higher than $695. North Java rates were $140. So, to receive a 60% loan and 40% grant (free money) was really fantastic or so you would think, wouldn't you?

Over the next six months or so, Chatfield Engineers were preparing design and bid documents. It was then noted that there were no accurate maps of the District. Chatfield also began working on the soon to be famous map. About September, the Town Board began to see and approve bills from the engineers. In December, Ron McCormick asked why there was a negative balance in the North Java Water District fund. Excuse me, Ron, did you just wake up? Where did he think the money for the engineers was coming from? The plan was to pay for the preliminary work out of the District's surplus. Then, when the grant money came in, the Water District would be flush again. OK ! That also raised the big question of the decade. When did

Moran get authorization to sign a contract with Chatfield
Engineers ? I really do not know. I do know that I would not
sign any contract without authority from the Town Board. The
Town Clerk, Janet Zielinski, attested to my signature on the
contract. I have looked at all the Town Board minutes and cannot
find a motion authorizing it. However, the bottom line, is that
each month the Councilmen reviewed and approved the bills
from Chatfield Engineers. We had opinions from two different
Town Attorneys and both concurred that the simple and right
thing to do was to authorize the contract at that point. The Town
Board refused to do that. They thought it better to show that the
Supervisor really did not technically have the authority. In any
event, they continued to review and approve the bills. So what ?

In December, the plans and the documents were forwarded
to all the State and Federal agencies for their approval. It was
then noted that the Water District had never really been extended
since 1931. That meant that the Town Board had to extend the
District to include all of the present users of the system. This
gave the opposition fuel for their fire. They distorted the truth
and implied that I was attempting to increase the size of the
district. What the hell did I care? I still really don't give a damn
who gets water up there or not. They used this map and district
extension issue to try and halt the entire project. Why? I still
don't know and probably never will.

This map was their loop hole. I am going to try to explain
the map and the problems. In order to have a special district in
a Town, it was necessary to have an adopted boundary map that
defined the district. The reasoning behind the requirement is
that in a special district, the Town is either taxing or using some
other method to raise funds and charge the residents of only
that special district.

To most people, our intention and our only intention was to
finally correct the district map to simply include all present water
users. Simple? No way, Jose. Those opposed to the project argued
and bitched about every detail of the map. It took months before
the Town Board had the courage to officially adopt the map.
Finally on July 8th, the map was approved and adopted. John
Meyer voted no. John voted no because several months prior,
he was accused of being sneaky and everything else. In fact, one
of the Commissioners just about jumped on the table because he
thought John wanted water. The ironic part of the whole incident

is that John's grandfather lent the water district their initial investment. Good pay back, huh?

Anyway the map also brought the opportunity for a permissive referendum. All that was required was that 5% of the residents sign a petition requesting that a vote take place on the issue. The petition was passed and signed and presented to the Town Board at the next meeting. We now were forced to conduct a vote that will surely go down in history.

But... it wasn't quite that easy. We now had to nit pick about who was going to vote. All the while this stuff is going on, the Rural Development people are hounding me as to what the hell is the problem. Do the people of North Java realize that there are many other communities looking for just such an opportunity? Madonna Barber, Supervisor of the Town of Eagle and her Town Board even came to one of our meetings. They asked if Eagle could receive the money if North Java refused it.

Because of elections and time restraints, the vote was scheduled for November 20, 1997 at the North Java Fire Hall. I was trying to separate myself completely from this issue. I made the big mistake of having Janet Zielinski in charge of voting credentials. How could she screw that up? Just get a list of the property owners from Real Property Tax Services and check that with the bills sent out from the Water District. After all, there are only 88 hook ups. How bad can that be?

That day I was on my way back from Albany, with Larry Nugent, Supervisor of Genesee Falls and Gary Weidman, County Highway Superintendent. My cell phone began to ring as soon as the voting began. Janet was not going to allow Clarence and Billy Sheer to vote. They were smack in the middle of the water district and everyone knew it. Janet had also disallowed some others to vote. The people were furious. Even a couple of the election workers were shocked that this was occurring in North Java. Maybe in the Dominican Republic or South America, not here in Java. The final vote was in. 35 against, 30 in favor of accepting the grant/loan. Keep in mind that there are about 100-120 eligible voters in the district.

In December, I asked the Board for a resolution to direct me to issue a letter declining the grant/loan from the USDA/RD. They did and I did too.

Within a month, we had another failure of the chlorination system that required an advisory to residents to boil their water again. In the 1/10/98 edition of the Batavia Daily, their own editorial staff wrote under the headlines of :

OPPORTUNITY KNOCKED, AND THEN LEFT JAVA

"... So now the district is left with a 65 year old system that has been plagued by leaks in recent years. And, despite the existence of a backup well, the reservoir serving the district runs low in summer dry spells.

There is no question the system needs improving, and badly.

Apparently, however, squabbles over who would and would not be included in the district and rumors about some Town Board members having ulterior motives, sank the project.

That's too bad.

Now, the water system still needs improvements; the first in what is likely to be a series of repairs has already been made. And the money will come wholly out of district's residents pockets.

As for North Java Water District residents, they'd well go back to the board and ask it to reopen the project and pray that another grant comes along. And meantime, they should keep their checkbooks and boiling pots ready. "

The North Java Water District became the laughing stock of not just Wyoming County, but the entire state. No matter where I went, people would joke about the famous Water District or their notorious map. Once I was at a Rochester Red Wing baseball game at Frontier Field and someone started hollering at me from the rows above where I was sitting. I had Cindy and the kids with me and here's this guy yelling at me about the North Java Water District. To keep his voice down somewhat, I went up to his row. He worked for a federal agency and I am not going to identify him. Anyway, he boisterously questioned, " What's the matter with the people in North Java? What don't they understand? For every dollar they spend, the federal government is going to give them back 40 cents." I don't know. Who cares. Let those who opposed it drink swamp water.

On May 29, 1998, I attended a ribbon-cutting ceremony at the new Wyoming County Community Action Building on Route 20A in Perry. Tom Mazerbo from the USDA/RD was there. Community Action had taken advantage of a Rural Development grant to build the facility. Mazerbo came up to me and asked how were things going. I said pretty good, now. He then asked about the Water District. I told him about some problems and recent leaks from the week before. Mazerbo then asked " why don't you just take the grant and get it over with?" I was stunned. I asked him if the grant was still available. Of course it is, he replied. I told him that I had sent a letter of declination. Mazerbo said the USDA never received it. Really? I still don't really know if the USDA/RD lost the letter or deliberately lost it. I do know that I sent it via U.S. Mail and I'm quite sure it did get to the USDA.

I had quite a decision to make. My first instinct was, to hell with it, I am not going to put myself through that again. I confided in some other people and the opinions were mixed. Some said you should at least tell the residents. Others said, "piss on them".

I wrestled with my decision the entire week end. As I said, I asked advice from friends and colleagues. Finally on Monday morning, I had made up my mind. I had a responsibility to notify the customers of the North Java Water District that the grant/loan package was still available to them. I simply could not hide it from them. Without seeming too sanctimonious, I would really be doing a disservice to the majority of my constituents, if I ignored the words of Tom Mazerbo. After all, it was still their decision. Right?

On June 2nd, I issued a letter to all residents, Water Commissioners and the Town Board explaining the chance meeting with Mazerbo and informing them that IF they wanted to reconsider their previous decision, they still could accept the grant/loan. I asked and pleaded with the residents to contact me or any Councilman with their opinions.

My proposal was quite simple. I said if a SUPER MAJORITY of the residents wanted the grant, the Town Board would reactivate the process. And guess what? I was accused of bringing up a dead issue. Why did I want this grant ? I was accused of never sending the letter to the USDA rejecting the grant. I must have something to gain for this. I will continue to bring it up until the residents get sick of it. SO MUCH BULLSHIT!!

Before the June 9th Town Board Meeting, I had received letters from two residents in favor of accepting the grant and also received telephone calls from twelve (12) more in favor. Don Roche stated in the June 9th Town Board minutes that he received about twelve calls, six for and six against. I provided names with my counts, conveniently, Don didn't remember. The USDA/RD office in Syracuse received calls from two residents and the Town Clerk, stating that the USDA should keep their money, the Water District does not want the grant/loan. Can you imagine that?

In fact, things got worse. Chatfield Engineers and the USDA refused to deal with Janet Zielinski, Clerk. Joanne Almeter was calling everyone from Washington to Albany to have the money deobligated. Earlier, in March, the Town Board received a letter from Fire Chief Doug George of the North Java Fire Company. The letter stated, " On the evening of March 24, 1998, I finally realized just how much foolishness there is in the North Java Water District." Can you imagine? Doug went on to state that Henry Rose, a Water Commissioner, informed the North Java Fire Company that they should not be using water from the reservoir to fill their trucks. I could not and still do not believe it. The Fire Company was more than willing to pay a water rate comparable to the residents. The main goal of a Fire Company is to save lives and minimize the amount of property damage. Many members of the Fire Company were also residents of the Water District. There was no water shortage at that time. Should the farmer that owns the ponds, refuse to let the Fire Company fill their trucks with his water? Who was Henry Rose acting on behalf of? Rose had no authority to either dictate or set policy. He was only one of the water commissioners. At the April, 1998, Town Board meeting a resolution was passed unanimously that instructed me to write a letter to Henry Rose stating just that. What the hell is the matter with some people, anyway?

At the June 9th Board Meeting, Herm and Esther Miller and Gordon Hildebrant spoke against the grant/loan. Also in attendance from the Water District were: Don Almeter, Ray Wilson, Neil Miller, Mark Eddy, Dave Meyer , Dick and Pat Anger and Chuck and Barb Eley. The Town Board unanimously authorized me to send a letter to the USDA requesting them not to deobligate the funds and thanking them for their patience in this ordeal. The Board also established a Committee to work as a liaison with the USDA and the Engineers. The Committee was chaired by Dave Meyer with Ray Wilson, Dick Anger, Trace George and Richard Spampata as members. As Janet Zielinski recorded in the Board Minutes, " reasonable people".

On August 12, 1998, the Town Board conducted a Public Hearing on whether to proceed with the project or not. It was again another unanimous decision by the Advisory Committee and the Town Board. Why not? The District already owed the

Town General Fund $9,000. At least they would get that back. Remember, they were still paying all of the engineer's bills with their own money.

The residents had until September 8th, to submit a petition requesting the Town to hold a public referendum on the question. If we did not receive a petition, it more or less was to be taken as approval by the residents. No such luck.

Joanne Almeter was still working behind the scenes trying to convince people that the project was no good. Almeter was quoted in the Daily News of 8/26/98, " Perry Road resident and North Java Water Adviser Joanne Almeter said residents have shared their thoughts once on the project, which includes about $209,000 in loan funding and about $200,000 in grant funding from the USDA/Rural Development. 'The people spoke', Almeter said, 'Doesn't it mean anything?' " Almeter was referring to the referendum that was defeated 35 - 30. Sure it does, Joanne, but doesn't the very first vote that was taken in March of 1996 count too? Remember, from day one, the Commissioners, Town Board and the residents were all in favor of this project. Does anyone really believe that I wanted to piss everyone off and pursue a project that no one wanted? Then in the same Batavia news copy, Almeter was again quoted, " 'Even if we borrowed $409,000 there could be a leak tomorrow. There is no guarantee.'" Excuse me, Joanne. A couple of corrections. First, the district was NOT borrowing $409,000, it was really going to borrow about $229,000. As far as the possibility of leaks and no guarantee, I have to say, WAKE UP, for Christ's sake. If we went to bid, awarded the bids with bonds in place and had the successful bidder approved by the federal government (USDA), I would have to surmise that the contractor installed the correct materials and completed the project properly. I would say, you betcha, we would have a guarantee. It had better not have any leaks. Anyway, Almeter was pounding the pavement to convince everyone that I wanted this project for some type of personal gain. See ya in church, Joanne.

The amazing fact in this petition was that the Town Clerk provided the actual petition to those requesting them. Janet Zielinski was quoted in the Batavia Daily of 9/9/98, " 'Town Clerk Janet Zielinski did not comment on which residents took the petitions. She said people do not have to say who they are in order to get a form, but she expects the petitions to come back with enough signatures for a possible vote.' " Amazing ! Janet

Zielinski, who did not ask who wanted forms, knew they would be returned and returned properly. I should also point out that Janet Zielinski never lived in the North Java Water District. But by God, she fought against the grant in every way imaginable.

Sure enough, the petitions were turned into the Town Clerk by the deadline. I had publicly stated many times, that if we did receive petitions, that I would consider them as a message from the residents to halt the project. Joanne Almeter was again quoted in the 9/16/98 edition of the Batavia Daily News, " North Java resident Joanne Almeter said, 'Residents are tired of dealing with the water issue. They very willingly signed it. They are sick of it.'" No shit, Sherlock. Everybody was sick of it.

So.. now we had another public referendum to allow the residents of the District to decide officially November 19th was the date. By the way, I did vote no on the motion to hold another vote.

This time, I wanted no fiascos like the last election. The advisory Committee immediately began working on a list of eligible voters. It took several meetings, but by God, we finally had it right. We were ready for anything. There were signs up in North Java, some people (guess who) were going door to door campaigning against the project.

Paper ballots were going to be used. There was even a controversy on them. Harry Brown, the Election Commissioner said there should not be numbers on them. Fine, we printed up new ones without numbers. How difficult should we make this thing? Of course, we held another public information meeting, the night before the vote. This meeting gave anyone interested, a chance to ask any questions and get facts, not rumors.

On November 19th, I and a handful of residents from the District were on hand to get the results. The residents by a vote of 48 to 21 approved the project and wanted the Town Board to accept the grant/loan and proceed. There were two people at the Fire Hall where the voting took place who actually accused me of fixing the election. My good friend Joanne Almeter again was quoted in the Daily News of 11/20/98 , " 'If it was voted down tonight, he (Me) would bring it back up until the people got sick of.'" Yeah, right. Remember, genius, I voted "no" on even having that damn vote. I WAS ALREADY SICK OF IT.

Now it's over, right? Not quite, yet. Two weeks later, Zielinski, the Town Clerk still had not filed the election results with the Board of Elections. I telephoned her and was cut off, with her screaming that the Attorney was going to handle it. Here we go again.

After the election was over, the election workers sealed the ballot box with the results inside. Arlene Witkowski, the Republican Representative and Gert Lefort, the Democrat Representative turned the box over to Janet Zielinski. Zielinski was quoted in the Daily News, " 'The last time I was blamed for how the election went. I didn't want anything to do with this election.'" Sorry, honey but that's your job as Town Clerk. As to why she did not open the box and report the results, Janet Zielinski said, " I don't think I have the authority to open something that is sealed." I had to call Gordon Brown, the Town Attorney. Gordon decided to bring in the election workers again, have them open the box and personally hand the results over to Janet Zielinski. We did it that way. It cost the Water District $222 in attorney fees, plus paying for the election workers and about a two week delay. Just plain old nit-picking and chicken shit.

In December of 1998, the Town Board voted to proceed and continue with the Advisory Committee to work with the engineers and the contractors. Finally, at our 1999 April Meeting, we awarded the water contract to D&H Construction from Arcade.

The project was totally complete by November of 1999, with the exception of restoration work on landscaping. It was also completed within 7 or 8% of the budget figure that was being used from the earlier time.

Today, the North Java Water District consists of complete new lines, chlorination system and a distribution system that is finally mapped. It will provide North Java with quality drinking water for years to come. Was it worth it? I really can't say. Ask the omniscient Joanne Almeter.

Chapter 38

Papal Smoke & White Socks

January 2, 1997, the Wyoming County Board of Supervisors held their annual organizational meeting. I was re-elected as Chairman and Bob Bowles was re-elected as Vice Chairman. Bob's vote was unanimous, mine was not.

Nelson George from Sheldon again was very vocal in registering his no vote. I don't think he had the same white socks on though. The Perry Herald of January 9 read, " Sheldon Supervisor Nelson George, who voted against Moran, was critical of Moran's administration and handling of the board's standing committees. He said the changes made by Moran in the Board's standing committees for 1997 flew in the face of recommendations made to the County Board by a consultant it hired. George said it cost the county $50,000 to have the Center for Governmental Research study the county and its operations and make recommendations to make it more efficient. The CGR study determined the county needed only six standing committees. At that time there were sixteen committees. "

The article continued, " explaining his no vote on Moran's nomination, Supervisor George said it was not a protest vote, but one that symbolized a leadership that vacillates and does not reflect or resonate managerial confidence". Somebody had to write that little speech for him. Nels just doesn't use vocabulary like that.

As is usually the case, what he said was not totally accurate. In 1992, the Center for Governmental Research (CGR) was contracted with by the Board of Supervisors. The purpose of the study was to review staffing and scheduling in several county departments. The Sheriff's and Social Service Departments were the main focus. The final report was 107 pages and the committee structure was mentioned on one page. Howard Payne, the Chairman in 1992, requested CGR to look at a proposal to reduce the committees from 16 to 6. CGR gave it their blessing but did no research on the proposal.

Jim Schlick, Bennington Supervisor, was livid when George's comments were made public. Jim also received a telephone call from one of his board members about whether the county was

Thomas R. Moran

spending money on consultants and then not following the consultants' recommendations. Jim and I talked about the problem and we decided that I needed to go public to clarify the issue. We felt that the county taxpayers needed to know all the facts. We needed to let the people of Wyoming County know that the Board of Supervisors did not spend $50,000 on a consultant to study the committee structure and then ignore their recommendations.

On January 15, 1997, the Batavia Daily News printed an article titled , " Chairman disputes supervisor's comments." The article went on and stated, "The Sheldon supervisor said he was not on the Board of Supervisors when the 1992 consultants report was done, so ' it could have been' correct that the bulk of the report did not specifically address the standing committees. " Well, then why the hell did you say it, Nels? Nels ended his comments with, " I made a point; we'll go on to the next thing."

I am glad that Jim Schlick convinced me to issue a rebuttal to his remarks. At least the people heard the truth. They then could believe whatever they wanted.

The one sided remarks that are printed in the press, are probably the most frustrating part of the job. Normally there is no sense in contacting the paper. They could care less. Journalists only need to print the facts and often one-sided at that to ruffle feathers and sell papers. Look at Geraldine Luce's off the wall articles. They aren't even factual but she is held to a lower standard because she's a wanna be journalist. But in this case, a supervisor either knowingly or unknowingly asserted the majority of the Board of Supervisors of being bumbling idiots. This had to be addressed. We were also fortunate that we had a reporter at the Batavia Daily with the class of Paul Mrozek. My door was always open to Paul Mrozek. I tried to give him the news as it happened. One time, Paul gave me hell for not telling him about a personnel problem with an employee. The employee was a Department Head. I told him that I did not think it was news worthy and the story should not be printed. Paul disagreed with me. His contention was that if the taxpayers are paying the salary, they have a right to know. I'm still not convinced. Paul Mrozek was and still is a good friend of mine. The very best to you and yours, Paul.

I'll stay with this topic a little bit more. If you work at Motorola and your boss is giving you a rough time, for whatever reason, you have two choices. Quit or take it. On the other hand, if you are a county employee, oh boy, look out. The employee can write a letter to the editor or ask someone else to write it. The hospital employees are probably the best letter writers that Wyoming County has. Check out the editorial page and see if you agree.

Another journalistic forum is the " letters to the editor." I don't care if it's Geraldine Luce or Mickey Mouse. What makes these people experts? Why would the person of average intelligence even half believe any of it? I think the letters are simply too often an extension of the " Rumor Mill" and grapevine. You rarely see a letter from an elected official disputing their claims. The reason is quite simple. Never get into a pissing contest with a skunk. You will not win. You will only sell more newspapers. But sometimes it must be done. For those of you who wish to continue to write, give us your opinions. Don't make false accusations and do not be mean. Remember, God has no use for mean people. If you read the Bible, you will recall how upset and angry Jesus Christ became with the merchants selling their wares in the Temple. Can you imagine how pissed off he is now, when he sees vindictive hypocrites in Church pretending to be the holy of the holies ?

1997 was a continuation of 1996. By that I mean, the County was still heading onward and upward with changes.

One of these changes was dealing with management salaries and it was a bummer. Prior to 1996, the Finance and County Operations Committee met for at least one full day to discuss any possible salary increase for the County's management personnel. Management was placed on Schedule D. Schedule D was an alphabetical listing of each department and each management position in that department. The first department was Office for the Aging and the last one was the Youth Department.

Typically, all union employees received annual raises plus an automatic step increase until they were at the top of the grade. Naturally, all step increases came with about a 2.5% salary increase. There was no way the Supervisors could ever match the union increases for those in management. They would have been blasted by the taxpayers, And management ran the County.

Usually in December or January, we would meet to consider the raises. Prior to Kevin DeFebbo's arrival there was no such thing as an evaluation. We would be in the committee room for hours, and sometimes the arguments got pretty nasty about who deserved a raise.

Sometimes we would agree beforehand that the County designate a certain amount on raises. But then, we'd be half done and realize that we had no money left. Sometimes, we would set a cap like 3% or 4%. That would work fine until a group of supervisors thought that a certain department head was underpaid or worth more than a 3% raise.

I hated these meetings. They had me using aspirins and antacids like candy. No one enjoyed the day. The bottom line was that the system failed the County and really was unfair to our department heads. There were many department heads who were being paid much less than their counterparts in other counties. Some even had union employees earning more than they did. When I was first elected Chairman, I promised the department heads that we would study the entire salary schedule.

At one of my NYMIR Meetings, I spoke with Stan Dudek, Orleans County Administrator and Nick Mazza the Livingston County Administrator. They did not have the same problems we did. Their salaries rarely made the papers let alone headlines. I really liked Stan's procedure in Orleans County. Their department heads were on a schedule that also provided a salary range from Step 1 to Step 5. I thought that was a fantastic idea. If the County was hiring someone with little experience, they would be placed in Step 1 etc. It also provided a mechanism to reward a department head for an excellent evaluation. Kevin was doing all the evaluations for the department heads. The department heads obviously were evaluating their own employees.

I talked with Kevin about my idea and he jumped all over it. Kevin and I decided to present it to the Finance Committee. Bob Bowles and Jim Schlick were anxious to see who was going to come up with the salary range and how. A private consultant was ruled out because of cost and we were not sure how the other supervisors would feel about some outsider telling us what our management people were worth.

I convinced Kevin and the Finance Committee that he and I could come up with it. Kevin was a little reluctant because he worried about my " open mindness ". I assured him that I could be rational and would not shut anything completely out but he too would have to be open minded. Kevin and Cheryl Mayer did all the background research. We had salaries for all department heads from counties similar to Wyoming County.

Kevin and I spent days sequestered in the committee room. Finally, we sent up white smoke like they do when the Cardinals select a new pope. We had a schedule and one that we both agreed was fair. Yes, most department heads received raises, but we did have two whose salaries were frozen. We also created a new schedule for those in management but who were not department heads. That was a little bit more difficult and probably should still be studied further.

Now, we had to present it to the full Board of Supervisors. One of the first concerns to arise was the step increases. Kevin assured the supervisors that an employee had to receive an outstanding evaluation in order to merit the step. He was not about to give too many 'outstandings' out. I also mentioned that the Supervisors were ultimately in charge anyway. If they felt Kevin had been too generous they would simply vote the increase down. For that matter, they could throw out the whole schedule anytime they wanted.

The vote was unanimous. 16 to 0. Even Nelson George voted for the new schedules. Maybe it was because they all knew that it was the right thing to do or Nels forgot to wear his white socks that day.

Chapter 39

Samantha

On February 27, 1997, my telephone rang just before six in the morning. It was Under Sheriff Ron Ely. Ron informed me that a seven year old girl was missing and presumed abducted in Wethersfield. It was raining like hell and I could only hope that this little girl was just lost in the rainy woods near her home in Hermitage.

Samantha Zaldivar was reported missing on February 26. Angel Colon was the last person to see her as she supposedly left for school that morning. At that time, Samantha was living in a mobile home trailer park with Colon, her mother Rachel Stra and two half sisters, Angela 4 and Cassandra 3 . Samantha was Rachel Stra's daughter from a previous marriage to Noel Zaldivar. Angela and Cassandra were Rachel and Angel's children. The Wyoming County Sheriff's Department, local volunteer fire companies and many others began to search the area around her home. They came up with nothing.

Ron Ely, Dennis Spink, Gary Eck, Steve Tarbell and others from the Sheriff's Department rose to the challenge. Ron Ely had a great relationship with the Federal Bureau of Investigation (FBI) and was able to receive personnel and technical assistance from them. Even though Sheriff Capwell ran an excellent department, they were not prepared for this.

The FBI immediately set up a command center in the Public Safety building. Kevin DeFebbo and myself were fortunate enough to be invited by Cappy for a look see. It was impressive. The FBI had set up phones, faxes, and computers spread over about three or four long tables. There also was a time line and detail posters hung around the wall. On these sheets of paper things were written like what movie Angel had seen on television. What time a neighbor heard a vehicle. All kinds of little details like that. And at the one end of the room was a huge picture of Angel Colon. Colon was the number one suspect from the beginning. Cappy asked me that day if the department could buy some needed equipment for the investigation. As an example, the FBI was willing to give the Sheriff, software to file all this information. The department did not even have a lap top computer. Of course, I said OK.

I spoke with a couple of the FBI Agents one day. I asked them how could Colon and Rachel Stra have maintained their composure. I could not understand how anyone might sexually abuse a little girl and then kill her and act as though nothing much happened. An Agent said that people like us could never rationalize it. Murderers, rapists, sex offenders are really animals that we will never comprehend. Colon would be at the courthouse almost on a regular basis. The first time that I saw him, he came in wearing a Miami Dolphins jacket. His facial expression was just blank. He looked like a wise ass punk. I tagged him as guilty right away.

Weeks went by with no breaks. Ron Ely and others were convinced that Colon buried Samantha in a quickly dug shallow grave. That upset me even more. Not only did it seem Colon killed a little girl but he didn't even show any remorse or respect with a proper burial. I was right in the middle of this. I always admired our employees in the Sheriff's Department, but now it was almost a case of awe. I mean, just think about it. Here you have your friends conducting a murder investigation working along with the FBI and District Attorney Stout. They all did it with such compassion and professionalism that they should have all received citations.

Some supervisors thought that I was becoming too involved in the case. Maybe I was. But because of my good relationship with Cappy and Ron Ely, I was being kept up to date in the investigation. Don't get me wrong. Not the gory details, just facts that eventually were made public. I remember one day walking to lunch with Anne Humphrey. We were right by Ace Hardware and she looked at me and said, " Tom, are you just giving the Sheriff's Department a blank check for this case?". I replied, " Please, Anne, don't even go there." Anne never did go there again and I thank her for that.

In early March, the Wyoming County Social Services Department removed the two little girls, Angela and Cassandra from the custody of Colon and Rachel Stra. The Social Services Department (DSS) had received a complaint about child neglect. During the incident of the removal of the children from the trailer, Colon got nasty and he was charged with obstruction of governmental administration and then resisting arrest. Colon was not employed, so D. Michael Murray was appointed to represent him. Colon ended up with a ' dream team' of his attorneys. A Court Order was then issued that banned Colon from any contact with his children. Colon vacated the trailer and moved to Georgia, then Florida. Colon and the family had lived in the Miami area before moving to Wyoming County around 1996. As far as Rachel went, after a few weeks in foster care, the girls were returned to her, for a period of time.

In late March, plans began for a massive search for Samantha and any evidence that could be found. This huge effort was coordinated by Sheriff Capwell and Jack Fisher of the Emergency Services. It was to be characterized as recovery of evidence and/or possible clues. We were not going to mention that anyone was looking for a body.

The search was scheduled for the week end of April 19 and 20th, 1997. At about 5:30 A.M. Deputy Garry Ingles picked me up at my home and we met everyone at the Fire Training Center on Wethersfield Road. The Sheriff wanted me as the public relations person. I was willing to do anything for the effort.

The search was planned by the Wyoming County Sheriff's Department, the N.Y.S. Forest Rangers, headed by Pete Liebig with assistance from all 19 volunteer Fire and Rescue squads, led by Jack Fisher. The Recovery Teams searched a 1 to 2 mile radius from the point where Samantha was last seen. Each team was supervised by a ranger and a member of the Fire Service. The teams were instructed to look for any evidence and/or clues in the disappearance of Samantha. The Search Teams also searched a five mile radius of road side ditches. There were five staging areas where volunteers would assemble and be given their areas to search. When they arrived back, pizza, wings and other goodies were provided. I think just about every merchant in the County and other areas donated food, pop etc. The five staging areas and their managers were, North Java (Bill Streicher), Letchworth (Gary Huff), Ames Plaza (Joe Lee), County Highway (Andy Merek) and Wethersfield Town Highway (Albert Kelleher).

My duties were fairly simple. Whenever the press, radio or television crews showed up, I would rush to that site and give them a prepared report and eventually adlib by day two. It was one of my first dealings with TV news reporters. Some were very courteous and one woman for R-News, in Rochester was just a plain pain in the ass. She wanted a helicopter ride. She wanted to know why we were not searching for the body. She wanted to know everything.

By Sunday evening after 1,000 volunteers searched the area until the last minute of daylight, their task for that day was complete. The search did not yield any evidence.

However, this unprecedented and most extensive search in the history of Wyoming County was determined to be a success in terms of response. All of western New York volunteered. Every law enforcement department in western New York had representatives. Some came from as far away as Seneca County. Three helicopters were used from Chautauqua, Erie County and the N.Y. State Police. Volunteer Fire Companies from as far as Livingston, Orleans and Genesee County sent searchers. Citizens from all over gave up their Saturday and Sunday to participate. It really was a community effort.

Angel Colon was still considered the number one suspect. Colon was being questioned by the Sheriff's Department with help from the FBI. Our guys were building a rock solid case. They had already secured evidence from the trailer, the Bronco that Colon and Rachel Stra had borrowed from her father, Bruno. They had testimony from key witnesses. Our friends, Gerry Stout, Sheriff Capwell, Ron Ely, Dennis Spink, Gary Eck, Steve Tarbell and the whole Department were becoming experts in homicide investigation.

Then things became very quiet. There were no more leads. The Sheriff's Department and Gerry Stout, the District Attorney were all becoming frustrated.

On May 23, 1997, Frank Conrad, a farmer plowing a field owned by his grandson just north of Shaw Road discovered the body of seven year old Samantha Zaldivar. Frank Conrad lives very close to the scene and very close to the Town of Java.

The Arcade Herald of 5/23/97 reported: " Frank Conrad said he was plowing the field when he saw something purple on the ground. When Conrad stopped and investigated further, he discovered the hood of a jacket sticking out of the ground, and when he pulled at the hood a small hand appeared."

As soon as Frank Conrad made the call to the Sheriff's, Ron Ely was on his way and he made a call to the FBI evidence collection team. I was on my way to Batavia with Cindy, Mike and Bridie to watch the Junior College World Series. Dispatcher Fred Ingles called me on my cell phone to let me know what was transpiring in Wethersfield. By the time I reached the parking lot at Dwyer Stadium, I had already received two calls from the press asking for more details.

Samantha's body was taken to the Medical Examiner of Monroe County in Rochester.

The preliminary results of the examination indicated that Samantha was sexually assaulted and suffocated in some way. Gerry Stout asked for blood and hair samples from Colon. D. Michael Murray said it would be up to Colon. Yeah, right.

In June, the Honorable Elaine Skotnicki, Town Justice for Wethersfield issued a bench warrant for Angel Colon for his failure to appear in Town Court relative to the charges from March. Colon was now somewhere in Florida or God only knew where. Again, because of Ron Ely's contacts, the U.S. Marshals were keeping a very close eye on young Angel Colon.

Colon was taken into custody by the U.S. Marshals in mid July in Homestead, Florida. He was then taken to Dade County jail. All this time, the Grand Jury was hard at work. Gerry Stout along with the Sheriff and FBI were presenting the evidence they had at that point.

On August 7th, the Grand Jury issued a 19 count indictment against Angel Colon for the murder of Samantha Zaldivar. Now all of the attorneys were attempting to reach an agreement on extradition. The bottom line was that Colon would not fight the extradition if he had an attorney with him on the plane from Miami to Buffalo. There was even talk of flying him to Buffalo on Con Air. Yes, Con Air is really an airline flown by U.S. Marshals transporting criminals and convicts all over the country. Ron Ely could not wait to get to Florida.

On August 12th, the Board of Supervisors held our regular monthly meeting at the Wyoming County Fairgrounds for the second year in a row. On the agenda was a Resolution calling for a salary increase for the part time Assistant District Attorneys. At that time they were, Mike Kelly, Dave DiMatteo and Keith Kibler. The increase was not just recommended by Gerry Stout. It also was highly recommended by Dennis Vacco, Attorney General of the State of New York. There was an excellent chance that this Colon case was going to involve the death penalty. Wyoming County could well be one of the first counties to have a death penalty trial. Under Governor Pataki's death penalty law, there were provisions to assist the counties both financially and with technical assistance. Of course to be fair to the other side, the State had also set up a New York Capital Defenders

Office. All concerned, urged Gerry Stout to clear his desk of all cases except the Colon case. Keep in mind that besides the usual court cases, the District Attorney was also preparing for a trial of Brian VanKuren, 21, who was charged with rape, two counts of burglary and two counts of assault in the Town of Eagle. It too, was a terrible case. The District Attorney's Office also handles all town court matters and charges stemming from any incidents at the state prison. The Assistant DA's all had private practices that were severely hurting because of the time now being demanded of them by their work load. The entire salary package meant an increase of about $24,000 total. $8,000 per ADA.

I was totally supportive of the measure for many reasons. I am not a prosecutor or district attorney. If those who are familiar with the positions and offices throughout the state, recommend that our DA clear his desk, who am I to argue? Gerry Stout was doing an excellent job in this case and all others. He even came to Public Safety Committee and updated the members on all items that he could. Gerry was also elected by the people of Wyoming County. Gerry's door was always open to all supervisors, if they had any questions or concerns. By this time, Angel Colon had D. Michael Murray, Norm Effman, and Patricia Warth and Thomas Dunn of the Capital Defenders Office, to represent him. I felt that we , the members of the Board of Supervisors should support our DA in this position. The pay increase passed 12 to 4. Voting no were Paul Agan, Attica, Anne Humphrey, Perry, Bob Bowles, Castile and Ron Herman, Wethersfield. Ron Herman was the only one to offer any explanation. Ron said, according to the Batavia Daily of 8/13/97, " .. Didn't think there was a back up of cases in the District Attorney's Office... I think we should see performance before we go to an increase." How about letting Colon walk, because our District Attorney was prosecuting some misdemeanor in Wethersfield? Is that the performance you were looking for, Ron? Alex Lane was quoted in the same article, " Warsaw Supervisor Alexandra Lane said she was originally opposed to the resolution but changed her mind and voted in favor. She said she switched because she felt the district attorney needed the support for the Samantha case. "

Shortly after Labor Day, Ron Ely and I think Gary Eck flew to Miami to escort Angel Colon back to Buffalo on 9/8/97. They all flew Northwest Airlines and accompanying Colon was Patricia Warth, from the New York Capital Defender Office, at his request, just to make sure Angel did not get hurt or anything. When they disembarked in Buffalo, they were supported by Sgt. Ed Till and Deputy Jason Mayer of the Wyoming County Sheriff's Department. Media from all over western New York also was there to greet the group. The Colon case was becoming more and more public. Escorting Colon through the terminal was no easy chore with all the onlookers in addition to the media. The Niagara Frontier Transportation Authority staff sent about a dozen or so airport police to assist.

On September 9, 1997, Angel Colon was arraigned in the Wyoming County Courthouse on first degree murder charges and 18 other counts in connection with the death of Samantha Zaldivar. Gerry Stout then filed a notice that he may seek the death penalty. Through Gerry's efforts and those of Dennis Vacco, Senator Volker, Assemblyman Reynolds and Governor Pataki, Gerry was able to receive help. Dennis Vacco assigned Diane LaVallee, Assistant Attorney General to help Gerry. The Death Penalty bill had just become law. I think one other trial was on going on in the state at that time. No one had tried a death penalty case in New York in years. The help was very welcome. Of course, the defense team objected verbally and in court. Imagine, it's OK to have two representatives from the State Capital Defenders Office, that are paid by tax dollars, but don't give any help to our local district attorney. It's just not fair, they said. Sorry, Norm, that's bullshit.

I should remind you that as I said previously, the Board of Supervisors' Offices were on the same floor as the Courtroom. The entire staff, including myself were witnesses to many of the court proceedings. It still sends chills down my spine when I recall the expressionless face and cold eyes, of Angel Colon. On the other hand, we were also witness to some of the horrific antics of the TV and other members of the media. They were mostly inconsiderate, rude slobs. They left everything from garbage, coffee cups to dirt and mud in the courthouse. And as you may remember they all used the one restroom that was on the second floor. The media invaded Warsaw. There were satellite trucks parked all over the village. They were interviewing people as they ate lunch. It was a true feeding frenzy. I hope this describes the picture accurately for you.

The next ten or eleven months was something of a mix between Perry Mason and the OJ murder trial. There were legal briefs, press conferences and more legal briefs. Angel Colon was in our Wyoming County Jail, housed with a couple of other perverts. Colon and Rachel Stra would have court appearances every once in a while for the murder case or even family court. We never knew when these were going to occur, until we arrived at the courthouse and saw the media all over.

At one point, we had a meeting between all parties on how in the world we were going to get a jury together. It was estimated that they would need to interview hundreds. Where were we going to do this? I actually called Brenda George from the North Java Fire Company and set a couple of dates. It was going to be very difficult. It was estimated that one of every five residents that were potential jurors, would be called. In a death penalty case, the prosecution and Judge for that matter has to be absolutely perfect. Even the defense cannot make a mistake. Any mistake and immediately, the accused has a right to appeal or worse. It was also felt that the Angel Colon murder trial was going to be about the first case in the new Courthouse.

The prosecution and the defense had expert witnesses from all over the country. There were volumes and volumes of testimony. Boxes of evidence. Computers, technical and medical equipment. The cost? Just to touch on it briefly, there were some injustices in the financing of a death penalty case. The state did set aside money to assist counties with a death penalty case. The defense team simply received reimbursement for their expenses. Not so with the prosecution. Wyoming County did receive help but we were extremely fortunate to have Gerry Stout, Dale Volker and Tom Reynolds on our side. A two million dollar murder trial could bring a small county to its knees. When is the price of justice too high? Just something to think about.

I had the honor of being friends with Gerry Stout, Al Capwell, Ron Ely, Mark Dadd, Steve Tarbell, Dennis Spink and many others. There is nothing that I could possibly say except that I admire each and every one of these people. They are truly qualified professionals and all of Wyoming County should be extremely proud of them and the job they all did in this case.

Angel Colon, his defense team, the prosecution and the law enforcement community reached a settlement. On August 13, 1998, 24 year old Angel Colon, entered a plea of guilty to the murder of Samantha Zaldivar. The first degree murder charge was reduced to second degree murder admitting to depraved indifference to human life in connection with Samantha's death. Judge Mark Dadd set August 26th as sentencing day.

Ron Ely and Gary Eck escorted Angel Colon from the jail to the Courthouse that morning. The Courtroom was packed. Besides the media and Courthouse employees, Samantha's grandmother, aunt and cousin all traveled from Florida. Bruno Stra, Samantha's grandfather was there as he always was. I always held a place in my heart for him. Bruno Stra was at every proceeding and how he controlled his temper, I have no idea. Many times, in disgust at Colon, I would want to shout out at him or physically harm him. Bruno controlled himself. He is a good man. Rachel was absent.

Colon was again emotionless. He was wearing a black and white pull-over short sleeve shirt. Just to show himself as a bigger wise guy, he had rolled the sleeves up to show off his muscles. Yeah, muscles used in the murder and rape of a defenseless seven year old girl who should have been giggling and getting ready for another year of her life.

The deal was pretty simple. Colon would plead guilty, Rachel Stra would receive no jail time and Colon would be sentenced to 25 years to life without parole for at least 25 years. I immediately accepted the sentence and felt that it was a necessary compromise. Others did not.

Gerry Stout became the target of criticism. There were the editorials, telephone calls and radio calls. Gerry decided to have a press conference and explain his case. He did a great job.

The district attorney had pieces of the bed mattress and bed rail as evidence. It was determined that there was blood and the DNA results proved the blood was Samantha's. There was also blood in the Ford Bronco that was used by Colon to take Samantha's body to the field. Colon was seen washing and hanging the floor mats thinking he had cleansed all blood from the materials. Not so.. the Sheriff's department can now do investigations unheard of ten years ago. I personally attribute our huge advances to Steve Tarbell and his dedication to forensic studies.

The expert witnesses had differing opinions on whether Colon deliberately suffocated Samantha or if he accidentally suffocated her, by placing a pillow over her face in an attempt to quiet her. To be convicted of first degree murder, the prosecution must prove to the jury that Colon intended to kill her.

Another key element of the plea bargain was that Colon waived all his rights for an appeal. That was huge. Wyoming

County had the killer and he was going to jail for at least 25 years, if he could survive prison.

Another positive aspect of the arrangement, was that Colon signed a statement admitting he injured Samantha(sexual abuse) and suffocated her in an attempt to quiet her after she began to scream and bleed. Colon also said that he cleaned up the bedroom and when Rachel came home from night school then told her that Samantha was sleeping. He said later that night, he picked up Samantha's body, placed her in the Bronco and drove to the field to bury her.

I know the public at that time felt Colon was getting off easy. I wanted to know why he would plead guilty and face 25 years to life. Who was he protecting? Was he doing it just to keep Rachel Stra from going to jail as an accomplice? Let's face facts, if Colon survives state prison, Rachel will certainly have a new boyfriend by the time he gets out. Why?

The bottom line of this case and the plea bargain, was that we had the very best professionals in control of this case for all those concerned. The public did not know all the details that they did. Instead of questioning if Colon did that or this, they received a signed statement from Colon admitting guilt. The plea bargain assured that there was not going to be a never ending slate of appeals. It was a win win for all, except poor little Samantha.

Those deciding the decision on the plea were Gerry Stout, Ron Ely, Assistant Attorney General Diane LaVallee and Harold Frank an investigator from the attorney general's office. Harold Frank was unbelievable. Every law enforcement officer that I ever talked to had nothing but the highest praise and thanks for his contribution in this case.

In conclusion, I hope Wyoming County never has to go through another ordeal like the Samantha Zaldivar murder case. God Bless Her in Heaven and thank God for Sheriff Capwell, Ron Ely, Gerry Stout, Norm Effman, Mark Dadd and all the others who worked so hard and tirelessly to bring this horrific case to an end with a measure of justice for her and a punishment for her murderer that, although practical, it does not and probably will not ever satisfy the public's desire to see Colon suffer as she did. I'm sure it will never be considered justice served, for she is innocent and dead and he is guilty and alive.

Chapter 40

1997 Elections -
Chicken Shit Dirt

The "rumor-starters" (a good clean name for that kind of people) were really busy in 1997. There were more lies about what I was doing than there were prayers being said at Sunday Mass.

Even before election time, they were started. I still would like to get into the head of somebody who decides to start a rumor for whatever reason. As I said before many times, do they actually wake up in the morning and say to themselves, well I think I'm going to start a nasty rumor about somebody today? Are they so stupid or mean that they do not understand the hurt they are responsible for? I just can't understand it. Not that I am anymore holy than anyone else, I simply could not bring myself to start or repeat a vicious rumor that I knew was untrue.

The " Java Six" were accusing me of embezzling money, stealing North Java water (God forgive), drinking two cases of beer before noon, lying (can you believe that one?), collecting a disability pension fraudulently, and many others that I really don't want to get into yet.

We, the Republicans, decided to hold our caucus on August 4th at the Java Center Fire Hall. There were 82 Republicans on hand plus a Democratic Judge, Mike Skrzypek, whom Joanne Almeter invited. That kind of a turnout was unprecedented, as far as I can determine. Our faction was out to nominate Sue Kozlowski in place of Janet Zielinski. We had also decided to oust Ron McCormick if he accepted a nomination. Carl Heterbring, the Republican town chairman and I agreed who better to conduct the caucus than Joanne Almeter. She did and what a terrible job she did. Once Carl and I recommended Almeter as Chair, she was elected by voice vote. Almeter then appointed her own tellers. The tellers would count the secret paper ballots. Almeter, keep in mind, ran the show that night.

Sue Kozlowski beat Janet Zielinski at the caucus. Therefore; Sue was the Republican candidate for Town Clerk. Ron Ring was nominated for Supervisor and I beat him. Ron McCormick announced that he would not seek re-election. Hip Hip Hooray ! Ron Falconer and Janet Miller were the Republican candidates for council members.

Janet Zielinski filed a challenge against the Republican caucus. Huh? Was she accusing her buddy, Almeter of conducting a questionable caucus? Her contention was that the paper work filed by Almeter was invalid and the caucus was improperly advertised.

The Board of Election scheduled a hearing for August 20, 1997 at 2PM at the Board of Elections office in Warsaw. In the Batavia Daily the Democratic Election Commissioner, Harry Brown was quoted, " She can file a petition with the Supreme Court on these objections." The Republican Commissioner, Herb Toal, was quoted in the same paper as saying, " Janet Zielinski brought a charge to the board's attention that Java's Republican caucus was wrong. As far as an election board, we have very little that we can say or do. " In the same issue Janet Zielinski was quoted saying, " I don't think I should really comment at this time ". Really, if I felt aggrieved I think I would have some comments. Almeter too declined comment.

Carl Heterbring was confused. Almeter ran the caucus, there were a record number of people in attendance, what the hell was the problem. And...... two days later, Zielinski received the Democratic nomination for the Town Clerk, anyway.

Once again, I was going door to door to campaign. My campaign platform was quite simple. The Town of Java and Wyoming County property taxes were not having an increase again. In the Buffalo News of 11/29/97, it was stated, " In 1995, a study by M&T Bank found that Wyoming County had the lowest taxes in the state. Next year, Wyoming County will drop its tax rate still another notch." I also ran on my record as a proven leader that achieved results. The transfer station was operating successfully for two years. Highway equipment was updated on a regular basis. I kept the residents informed by issuing my newsletter monthly. The Park was being developed with no tax dollars being budgeted. I even applied for grants for the transfer station, records management, park and of course the damn water district. What else could I do?

How much more was I expected to do?

Once again, it was political dirty tricks time and someone sent a really horrible letter to town residents two days before the election. One resident called me so upset that she just wanted to reassure me that no matter how she WAS going to vote, she was now not only voting for me but encouraging her friends and neighbors to vote too. The letter was just shitty. Shitty material and written very shittily too. I will tell you one paragraph that was absolutely absurd. In 1997, there was a young man that was accused of deliberately infecting females with the AIDS/HIV disease in the Jamestown, N.Y. area. This paragraph implied that if the Town Park was developed, Java too might experience a tragedy such as that. Is that ridiculous or what?

Don Roche was also going door to door. He was preaching that he was responsible for the good financial condition of the Town and its improved highway equipment. Right, Don! Check it out. I mentioned earlier that Don Roche supported the idea of setting aside money for highway equipment. He also urged the Board not to build the salt storage building near the highway and instead place it back further from the road. He was right. And of course Don Roche was whispering as only Don could do.

I always liked and respected Don. Until now... politics had taken that friendship away. Instead, rumors and allegations had taken the place of truth. I was getting sick of campaigns. Cindy was even more hurt than I was. Ron Falconer said it best, " We have to agree to disagree". Shit, the first few years in office, the entire Town Board would stop at the JCT or Sad Dog Saloon for a few beers and some euchre. Now, all of a sudden, we could not do that and instead some had to bad mouth others. Now what was that all about? Java is a small town and there is no need for that type of politics. The Java Six never confronted me personally. They would only do it behind my back or as a group in front of an audience. Kids stuff. Why not call Moran and say, " Hey did you use North Java water to fill your swimming pool ? " You would have got a big NO for an answer but I guess you didn't ask because you already knew the answer. At one Zoning Board meeting, Mark McCormick made a reference that I was receiving a free pass at Archie's Chip and Putt Golf Course. At the next meeting, I provided copies of the canceled checks.

Election night was planned as a huge party. I had an Elvis Presley impersonator scheduled to appear at the Sad Dog Saloon. Dave Hackett as usual was very generous. I invited everyone from Town and Sue Aldinger, Kathy Kuchler, Sally Meeghan, Lucy Sheedy and many others from the County. I know it was a little presumptuous. But what the hell.

I beat Don Roche by a little over a 100 votes. So it was getting closer. I still loved the job but I really hated the rumors, allegations and downright lies. I really did not know if I was going to run again or not.

Ron Falconer and John Meyer won as Council members. Oh yeah, Charlie McCormick was a loser again, this time as a candidate for council. I think he was the low vote getter among all of us. And... yes, Janet Zielinski beat Sue Kozlowski. Zielinski ran as a Democrat because Sue beat her out at the Republican caucus. At least, we were going to have a reasonable Town Board.

In the County, Howard Miller beat out Alex Lane in the Town of Warsaw. Howard Miller served as Warsaw Town Justice from 1972 to 1991. Howard was quoted as saying, " I hope to be more of a part of the solution." And he was. Howard Miller was a former military man and he also had a great sense of humor. And, my dear friend Ken Lowe lost his reelection bid in the Town of Covington to Wil Guthrie. Ken was one of the kindest and nicest people on the Board of Supervisors. I still owe an awful lot to Ken and his wife, Fran. Just to show you what kind of people they are, one time, Cindy and I were going to meet them at their house in Covington. It was a warm sunny morning. When I pulled into their driveway, there was Ken and Fran rocking in a glider on the side of the house and holding each other's hands. Imagine, after 50 plus years of marriage and still showing public affection. How can anyone say anything but good about them? What did Ken get after years of public service? Nothing. Covington never even had a testimonial in his honor. I guess Jim Schlick and I know what that is all about.

Earl Dominesey from Sheldon was another welcome addition. I knew Earl before he was Supervisor. Earl was also the Sheldon supervisor from 1974 to 1981. I cannot say enough good about Earl. Earl was a Democrat. But.. Earl always based all of his decisions on what was best for Wyoming County. Party politics had nothing to do with it. Earl asked little in return. In fact, after the 1997 elections, he telephoned and requested a meeting with me to discuss the state of Wyoming County and the Board of Supervisors. He wanted to be informed and educated before January 1st. Because things were so tense in Java and Sheldon, we decided to meet at Earl's Restaurant on Route 16 in Erie County. This way, nobody would see us. See how bad things were getting. I appreciated Earl taking the time for what I would call a re-orientation. I also appreciated Earl's friendship while on the Board and after. God Bless Earl and his wife Jean and their family.

With the absence of Nelson George and his dirty white socks, my re-election as Chairman was unanimous in 1998. The main goals for 1998, were the completion of the new courthouse, decisions on the renovation of the old courthouse, continuing the reform of the workers compensation program for the county, towns, villages and school districts, trying to keep the state in line and of course holding down property taxes.

In the Batavia Daily News of 1/3/98 this quote appeared:

" *'I was quoted last year as saying this is a fun job even on the worst day,' Moran said before a packed board room Friday, (Organization Meeting on January, 2 1998) ...Well... I still feel that way. Looking back on 1997, I think we can all agree that it was a very good year. "*

Chapter 41

The Year of Natural Disasters

Back in 1995, Jack Fisher, the Director of Emergency Services, informed each Town in Wyoming County that they should have a disaster plan, in place. The purpose of the plan was to allow for a coordinated effort by all government services in case of a disaster. The County also adopted the plan. Article 2-B of the New York State Executive Law provided that the chief elected officer of each municipality had the authority to declare a state of emergency and coordinate and supervise all activities. Jack Fisher was a very informed and dedicated individual who did his very best in his position and on behalf of the county. Wyoming County was at least some-what prepared.

In January of 1996, my very first year as Chairman of the Board of Supervisors, Warsaw, Pike and Genesee Falls experienced a rapid thaw of snow and heavy rains. Jack Fisher immediately greeted me at my car in the parking lot of the courthouse. Jack then drove me around to see first hand the effected areas. The most severely flooded locations were Pike and Genesee Falls at the river. I arranged for a meeting with Sheriff Capwell and Gary Weidman, the County Highway Superintendent, to meet with Jack Fisher and myself. It took about ten minutes to decide that I should issue a state of emergency declaration for those towns. Some thought that declarations of emergency were too much like grandstanding and over dramatic. They were not. The County and the towns have a responsibility for the safety and welfare of its residents. It also provided for total documentation of the event and was reported to the State and sometimes Federal governments, in case any federal funds were forthcoming.

January 9, 1998, Disaster Number One: Wednesday night, the 7th of January, the temperature began to rise. By Thursday, snow was melting very quickly and then the ice storm began. By early Friday morning, there were over 5,000 homes, businesses and farms without power. There were hundreds of structures flooded. Many roads were impassable.

Jim Reger was the new Emergency Services Coordinator just taking over on 1/1/98. What a baptism he got. After talking with Jim, we decided that Sheriff Capwell and Gary Weidman should meet with us. Again, it was decided that I should issue a state of emergency throughout Wyoming County.

Most farms have the luxury of generators, but there were many who did not. Reger and the Volunteer Fire Companies did a superb job getting more generators. It was a terrific hardship for many dairy farmers. Travel in certain parts of the county were extremely hazardous due to fallen branches, trees and downed power lines. The Wyoming County Chapter of the Red Cross opened shelters in several Fire Halls as well as Attica Central School.

Through the powers of the Chairman of the Board, I designated Jim Reger as the officer in control. Jim supervised the operation of the volunteer fire and emergency services and worked closely with the Sheriff's department, County Highway and other local government agencies.

By Sunday morning, all power was restored except for about 250 homes. The temperature was again in the 30's and things were beginning to get back to normal. On Monday, January 12th, I lifted the state of emergency and we all began to attempt to secure some financial assistance for those needing it.

On June 2, 1998 the unbelievable occurred. It was a stormy and unsettled day, with typical thunder storms and high humidity. There was a Finance Committee meeting and a County Operations Committee meeting in the afternoon. The Java Center little league team's game was postponed on account of the rain. At about 6:30 P.M. I was on my way from Java Center to Kathy Wilson's house in North Java for some park business. When I approached the five corners intersection of Routes 78 and 98, the brightest and most brilliant rainbow I had ever seen was on the eastern horizon. I can still see that rainbow. The colors were magnificent, then I received a call on my cell phone that a tornado was reported to have touched down in Orangeville!

I turned the car around and headed for my home. I was on the phone for the next few hours with Jim Reger, Sheriff Capwell and Gary Weidman the Highway Superintendent. Again, it was decided to declare a limited state of emergency in the Towns of Perry, Orangeville, Warsaw and Castile.

The official report read, " Shortly after 6:30 P.M. a tornado touched down in the Town of Orangeville traveling east affecting a path   mile wide and 15 miles long, lifting off east of Perry. " The path of the tornado ran in an east-west zig zag pattern starting around Wethersfield Road, then north to Hermitage Road and Liberty Street near the Orangeville-Warsaw border. It continued across the Oatka Valley in South Warsaw, up the east side of the valley at Keeney Road, then to Oatka Road and Silver Springs Road and into the village of Perry.

There were about 10,000 residents without power and numerous homes and farms that received substantial damage. Travel was limited and almost at once, residents from all around became curious and ventured onto the roads to make matters worse. The Red Cross was again in action and opened shelters in the Perry Firemen's building in the Village Park. We also imposed a curfew in the village of Perry from 6:00 P.M. til 6:00 A.M.

I think it was about eleven o'clock when I finally got off the phone. I made arrangements with Gary Weidman to meet at the courthouse early in the morning to travel the path of the tornado. Gary and I headed out very early. All of the roads in the wake of the tornado were closed. Gary drove and he had to maneuver the car around trees, power lines and other debris.

I had never seen anything like it. And I hope I never do again. As we drove from touch down, we could see the extensive damage. The Herman barn on Hermitage Road was destroyed. The Rood storage building could be seen in the woods 1/4 mile away. The Stoffer home no longer existed. You could actually see the path of the tornado through the woods and fields going into the valley. On Keeney Road, several homes suffered serious damage including Howard Miller's home. The eeriest site was the Wilkie Farm on Silver Springs Road. The barn was gone but the stanchions were still there. There were reports that some of the cows were still standing also. When we went over the hill towards Silver Lake we could again see exactly where the tornado touched down. It seemed to bounce up and down along its path of destruction. Witnesses stated that it went right across the lake and headed for the Washington Street trailer park. At least four mobile homes were totally destroyed and many others suffered severe damage. The roofs on Burt's Lumber and Daryl's Pizza were lifted off.

Gary and I met Jim Reger and the Perry Fire Chief at the trailer park. Anne Humphrey was also there. I talked to several residents and I could not believe their resolve. They were taking it much better than I was. I had a queasy feeling in my stomach. I felt that I had a responsibility and duty to these people. I was determined to do whatever was necessary to obtain financial help for them.

Upon arriving back at the office, I telephoned, Congressman Bill Paxon, State Senator Dale Volker and State Assemblyman Tom Reynolds. All were very receptive and all expressed a willingness to sponsor any movement for assistance. Having just returned from the scene, I was still quite emotional and all three could sense the urgency of the situation. In fact, while I was talking to Reynolds, I told him that Wyoming County was going to require about $1 million for disaster assistance. Tom indicated that he would do everything he could, but he could not promise anything yet. It was the day after the state of New York GAVE, not loaned, Erie County 43 million to renovate Rich Stadium (Buffalo Bills) . I then told Tom Reynolds, " You remember the $43 million that you appropriated for the Buffalo Bills? , well... give us one million and give them the other 42 million." Dale Volker and Mark Reiman from his office made arrangements to meet with Anne Humphrey and myself the following day for a tour of the damage. Dale was flying back from Albany so that he could see first hand what the tornado had done. Dale was visibly moved by the damage.

It was amazing that there were no serious injuries. Through the combined efforts of Paxon, Reynolds and Volker we were able to secure financial help. Governor Pataki also declared a state of emergency in those Towns. Marty Mucher and Alan Bliss from Wyoming County Community Action spear headed the movement. The Board of Supervisors held an emergency session to officially request the $1 million. Alan Bliss began his year long work on disaster relief.

On July 2nd, the Board of Supervisors held another emergency session to accept $633,000 in relief aid for the tornado. That money could not have been received without Tom Reynolds, Dale Volker, Bill Paxon and Jim Reger and Alan Bliss. Jim and Alan did all the damage assessments and paper work. Dale, Tom and Bill made sure it happened.

Alan Bliss coordinated the administration of the grant. He personally contacted each resident and helped in completing the forms. Just as a side note, one resident had the audacity to write the Governor, Volker, Reynolds, Kevin DeFebbo, Howard Miller and myself complaining that he apparently had a problem with some of the financial income questions that were on the form.

He thought they were invasive and " big brother nosiness". Oh well.....there's always one.

In the early morning hours of June 26, 1998, thunderstorms began in the Town of Arcade. When they were over in less than 2   hours, Arcade received over 5 inches of rain. Cattaraugus Creek is usually at one and a half feet, by early afternoon it was at 12   feet. Cars, pets and even a portable toilet were floating down the village streets. Again, the damage was severe.

A serious drama took place on Water Street in the village. According to the Arcade Herald of 7/2/98, they reported: " Pat Domes and her son Michael had anxiously watched the flood waters rising. As they struggled to get into their car and head for higher ground, the water came over the bridge and quickly began to fill their car with water. Volunteer firefighter Ernie Saari saw what was happening and three other firefighters, Don Myers, Gary Gradl and Vic Husted joined him as he went to their aid. By this time, the car started to float, and the current had pushed the car sideways, jamming the passenger side of the vehicle against the garage. The current, was estimated at between 15 and 25 mph, held the passenger side fast. ' The car only had about six inches of its roof showing' Gradl says. '" All I could see were their faces turned up in an air space at the roof and a cat she was holding up'. Michael Domes described his experience, ' The car filled up as we got in', he says. ' We were hoping the door would open and we said a little prayer. After a while, I could see the firemen were having a hard time getting us out.' ' We were using hoses and a rope line and we were still worried about being swept downstream,' fireman Vic Husted says. ' It seemed like an eternity'. As firefighters struggled to free the Domes, village employee Dan Laird and police Sergeant John Rix drove by in the village pay loader. ' When I saw Don and Gary up to their necks in water, I knew they were in trouble' Rix said. ' They were in full turn out gear and when I looked at their faces, I could see they were in trouble'. Using the pay loader, Laird lifted up one side corner of the car, releasing the pressure on the door. Immediately, the inside pressure forced the door open and the Domes were helped onto the bucket and taken to safety."

The gentlemen above are true heroes. There were also volunteer heroes from 22 other Fire Companies from Wyoming, Cattaraugus, Allegany and Erie Counties.

156 homes and 22 businesses experienced damage from the flood waters. The Red Cross was again summoned and responded as usual. The Red Cross provided emergency shelters, clothing, food and other essentials.

Jim Reger, Alan Bliss and Supervisor Doug Berwanger coordinated the relief movement. Building inspectors from adjacent counties and the State all arrived in Arcade to assess the damage. Another State of Emergency was declared and followed up by one from the Governor. Disasters and states of emergency were becoming far too common.

On July 8, 1998 it began raining on the other side of the County. This time the Tonawanda Creek was the main focus point. My parents were visiting from Florida so I was home that day. Here we go again, I thought.

The telephone began ringing in the morning. This time Attica, Bennington, Sheldon, Warsaw and Orangeville received over six inches of rain in a matter of a few hours. Another state of emergency. Another disaster. This time, we were not so fortunate. Two people drowned in Attica. Again, that queasy, nauseous feeling. Terrible !

In Attica, people were evacuated from Prospect, Washington, Water and Exchange Streets. Jim Reger, the Sheriff's Department and all of the County's volunteer fire service were on duty again. By mid afternoon, it seemed the worst was over. Then it all began again. This time another three inches of rain. Earl Dominesey and Suzanne West both called me around dinner time. Centerline Road from Sheldon across Route 98 in Orangeville was a total mess. I drove to the scene.

I just could not believe what I saw. Centerline Road looked like the Niagara River rapids. The bridge in Johnsonburg was impassable. There were people stranded in their homes as if they lived on an island in the center of a raging river.

Jim Daniels, the Orangeville Highway Superintendent was also present, along with County Superintendent Gary Weidman. Immediate action was necessary. Fortunately Ed Hulme was there. I authorized Ed to do whatever it takes to provide for the safety of those residents. There were probably about 100 volunteer emergency service personnel. They were performing above and beyond the call of duty. I always appreciated the efforts of the volunteers, but after witnessing their actions during these disasters, the word appreciate just doesn't cut it any longer.

All Americans should be grateful to them and even more proud of their efforts and selflessness. May God Bless them all !

Earl Dominesey, Suzanne West, Jim Schlick and Paul Agan began to take corrective action at once. A committee was formed to assess all of the creeks and streams in the county. The objective was and still is to identify potential problem areas and clean them up. Much of the flooding on the Tonawanda Creek was due to trees, limbs and other debris blocking and actually damming up the waters. The County is now appropriating money every year for stream stabilization to prevent or minimize damage by future flooding. Of course, it is never enough. The Board of Supervisors tries to do what they can with what they have.

This time, even President Clinton declared Wyoming County as a disaster area that made it eligible for federal funds.

All of the county officials were becoming far too familiar with the offices of the State and Federal Emergency Services. The State and federal agencies held two emergency meetings on how to apply for financial assistance. Senator Volker publicly praised Wyoming County and our handling of the disasters. We were looked on as examples of total coordination and cooperation among county department, local governments and the volunteer service.

The Red Cross of Wyoming County worked their butts off. Their training and experience paid off in spades. The executive director, Dale Palesh was a blessing to all of us. I was beginning to feel guilty calling on her all of the time. Dale and her volunteers worked not only with the victims, but also with Jim Reger and all of the other emergency services people. We had a great rapport with her and the Red Cross. On July 14th, the Board of Supervisors presented Dale Palesh with a proclamation recognizing their efforts through all of the disasters. I also declared that the remaining Mondays before Labor Day, were to be " Dress Down" days. For a $5 donation, county employees could come to work in casual dress attire. The Red Cross's financial condition had suffered quite a strain and we hoped to replenish some of that.

Before I close the book on this chapter, I'd like to commend Jim Reger. Jim was new on the job as of January 1, 1998. He suffered quite a bit of good natured ribbing about his being the cause of these disasters. In fact, I said publicly that if we had one more disaster, he was going to be fired. From the very first ice storm, Jim rose to the test and got better and better. Wyoming County is truly fortunate to have a man like Jim Reger as its Emergency Services Director. Thanks, Jim !!!

By the way, on September 25th, Mother Nature took one last swipe at Wyoming County, a mild earthquake was felt at 4:24 P.M. I was in my car, so I never felt it.

Chapter 42

Politics at its Best, Politics at its Worst

On February 25, 1998, Bill Paxon's Office called me to inform me that Bill was announcing his retirement on February 26th at the Holiday Inn in Batavia. My first reaction was total shock. I admired Bill and was always grateful for his representation and prompt replies and actions on all issues that affected Wyoming County and Java. I had never known a better congressman. Bill Paxon was also among the leaders in the Congress and had even been mentioned as a Vice Presidential candidate. Bill was at one time an ally of Newt Gingrich. Sometime in 1997, he and Gingrich had a falling out for some reason. That is Washington politics. They don't get any better than Bill Paxon. He was and is honest, dedicated and loyal to all of his constituents. The district and Wyoming County was losing a very dear friend and advocate.

Tom Reynolds was also going to announce his intention to run for Congress in place of Bill. That was great news to me. Tom Reynolds was also a true friend of mine and a friend to Wyoming County. Maybe we were losing Paxon, but in a short time, I knew that we would be very satisfied with Reynolds. Who was going to replace Reynolds? Tom Reynolds had in a few short years, become the Republican Leader of the New York State Assembly. Tom was the number three man in New York.

Suddenly it hit me. I could handle this assembly position. There was no doubt in my mind. What the hell, I had been involved in state politics, campaigns and personally witnessed the games that were played in Albany. I could definitely handle this challenge. Cindy thought it was a great idea. Reynolds had always given me advice on politics and I was going to ask him what he thought.

Thursday, the 26th, there was a huge press conference with Bill Paxon, his wife Susan Molinari and their baby. After Bill announced his decision not seek another term, Tom Reynolds immediately announced his desire to become the Congressman from the 27th Congressional District. Tom came up to me afterwards and said that he would be in Warsaw, the next day to announce his candidacy in Wyoming County. I asked him to set aside some time for me, personally. He said sure.

After I left the press conference, I began to call my friends, colleagues, and supporters for their thoughts. I contacted Jim Schlick, Doug Berwanger, Gus Petrie, Ken Lowe, Ross Roberts, Carl Heterbring, Dave Hackett, Sue Aldinger, Janet Coveny, Eric Dadd, Jim Hardie, Arlene Witkowski, Donna Schofield, Ron Ely, Sheriff Capwell and many, many others. I tried to reach Howard Payne but he and Loretta, his wife were vacationing in Florida. Everyone that I reached told me to go for it. They were unanimous. I then rested my decision on Tom Reynolds. I needed Tom's support. If he was against me or even neutral, I was NOT going to run. I could not wait for the next day. On Friday, February 27th, Tom Reynolds was in the old family courtroom in Warsaw to announce his intentions once again. After that announcement, he came up to my office and we spoke behind closed doors. Sue Aldinger, Kevin DeFebbo, Cheryl Mayer, Kathy Schwab and Janet Coveny all knew that my decision was going to be based on my conversation with Reynolds.

I opened up the discussion and asked for his opinion on whether I should seek the nomination for the 147th Assembly District. He was overwhelmed. Tom was really enthusiastic. I was on cloud nine. He talked of how we could work together between the state and Washington. He thought it was a natural fit. Instead of Paxon and Reynolds, it was going to be Reynolds and Moran. He shook my hand and gave me a huge hug. He was just as happy as I was. Then he got very serious and advised me as to how handle the County Chairmen (Republican Party). He told me to reach out to every one of them and also every Committeeperson for all of the counties. He gave me some pointers and contacts. We talked for over 45 minutes.

As soon as he left, the entire staff knew what my decision was. After all, if Tom Reynolds was encouraging and supporting me, what more could I ask for?

The 147th Assembly District encompasses all of Wyoming County and parts of Genesee, Livingtson, Erie, Cattaraugus, and Allegany Counties. That afternoon, I called every Town Supervisor in Wyoming County to let them know that I was scheduling a press conference on Monday morning, March 2nd to announce my intention to seek the assembly seat vacated by

Tom Reynolds. I also called my very good friends Dennis House, the Chair from Livingston County and John Walchli, the Chair from Allegany County. I also spoke with Ed Burdick from Allegany. I also contacted my " good buddy", Jim Maloney, an attorney. They were all behind me. Jim Maloney was a classmate in law school of my very good friend Paul McQuillen. I had appointed Jim as Town attorney. I also gave a very high recommendation for him to Eric Dadd, who hired him as an Assistant County Attorney. I also introduced him to Tom Reynolds who was instrumental in having Maloney appointed as Counsel to Senator Mary Lou Rath. When Jim left Senator Rath, I also hooked him up with the New York Municipal Insurance Reciprocal to represent them in various litigations. Jim agreed to be my campaign manager. I also contacted the County Republican Committee Chairs, Carole Butler, Wyoming, Bob Heaney, Allegany County, Lowell Conrad, Livingston County, Amy Torrey, Genesee County, Jerry Moriarity, Cattaraugus County and of course Bob Davis from Erie County.

I was on the telephone the entire week-end. Everyone was excited. Imagine finally an Assemblyman from Wyoming County! On Monday morning at the Courthouse I was going to make my announcement in the Chambers of the Board of Supervisors. The Buffalo News reported that there were over 30 County officials in attendance. I think every Supervisor was there to show their support. Hank Bush was there also. It was a great morning.

Carole Butler was absent so Jim Schlick, as Vice Chair of the Republican Committee introduced Carl Heterbring, the Java Town Chair who then introduced me.

I began my speech with a baseball analogy. " Lou Gehrig said it and so did Mickey Mantle and now I am going to say it, today I am the luckiest man on the earth". I also said, " Opportunity is knocking on my door but it is also knocking on Wyoming County's door, I think we had better answer it ". I vowed to represent the entire district and stated that I could make a difference. I focused on less government and lower taxes.

By the end of my speech we had some more candidates. Dan Burling, the Vice Chair from Genesee, Rod Bennett, Legislator from Allegany and Gregory Parker from Livingston County had all thrown their hats in the ring. Rodney called me that afternoon and told me that he was going to withdraw from the race in a few weeks and endorse me. I also attempted to contact Jess

Fitzpatrick, the Legislative Chair in Cattaraugus County. Then, I received the first of many interesting phone calls. Charlie Nesbitt, an assemblyman from Orleans and Genesee County called. Now, I knew Charlie but we were by no means buddies. Charlie encouraged me to ask for a convention to decide this race. A convention would include every Republican committeeperson from the entire district. Each committee-person would have the number of votes that George Pataki received in the last election. The majority would receive the nomination and if an agreement could be reached, there would not be a long and expensive primary. Interesting.

I also recruited my very good friends, Paul McQuillen and Mario Alaimo. Paul was best man at our wedding, fellow ConRail employee and real buddy. Mario was a friend of mine from the days when he worked for Tom Reynolds. Mario was experienced in state politics and all issues concerning the assembly. Mario was then working for the Erie County Board of Elections. The next Saturday morning we had a campaign committee meeting. Jim and Helene Schlick, Anne Humphrey, Doug Berwanger, Bob Bowles, Sue Aldinger, Donna Schofield, Carl Heterbring, Bill Holt, Jim and Betty Hardie, Herb Toal, Arlene and Mike Witkowski, Mark Cali from Perry were among those in attendance. Donna Schofield was appointed as Treasurer. Doug and Jim Schlick were like co chairs. Maloney said he would be better qualified to serve as a legal advisor with Paul McQuillen. In fact, Paul took me personally to Carlson's Photography immediately for a picture so that Hogie's Quick Print could begin printing the palm cards to distribute to committee people. Mario was the key person in this campaign. This campaign was off and running, full steam ahead.

Jim Schlick and others solicited financial donations. There were several fund raisers. Gary Boorman was gracious enough to donate his office space on Buffalo Street in Warsaw as my campaign headquarters. Jim Schlick and Don Joller secured office furniture, refrigerator, microwave and many other items. We were moved in within ten days or so.

Things were looking great. Reynolds was also in touch on a regular basis to provide advice and ask how I was doing.

My committee was awesome. They demanded that they be allowed to do all the work. They ordered the materials, printing and scheduled fundraisers. They wanted me to reach out and contact every committee person. Cindy and I were both completely overwhelmed and humbled by the out pouring of volunteers, work and donations. It was, and still is, a very emotional topic.

I visited the Allegany County Republican Chair, Bill Heaney first. Heaney lived in Belfast and was a school teacher. I went to his house for the initial contact. The reception was very good and he also reported that Rodney Bennett was not in the race for the duration. Heaney gave me a ' proud to be Republican' button, which I still have today. Big Deal ! I then visited Jerry Moriarity in Franklinville. I was very impressed with him and thought he was sincere and a real gentleman. Lowell Conrad was next on my list. Conrad was the Livingston County Chair and ran a very small television and appliance store in Geneseo. I guess he may have been a vacuum cleaner salesman in his prime. His reception was not quite as warm. It was more like Carole Butler's lack-luster response to the whole thing. Like" Oh, really, that's good."

Bob Davis was impossible to see personally but I spoke with him on the telephone. Davis was a very busy man. In fact I usually dealt with Bob Lichtenthal, his vice chair who surprisingly ended up being appointed to the Erie County Water Authority as Chairman. Here's a funny story about the first time I met Davis. I was in Albany to attend a County Board Chair reception for state legislators. Tom Reynolds was not able to attend but he sent his point man, Mike Brady. Mike apologized for Reynolds and told me that Tom would like me to come to a restaurant called, ' The Sign of the Tree' in the Empire Plaza about 10:30 P.M. I was going to have dinner with Jim Maloney, who was working for Mary Lou Rath at the time. At dinner, I mentioned the invite to Maloney. He went nuts. He said we had to go. I really wasn't going to. It was snowing, it was late and we had already had a few beers. Maloney said he would drive. OK, then we'll go.

Maloney and I arrived at the bar about 10:30 P.M. No one was there. However, shortly after our first beer, in came Tom Reynolds and an entourage of about 30 or 40 people. There were other assemblymen, (including Charlie Nesbitt) staffers, Erie County legislators and of course Bob Davis. Tom passed out cigars to all and introduced me to just about everybody, including Davis. Then Bob Davis sat down at a corner table with his back to the wall. This way, he could see everything and everybody at the bar. One by one, those in attendance went to his table to pay him homage and praise. After all, this was Bob Davis, the Erie County Republican Chair. Again, Big Deal ! He put his pants on the same way that I did. Maloney went over for his few minutes in the sun? "Aren't you going over, Tom?", Maloney asked. No. Why would I genuflect before the Erie County Chair? I had just met him and wasn't really that impressed. I mean, he was not elected by the general population, he had no real stake in the operations or conditions of Wyoming County. Looking back, I probably should have kissed his ass. It was quite a night of politics, beer and cigars. I had a great time and met some other great people. However, some of these political party Chairs believe their shit doesn't stink. They want all republicans to honor and obey them. Lowell Conrad actually told some one that I should come back over and kiss his ring again. Right, and I did. I went over a second time and he questioned me in detail about some things that he had heard from none other than Joanne Almeter. Oh great. Lowell also told me that he was very experienced with primaries and conventions. After all, he said that he was personally responsible for the election of Jerry Johnson as State Assemblyman. Conrad told me that he made Jerry Johnson what he was today. Of course at that time Johnson had not been arrested, convicted and spent time in prison for weird things he did. In fact at this writing he is in the Steuben County Jail serving a two year jail sentence. Way to go, Lowell baby !

Unfortunately, Carole Butler was completely lost in this whole process. She was so bullshitted by Davis , Heaney and Conrad that she couldn't see reality from bullshit. They were all just great people to her and people who should be admired by all the little people on earth. Carole never attended any of our campaign meetings and only attended the fundraisers as free ' comp' (complimentary tickets). If you are not aware of it, all party chairs receive free tickets to fundraiser events.

The first fund raiser was at the Sad Dog Saloon in Java Center. Where else would my first event be held? After all, that's where it all began. That's where my friends and supporters were. That's where it was at. We had a huge turn out and the entire committee did an excellent job. Carole Butler was physically there. Most of the supervisors were also present.

Warren Schmidt from Cattaraugus County was also in attendance. Warren and I had known each other for some time. Warren was working for Tom Reynolds as the Cattaraugus

County representative. He attended all the meetings concerning the West Valley nuclear plant. Warren was also a very experienced campaign organizer.

Warren made up some campaign buttons. However, he eventually was forced out of the campaign by Reynolds' chief of staff, Sally Vastola. Sally thought that if Warren was working on my campaign, it would give the appearance that Tom Reynolds was endorsing me. That should have told me something, but it did not register with any of us.

Doug Berwanger held a fundraiser for me at the Arcade VFW. Paul McQuillen, Carl Heterbring and Jim Maloney held a " Roast " at Byrncliff Resort in Varysburg, also. That was a great night and a fun night. Maloney was the Emcee of the event.

Ron Ely, Anne Herod, Anne Humphrey, Norm Effman, Paul McQuillen and my son, Kevin all spoke. Kevin recalled a little league baseball game, where I said something like, " Go high and hard into second base to break up the double play". Kevin was only about 9 years old then. Anne Herod and Anne Humphrey gave me an Honorary Degree in Feminist Studies, which I still have today. I was always accused of being a bit of a chauvinist. I never viewed myself that way and I think I was a hell of a lot more liberal than some of my counter parts. Norm mentioned the Native Americans and how much I admired and respected them that I would donate on a regular basis. That story stemmed from my habits while traveling to and from Albany. I would almost always stop at the Turning Stone Casino which was operated by the Oneida Indians along the Thruway. Usually, I lost to them. Sometimes, I won though and it kept me coming back. Ron Ely told the story of following me to a Republican Committee meeting one winter evening. He said that he could not understand why this car in front of him was going so slow. He insisted that I was doing no more than 20 miles per hour. Ely gave me one of those orange triangles that are tacked up on the rear of farm wagons. What Ron did not mention was that it was on Wethersfield Road and it was snowing and blowing. There was also about 2 feet of snow on the road. We all had a great time. After that event Jim Maloney vanished from the campaign and seemingly almost from the earth.

The biggest event that was scheduled was " ELVIS IN NORTH JAVA", on May 1st, 1998. A tremendous amount of work went into it. Terry Buchwald, an Elvis impersonator from Buffalo performed. Cindy, Donna, Arlene and the whole committee did

a great job. The North Java Fire Hall was decorated to the hilt.
Moran for Assembly signs and banners. There was a huge crowd
and it felt great. Even some girls from Doctor Fields, my dentist's
office showed up. I thought that they were Yankee fans not
Moran fans! Can you imagine, even my dental hygienist. It
doesn't get any better than that.

The wheels started to turn. Assemblyman Nesbitt was trying
to convince everyone that a convention would not only prevent
a primary but it would also unite the party and generate
enthusiasm. I can still remember all the debates we had about
accepting the decision of a convention or not. After all, Wyoming
County had one third of all the voters in the entire district. That
meant all we had to do was get 25 to 30 % of the rest of the
district to win the whole thing.   We spent hours trying to reach
a decision. A primary was estimated at costing us about $40,000.
That meant our committee would have to raise $40,000 for the
primary and of course more for the general election, if we won
the primary. Finally, we agreed to listen to the chairs and get
their rules for this thing and also see what the other candidates
thought of this.

The summit meeting was scheduled for 6 PM, March 26th,
at the Omega Restaurant in Geneseo. I was to only come along
with my county chair, Carole Butler. I should have known it
was going to be a bad night when the restaurant was not even
prepared for our group. Instead of dinner, all they had available
was sandwiches. No thanks, Lowell, I'll pass. Great job. The
most important political meeting in twenty years and you're
going to serve peanut butter sandwiches. Jesus Christ. Well...
Dan Burling, Rodney Bennett, and Greg Parker and myself were
there. The County chairs all kissed and hugged each other and
introductions were made.

Bob Davis ran the meeting. King Davis represented two
towns in the entire district (Sardinia and Concord).   Davis
outlined the guidelines for the convention. It was agreed to have
the convention on May 6th. Each Town Republican Committee
person would vote. The candidate receiving the majority of those
present would receive the nomination. The losers agreed not to
force a primary in September. There was some discussion on
the location. Finally it was agreed to have the convention at
Pioneer High School in Yorkshire.

Then Davis asked each of the candidates if they agreed and
would not run a primary in the fall. Dan, Rodney and Greg all

agreed. Davis asked me and I said that he would have to give me two or three days to consult with my committee. "Holy Shit!", Burling yelled, "you mean I just spilled my guts and you still won't agree?" I replied, " That's right. I have a committee that has worked very hard for me. I feel that I owe them an explanation and want their agreement in this process. If you can't wait, the hell with it and let's just go to a primary". Davis, intervened right away and said fine, you have until Monday. Then Heaney wanted to know why I was still scheduling fund raisers? I asked why not, I'm in this race to win it. I don't know why he was concerned, he never contributed, anyway.

I had my own thoughts about a convention. It was definitely a good thing for the Republican Party. It would show unity and support for the candidate. It would be an exciting convention and a fantastic campaign. I had encouragement from many leaders through out the state and in all of the counties. Without mentioning names there were even organizations, fellow assembly members and staffers that were expecting my arrival in Albany. A primary would be held in September which was almost six months away. Only Republicans would be able to vote in a primary and the most difficult part of a primary was and is a very low turn out. You almost have to beg people to vote in a primary. Finally we agreed and I made a commitment to the County chairs and fellow candidates that I would abide by the decision of the convention.

I contacted each and every committee person by telephone several times. I also sent them weekly letters to express my views on taxes, state government, law and order and other issues that a state representative should be informed about. I also hosted meet Tom Moran meetings in every County. The very first one was in a snowstorm in Ellicottville. There were also events in LeRoy, Darien, Machias, Alabama, Arcade, Rushford, Springville and throughout the Assembly District.

We also ran an aggressive door to door campaign. I visited the home of every Republican Committee person in the entire 147th Assembly District. I put thousands of miles on my vehicle, ran through a set of brakes and about twenty pounds of dog biscuits. Having gone through many door to door campaigns in Java, I always had dog biscuits in my pockets and an additional supply of them in my vehicle. And.. I mean big dog biscuits. That way, when I encountered a dog, I would always offer them a biscuit. Most would take it appreciatively. Others would not.

Jim Schlick and I were going door to door in Genesee County one beautiful sunny afternoon. I pulled into the driveway of a committeeman. The garage door was open. Jim says that it doesn't appear that anyone is home, go leave them a note. You see, I would usually send whoever was riding with me to the door first to scout for large and vicious dogs. This day, I said OK. I had just entered the garage area when a huge dog that might have weighed 150 pounds came leaping and lunging toward me. I threw him all the biscuits that I had in my pockets and ran for the car. I ran as fast as my little chubby legs could take me. It must have been quite a sight because when I finally was safely in the car, Jim was sitting in the passenger side completely doubled up with laughter. My car was loaded with bags of dog biscuits, boxes of campaign literature, palm cards, buttons, stickers and pens. It was quite a sight. We also stopped wherever there was a group of people to spread the good word. I listened to all and jotted down notes. I was having a ball and I was really enjoying every minute of it. I have always liked people and this was heaven.

Jim Schlick traveled with me to all of Genesee County. Mark Cali from Perry went with me to visit the people in Livingston County. Carl Heterbring, the Java Town Republican Chairman and I went to Allegany County. Mario went with me to Erie County several times and we had meetings both in Sardinia and Concord (Springville). One of our best days was in Cattaraugus County. Doug Berwanger, the Arcade Town Supervisor and I left early one morning. Catt County is a huge area of the 147th Assembly District. It spreads from Machias, Yorkshire, Delavan south to Ellicottville, as far east as Persia where you could actually see Lake Erie. It truly is as their motto says, " Naturally Yours". The people are great. We visited with everyone. We even stopped at the Tops Supermarket in Springville. One of the best stops was at the East Otto Town Highway Garage. When we walked in, Doug announced that he was with the next New York State Assemblyman, Tom Moran. We shot the bull with those guys like we had known them all our lives. It was fantastic. As I said, we left early morning and finally stopped at the last house around 6:00 P.M. We were now almost to Gowanda. We decided to stop for a cold beer at the Palm Gardens in Gowanda. There were patrons from the 147th District there and some were not from the 147th. Who cares? . Doug and I are both natural campaigners and we had convinced them that I was going to be the next

Assemblyman for the 147th. At the gardens, there were also four or five construction workers sitting at the bar. When they heard that we were from Wyoming County, they wanted to know about Angel Colon, the child murderer. We were telling them about the money involved and everything. One of them said that if the Sheriff could just announce that Colon was going to be released at noon on a certain day, all of western New York would show up and take care of Angel Colon in a cost efficient manner. Then, we decided to stop at the Springville Moose Club and finally the Springville Vets Club. Again, the reception could not have been any better.

Mark Cali and myself went to Livingston County several times. The most extensive campaign trip was on Good Friday in the morning. I met Mark at his office in Perry and off we went. Our first stop was to see a really nice lady, Judith Patrick in Leicester. Judith's concern were not unlike any others. She was worried about agriculture, property tax, abortion and all the other key issues for a conservative Republican. We had a very nice visit. When we left Judith's house, I received a telephone call from Tom Reynolds in Albany. Because of the reception or lack of on my cell phone, we had to drive to the crest of a hill. Once I had a good signal, I pulled over and chatted with Tom about how my campaign was going. He made it a point to say hello to Mark, who was obviously sitting next to me in the car. We talked for quite a while and he gave me some more advice and pointers. We thought it best to be finished before noon because of the solemnity and religious importance of Good Friday. Our last stop was Norm Gates' barn in York. I knew Norm from the Association of Towns and always admired and respected him and his views. Again, a good Republican Committeeman and Town Chairman. While we were there, Dennis House, the Town Supervisor and Chairman of the Livingston County Board of Supervisors showed up. We all had great conversation. Dennis was another great Republican and a respected leader through out the state. I served with Dennis on many boards including GLOW(Genesee. Livingston, Orleans and Wyoming County) PIC(Private Industry Council, Waste Management, Board Chairs and the New York State Association of Counties. I cannot say enough good things about Dennis. Dennis and Lowell Conrad were not seeing eye to eye. Conrad thought, as do some other political party leaders that they should be calling the shots in the towns and counties. They should decide appointments and who gets what jobs. Why? I have no idea. Maybe they're just on a power trip. Most of these people were NEVER elected, just appointed. I once told Carole Butler that if she wanted to vote or choose who gets what job, she should run for Supervisor and vote as a Member of the Board of Supervisors. Anyway, it was another good day.

An interesting side note. Almost immediately after we decided to agree with a convention, I received a telephone call from an individual in LeRoy. He would not give a name, only that he was truly concerned and supported me. The gentlemen always called at the office in Warsaw. Had he ever called me at home, I would have learned his identity via my caller ID. To this day, I have no idea who he was. He would not even tell me if he was a committeeman or if he had ever met me. No clues, see what I mean? I affectionately called him my Genesee County mole.

In any event, he would tell me that the cards were stacked against me. Burling had my personal and financial records. Alliances were being formed. Deals were being made. All kinds of little tid bits. He then told me that Jim Maloney was not on my side. Jim Maloney had allegedly cut a deal with Bob Davis. Interesting, huh? Remember, Maloney and myself were buddies. I mean, after all, I had made the connections that allowed him to be where he was. The mole also told me that a county legislator race in Genesee was the key to this whole thing. Willie Brooks was the incumbent Legislator representing Alabama and Oakfield in Genesee County. Matthew Betters challenged Brooks in the 1997 Republican Primary and things got nasty. There was supposedly a connection. My mole also called the day of the Convention and said that it was too bad. He thought that I had run a good clean race and it was a shame what was going to happen. I still was a little apprehensive. Was I being set up by this guy? Was someone trying to play mind games? I just could not figure this cloak and dagger thing out. Many of my closest advisors were updated by me whenever he called.

It was a grueling six weeks of campaigning door to door, telephone calls, meetings and writing to all the committee people in the 147th. I actually lost weight through it all. I was on the run from early morning until late at night. Surprisingly, only Ellicottville, Caledonia, Sardinia and Concord (Springville) ever actually took me up on my offer to speak and answer any questions. Virginia Burnside scheduled a meet the candidate night in Caledonia. I think the whole Town Committee was present including Virginia, Dan Pangrazio, Pamela Sinclair and Pam Rychlicki, They too were very friendly, warm and gracious. The Caledonia meeting was actually in a format of a debate. Mark Cali and I went to that. I explained my position on the issues and then answered questions. Mark and I both agreed that my performance was better than the other candidates.

Rodney Bennett, God bless him, focused on the agriculture issues. Parker from Livingston simply stated that he thought he could do a good job. Burling dwelled on the hard times that his drugstore was facing. My speech highlighted what we had accomplished in Wyoming County. I believed that taxes, and particularly property taxes must be reduced. State government must continue to be more responsive and far less intrusive. We must continue to promote welfare reform. Crime and punishment must go hand in hand. Agriculture and more importantly the dairy industry needed much more support from both the State and Federal governments. Most important, we needed to stop all unfunded mandates. Unfunded mandates simply mean higher property taxes.

I also promoted the concept of forming an alliance with other Assembly Districts in western New York. If all similar assembly districts united behind three major issues, a great deal could be accomplished. New York City assembly districts do this as normal operating procedure. Mainly because they are all Democrats. So what? Forget Democrat and Republican for a few moments and focus on what's best for the residents. I also made them aware of my very good friends in the Adirondack Region. Counties, towns and villages in the Adirondack Park formed an organization and stand united on important issues that affect their localities. Remember that I mentioned George Canon from Essex County? George is a leader in that organization, along with Jean Raymond, Theresa Skyward, Tom Mason, Dale French and many others. They forget their party politics when it comes to what's good for their region. Other upstate areas are just too busy playing the political game in Albany. For Heaven's sake, check out how your local Assemblyman or Senator votes. 99.999999999% of the time, it's the way their party leaders tell them to. I agree that you will always have the occasional party line vote, but should every vote read the same count. Do they think we are that stupid?

As further proof of the games and chaos going on in Albany, during the campaign I was in Albany to fight for reimbursement due to Wyoming County of about $350,000 from the State Education Department. I went over to the Assembly Chambers to enjoy the side show and was greeted by an Associated Press reporter who had heard of my candidacy for the 147th. He interviewed me at length and we had a really good conversation. The article appeared throughout the State and was in the local Batavia Daily News of April 4th, 1998. The title of the article was " Will 'luckiest man' feel same after getting dose of Albany? ". It went on to read.. " Moran's excitement seems genuine. Moran, the would-be state assemblyman says he is not daunted by the prospect of how he will be treated as a Republican assemblyman. ' I know it's difficult and you are only one small voice, but I think that one small voice can make a difference, ultimately,' he said. ' I realize at first you may not be recognized or respected to the extent that one has been there longer is. But over time, I am confident that I will make a difference'".

The gist of the article was that a Democratic Senator, from Rochester, Richard Dollinger had sponsored a bill aimed at reducing property taxes for disabled residents in the Rochester area. When the bill reached the Senate floor, Dollinger's name was omitted and replaced by Republican Mary Lou Rath, who did not even represent these people in Rochester. Manhattan Democrat Franz Leichter said, " One of our colleagues was treated here in a very petty, shameful manner. His bill was stolen. Somebody else put their name on it without even the courtesy of telling him. It's so petty. Aren't we here to serve the people of the state? " See what I mean, Bullshit and games.

On Tuesday, May 5th, 1998 John Carberry of the Batavia Daily News printed an interview that was conducted in my office in Warsaw.

" *Coat off, sitting behind his desk piled high with papers in the Wyoming County Courthouse, Moran reveled in his office decor, a testament to his Republican faith. Behind him perched a campaign poster for former New York Republican Governor Nelson D. Rockefeller. Across from Moran's desk was another poster, this one promoting the Nixon-Agnew team. A third wall was lined with signed photographs of current Governor Pataki, former 147th Assembly District and retiring Congressman Paxon and Tom Reynolds.*" The article goes on... " *Moran said he has the record to prove he can succeed Reynolds*

as a leader among Assembly Republicans and a team player in Albany.
' We fought the state's Office of Court Administration for four or five
years and now we're building a new courthouse for $4.5 million instead
of $9 million.' He also boasted of defeating the Albany bureaucracy in
Wyoming County's two year battle over the state mandated pre school
handicap programs. Moran said state officials hedged on their promise
to pay for 60% of the programs by offering $52,000 instead of the
$350,000 local officials said Wyoming was due. ' As of two weeks ago,
we started receiving the checks,' Moran said, ' for all the back money'.
Moran said the lesson he learned as a supervisor, county official and
admirer of Pataki and Reynolds is to ' cut taxes, have less government,
and whatever government has got to be more responsive'".

All this time, life was going on and county and town business was going on as normal. I was very fortunate to have Bob Bowles, Jim Schlick, Doug Berwanger and Anne Humphrey to assist me in the County. I was giving them additional duties and they were thriving on it. In fact, the result was that they and the Board of Supervisors was becoming a true team. All the Board members were now allies and players on the same team. We were working together, campaigning together and even socializing together. What more could you ask for? I have to say, the ordeal made us all better supervisors and better friends. We had the luxury of spending time with each other. After the meetings, we would go to my campaign headquarters at Buffalo Street in Warsaw. There was always pop and beer in the fridge. Sometimes we even stayed a little longer than we should have. But...... we were having fun and thought we were working for the good of Wyoming County and the entire 147th Assembly district.

There were hours of preparation for the actual convention. Nominations had to be chosen, speeches had to be prepared and of course we needed pomp and circumstance. A victory party also had to be planned. After much deliberation, we had made the difficult choices.

To say that I was honored by the nomination process is a huge understatement. I was humbled and overwhelmed. Mark Cali, the Town Republican Chair from Perry was going to nominate me with seconds by Undersheriff Ron Ely and Anne Humphrey, the Supervisor from Perry. The Committee planned for the convention in ways you just could not imagine. We had signs, buttons, banners, and balloons. We also scheduled a victory party at the Arcade VFW.

So..... there we were. May 6th had finally arrived. It was an absolutely gorgeous day in Western New York. I went to Warsaw for the morning to perform my daily duties as Chairman of the Board. I met with Kevin DeFebbo and recited my speech for that evening. Kevin thought it was great and that I had done a really good job with the delivery. The Wyoming County Office of the Aging was having a senior lunch program at the Warsaw Village Park. I attended and gave a short speech. You can imagine my nerves that day. Shortly after lunch, I went home to prepare some more and try to relax. Besides the delegates that were coming, many, many of my friends and supporters were also planning to attend. It was quite an event.

I think we arrived at Pioneer High School about 6:00 P.M. (an hour early). That gave me enough time to personally greet each delegate as they arrived. The school and auditorium was decorated to the hilt. A band from Rushford (Allegany County) was already playing patriotic music at the entrance. Long cafeteria tables were set up and manned in the foyer to sign in each delegate and guest. Dan Burling arrived in a huge bus with his supporters. Rodney was already there. I never did see Greg Parker until later. Paul McQuillen, Mario Alaimo and myself worked the crowd. Many delegates were already seated in the auditorium. Jess Fitzpatrick from Cattaraugus County was one of the first people that I encountered in the auditorium. Jess was the former County Republican Chair, a Town Chairman and was also the Chairman of the Cattaraugus County Legislature. I had known Jess for years and we respected each other. When I went over to say hello, Jess said, " You're screwed. It's all over". I said what are you talking about? Jess then told me that deals were made, Dan Burling was going to win and it was too late for me to do anything about it. I relayed what Jess had said to me to Paul, Mario and Jim Schlick. They immediately went around to visit the other county delegates. Sure enough, it was over. I will never forget the look on Mario's face after he talked to the delegation from Springville. You have to know that I had thought we had support in Erie County. After one of our meetings in Springville, the entire committee had picked up my buttons and many even wore them out of the building. Livingston County was split, of course Genesee was united for Burling, Allegany likewise for Bennett. How was Wyoming County, you ask? Well let me tell you. I had the vast majority, no doubt about it, but Burling did have some support in Attica, Sheldon and Castile.

Why? Who knows. So, now it was down to Cattaraugus and Erie County to determine who the candidate was going to be and they had already made up their minds. So... why bother with the charade and the hoopla? Well... I had made a commitment that I was going to abide by the decision of the convention and I was not about to renege on it. I did try to inform everyone that I did meet that we were not going to win this thing. Many of my supporters never got that word until later.

I did get a pleasant surprise prior to the start. There at the entrance to Pioneer High School and my moment of glory were my parents. Yes, my parents actually flew up from Florida to be witnesses to this historic event and their son's participation in it. It really was a great feeling. I thank them for their love and their concern.

Just about on time, Bob Davis called the convention to order. Davis appointed Jerry Moriarity from Cattaraugus County as the Parliamentarian and Bob Lichtenthal as the Sergeant of Arms. Then Davis stated that he wanted to recognize an individual that had come to him earlier and asked for permission to address the assembly. The Chair then recognized Greg Parker from Livingston County. Parker's thirty second speech was to withdraw from the process. Now, what the hell was that all about?

The candidates had met just prior to 7:00 P.M. to draw numbers for the order of nominations and speeches. The order was Moran, Burling and Bennett. Why didn't Davis tell us all that Parker was withdrawing or did he tell Burling and Bennett and just forget about me?

Mark Cali nominated me. Mark said the loyalty, respect and trust were my greatest qualities. He did an excellent job and I was extremely proud. Ron Ely, the Undersheriff was the first second to my nomination. Ron said, " as a 30 year law enforcement officer, that I would make the criminals do their time and hold them accountable for their actions". Anne Humphrey, Supervisor from Perry was next on the agenda. This was probably the most emotional speech for me. Here was one of my friends and fellow Republican member of the Board seconding my nomination for the New York State Assembly. How could I possibly be more proud and humbled by these speeches? Anne said, " I admire his leadership, understanding and concern for the people that he serves. Tom is the kind of man that understands building a park for children can sometimes

241

be just as important as building a bridge for a road." I can never, and I mean never, describe how I felt that night. Not only did I have hundreds of loyal supporters who thought that I would be a good Assemblyman, but I had nominating speeches that were made by three great friends and individuals whom I admired and were worth admiring.. WOW !!!!!

Now it was my turn. As I approached the podium, I could not even hear the cheering and screaming for Moran. I walked the aisle thinking that it did not really matter, it was over. Should I stand up and yell, KISS MY ASS? NO WAY!!!! I was determined to demonstrate that I really was a viable candidate, that I knew the issues, and yes, I could handle the job as Assemblyman for the 147th District.

"Chairman, Chairs, fellow committeemen, ladies and gentlemen. Let me begin by saying that I stand before you - the delegates of our great Party- feeling both proud and humble. In recent weeks, I have criss-crossed the 147th Assembly District several times. I've spoken with Bob Eich in the Town of Alabama, visited with John Marsh in Sardinia and Doug Morgan in Freedom. I've had conversations with Ron Priest in Otto, Bill Curry in Fillmore and Howard Sager in Perrysburg. I've even met Dan O'Shea's dog named Bear. I'd like to thank each and every one of you personally for the thoughtful, patient and yes the kind consideration you have shown me during my campaign. I am concluding this part of my campaign with renewed admiration and respect for the people of the 147th District.

Through the efforts of Tom Reynolds and Governor Pataki, our district has been kept at the forefront of New York State's proud reemergence. They have become a unique and very effective partnership in Albany. I am committed to creating and maintaining that partnership - a relationship that will us to be a part of the Governor's team. Together we can achieve an even greater future for New York State.

But the key to realizing the future is making important changes in the way state government works. It must be more responsive. It must be less intrusive. Too often, unfunded mandates result in higher taxes. We must always work toward easing the burden of all taxpayers. Those on fixed incomes, senior citizens, those in the agriculture community, for the small businessman and for all New Yorkers.

Welfare reform has produced a dramatic and long overdue reduction in welfare spending. The state has cut the welfare rolls by more than million people. Workfare does work. All able bodied recipients must be obligated to work. As Governor Pataki has said, Welfare was meant to be temporary assistance not a way of life.

We need to take a more aggressive approach to crime. Our neighborhoods and communities need to be protected through tougher laws which deny parole to violent criminals. You do the crime, You're going to do the time. As your assemblyman, I will press relentlessly for just such laws. We must also work to even out the amount of state and federal revenues available to localities for criminal prosecution and criminal defense. Currently all counties receive aid to criminal defense but, only half of all counties receive aid to prosecution. We are in essence providing more resources for criminal defense than our district attorney. We must do better.

During my 13 year tenure on the County Board of Supervisors, three as Chairman, I have traveled to Albany many times on behalf of my constituents. Those years of experience have taught me how state government works. In Albany, I challenged the state Education Department and I was able to recoup $350,000 in payments due our County for reimbursements to the Pre-K Program, leading to reforms in the process. I successfully challenged the Office of Court Administration's requirements for courthouse improvements. The result will be an attractive, functional facility aimed at meeting the specific needs of Wyoming County. Not the 'one size fits all' mandates of the state Office of Court Administration. That alone reduced court costs by 50% and saved our taxpayers more than 4 million dollars.

During my tenure as Chairman of the Finance committee and later as Chairman of the Board, Wyoming County has not been assessed a tax increase in eight years. In fact, Wyoming County property tax rates are the lowest in the state. I am very proud of this accomplishment. This has allowed county government and the private sector to enhance the pace of economic development which in turn improves the quality of life for all the people of our district.

As Chairman of the Board, I have also had the honor of serving on many state wide boards such as the New York State Association of Counties and the New York State Association of Towns. I have found that some regions in the state exert more influence than others in state government. The difference is not based on population. For example the Adirondack region stands as one and speaks with one loud, united voice. Their voice is heard in Albany. We, in western New York, and in the 147th Assembly District, must stand united and strong on significant issues of common concern, if we are to carry on the initiatives *and legacy of Tom Reynolds. We can begin, right here, right now at this convention.*

Together, we can be a force to be reckoned with.

Now in closing, I know we will all miss Tom Reynolds in Albany and wish him well and God speed in Washington. As your Assemblyman, I will continue Tom's work. I will represent you as effectively and vigorously as Tom has done in the past. The goals I have set forth will be difficult to achieve and the challenges will be many. I am ready, willing and eager to meet these challenges head on.

Together we can make a difference. And.. So... tonight, I am respectfully asking you, the delegates of the 147th Assembly District, for the honor, for the privilege, and the awesome responsibility of becoming the endorsed republican candidate for the 147th New York State Assembly District. I thank you. "

Well, you should have seen and heard the boisterous demonstration that followed. Keep in mind that the majority of my supporters did not realize the outcome was already decided. There was a standing ovation, balloons in the air. It was just unbelievable.

Burling was next and he focused on all the bad things that were wrong with New York. He did also mention that he too was tough on crime. In fact, he even said, " If you do the crime, you'll do the time." Hmmmmm. Bennett was last and did a good job.

Davis then called a recess for the purpose of conducting balloting. The process was that each County Chair would caucus their delegates and give a total to the Chair. After a short period of time, Davis summoned the candidates to his throne. The votes were in. We had a winner on the first ballot. Dan Burling was the winner. Davis asked me if I would address the convention and make a motion to unanimously endorse Burling as a show of unity. I, of course, as a loyal Republican agreed. Bennett was going to second the motion.

Now keep in mind that the majority of my supporters still had not received word of the outcome. I still apologize today for that lack of communication. Can you imagine their reaction when Davis asked me to come forward to address the convention? Many thought then, that I was in fact the winner. They went totally nuts. They would not stop cheering. I had to yell and scream for them to sit down. Then you could have heard a pin drop when I made a motion to endorse Dan Burling.

Like I said, we still had scheduled a party to be held at the Arcade VFW. When Cindy and I had arrived, we were greeted by cheers and hand shakes. It was another great function. I would not trade the experience for anything. I had also told Tom Reynolds, Bob Davis and many others that they too were invited. This upset some of my committee but I felt that they should be invited. And show up they did. Tom introduced me at the microphone and he was very gracious and sympathetic. I made my concession speech but also stated that we should all be proud of how far we went. After all, in spite of the perception of Wyoming County as rural and the lack of enthusiasm from our Chair, Carole Butler, we still were indeed a force to be reckoned with.

It was a very long night full of remarks like, what the hell happened? How could we lose this convention? What was going on ? Who sold us out?

The next morning I woke up with a very large hang over. It was another great day, the sun was shining, my parents were there. I decided to enjoy what we had.

The next week or so, I was contacted by people from all over the state. They were giving their sympathy and congratulations that I had made a valiant effort. We were all told that we had the best group, the best speeches and were deserving of it. I even heard from the Genesee County mole who gave me an ' I told you so'. There were a couple of people that I did not hear from.

Jim Maloney was no where to be found. He had fallen off the face of the earth. Guilty? Ashamed? You bet your ass. Something was wrong, that's for damn sure. It's funny and sad how you can have a good buddy or think that you are buddies, only to be betrayed. I guess he has to live with it and this world is made up of all kinds of people. I did run into Maloney later that summer.

Jim Schlick, Carl Heterbring and myself were representing Wyoming County at a Tom Reynolds Fundraiser in Buffalo. It was a luncheon for Tom and his closest 1,000 friends. Well, being from Wyoming County, we were early. The staff was not prepared for that. We were wandering around and found a 'Reynolds for Congress' sign outside of a door. When we entered, we were greeted by a bartender offering free drinks and snacks. Sure, why not? This was kind of nice. We were wondering why there were only a hand full of people, there. A few minutes passed and in walked Tom and the Republican leader of

Congress, Dick Armey from Texas. Soon we found ourselves in line like a bunch of kids waiting to get their pictures taken with Santa Claus. I still have the picture today. Obviously, we then knew we were in the VIP Reception that cost about $1,000. It really was an honest mistake. Tom or his staff could have asked us to leave but they didn't. They probably had a few laughs over it anyway. Later, Dale Volker told me that Reynolds used to crash the VIP receptions too.

We were then told to enter the main dining room for lunch. My God, the place was packed. We were looking for a table when I bumped into Maloney kissing Davis' ring again. Davis gave me one of those obligatory warm hand shakes and said, " say hello to your old buddy, Jim ". Yeah, right. I said something like, Jesus Jim, I thought maybe you went to take a shit and the rats got you. Then, I asked Jim if my back was bleeding? That is the last time that I ever spoke to Maloney. Think about that. He made his bed and he will forever be branded by me that way. Too bad, because he really is a very bright man who could go a long way even without selling his soul.

The other person that I did not hear from until the Buffalo Sabres were in the semi finals against the Washington Capitals was Tom Reynolds. Tom was trying to reach me for several days, but I was not quite ready to talk to him. The day before one of the first home games, I picked up the phone and it was Tom. He wanted to know how I was doing. He said that he had heard that some people thought there was horse trading going on at the convention. I then said, " Tom, there was more jousting and dealing then goes on at the Springville auction on a warm July Wednesday."

Tom Reynolds is still my friend. I really do not believe that he had any idea about what was going down until a few days before the convention. He's just too good of a man for that. I know some will argue but I am here to tell you, NO. Tom also picked up in Congress exactly where Bill Paxon left over. We in the 27th Congressional District are fortunate to have Tom Reynolds. I still would do anything for the man. He has always been my mentor and my political hero. Thank you, Tom Reynolds.

So.......... What the hell really happened and why?

Within a couple of weeks, the Genesee County Chairman of the Legislature, Roger Trifthauser scheduled a pep meeting between Burling, Jim Schlick, himself and me at the Attica Hotel on a Saturday morning. At first there were only four of us at the table in the back room. Roger is a very excitable and animated person. Usually, his excited personality bounces off the walls. I like Roger a lot. He's fun to be with and very exuberant about everything. Burling wanted my support. Many were still unsure if I was going to run a primary race or not. Then, Then they spilled their guts. They sang like canaries. Burling had the luxury of strategy from the RAC (Republican Assembly Committee, chaired by Charlie Nesbitt). How could that be? Well, Roger and Dan went on about the Willie Brooks legislative election in 1999. Matthew Betters was running against Willie Brooks in the Republican primary in September of 1997. Brooks was an eight year veteran and Betters was a rookie. Brooks was really concerned. Brooks and some of his friends on the legislature asked Albany for their help to stall the Betters candidacy. It seems that the RAC was a little involved in that primary. Obviously RAC, had no business being involved in any way with a county legislator's election campaign. RAC, its staff and its money was there to fund and elect Republican candidates for the New York State Assembly. Enter Eric Dadd and Norm Effman from Wyoming County. Eric and Norm had no idea what was happening. Here were Jim, Roger, Dan and me all smoking cigars and drinking beer. I take that back, Roger didn't have a cigar or a beer. It seems that when the heat was really being poured on, Tom Reynolds and Charlie Nesbitt called Roger and Dan. They told Roger and Dan, that they could not be involved in this and that someone would have to come forward to take the blame. OK! Burling agreed that he would and he did. After hearing that and talking to some people, I decided to investigate the matter on my own.

I went to the local office of the Batavia Daily News in Warsaw. I bought EVERY issue from September to November of 1998 that had reference to the Brooks controversy. In an article by John Carberry in the 9/8/97 issue Carberry wrote: " Pinocchio may have learned right from wrong and became a real boy, but among Oakfield Republicans today, he's an orphan. The legendary long nosed puppet appeared on a campaign mailer sent to Republicans in the 1st County Legislature District Saturday, accusing GOP primary challenger Matthew Betters of lying about his record. The move has Betters, who faces eight year incumbent Legislator Wilfred Brooks in Tuesday's primary, crying foul and wondering who paid for the negative attack.

Brooks denied any prior knowledge of the attack mailer. So far no one else has claimed responsibility. ... The post card, mailed first class from the Buffalo Post Office Friday, has a cartoon image of Pinocchio staring at his elongated nose. Underneath the image, the card reads: ' Matt Betters vs. The Truth'."

In the October 14, 1997 edition of the same Batavia Daily News, Carberry writes:

" The committee that poured more than $3,500 into an effort to derail Legislative hopeful Matthew Betters' campaign was formed to combat Betters' unlimited financial resources. " That according to Legislator Daniel Burling, who stepped forward to represent the Committee for Genesee County Endorsed Republicans. "

" The party can't be involved in a primary race, that's why this committee was formed, " Burling said.

So who was this new committee? Well the plot thickens. In the 10/1/97 edition of the Daily News, Carberry wrote:

" According to records filed Monday at the Genesee County Board of Elections, a September 6 postcard that accused county legislature district No. 1 Republican primary hopeful, Matthew Betters of lying about his record was paid for by a new political body called Committee for Genesee County Endorsed Republicans. ".... " Brooks said he took no part in planning the pre primary attack." " I was not aware of it " Brooks said.

Carberry goes on, " The Endorsed Republicans may be a new independent political committee but it's funded by some faces likely familiar to Brooks and other Genesee GOP members."

" According to the September 19 disclosure statement filed at the Board of Elections by Endorsed Republicans Treasurer Jean Burling (Dan's wife) the county's three state Legislature Representatives , Sen. Mary Lou Rath, and assemblymen, Thomas Reynolds and Charles Nesbitt each contributed $500."

" I'd do it again", Nesbitt said recalling help Brooks gave him during a Republican primary in 1992. "I'm pretty flattered that my opposition felt they had to bring in state officials", Betters said.

Carberry goes on, " Jean Burling's statement also shows money coming from Legislature Chairman Roger Trifthauser and Legislator Daniel Burling also contributed more than $100 each. No one who gave $100 or more, lives in Oakfield or Alabama."

The expenditure portion was even more intriguing. It listed
Jeff Williams as the campaign consultant who received $250 for
his services.

The first time that I ever met with Jeff Williams, he was
working for Tom Reynolds in Genesee County. Then he sort of
disappeared. Next he popped up as the Niagara County
Legislature Clerk. In September of 1998, the New York State
Association of Counties held their Fall Conference in Buffalo.
On Monday, September 14th, Jeff approached Kevin DeFebbo
and myself prior to a meeting at the Buffalo Hyatt. We chit
chatted for a few minutes when I asked him how he was involved
in the bitter primary. Williams told us both that Charlie Nesbitt
said he better get to Genesee County and help out Willie. I then
point blank asked him who the hell was responsible for being
the author of the Pinocchio cartoon. Proudly, he said, " I did it".

Now, here was politics at its worst. I'll let you, the readers
be the judge in this affair. You decide. Did lies and accusations
coming from my Java opponents really influence the voting of
the delegates?   Did Albany Republican Assemblymen
owe Burling, because he took the heat for this? Did Nesbitt owe
Genesee County because he screwed them out of having
an assemblyman from the County in 1992? Or did he just owe
Willie? Did Mary Lou Rath order Maloney to get away from the
Moran campaign or did Davis promise him more?   Did Davis
really tell the Concord and Sardinia Committee how to vote ?
Was Cattaraugus promised something else? Was Allegany
County really content with having Bennett as Burling's " Ag
representative" ? Wyoming County would be the logical place
to have an Ag Representative chosen from. Annually, Wyoming
County is either number one or number two in the state for
milk production.

I've drawn my own conclusions as you will , too. All I can
say, in many respects, is it was a wonderful experience and I
would do it all over again with one exception. NO MORE
CONVENTIONS. Conventions simply allow too many
opportunities for wheeling and dealing in smoke filled rooms.
And usually the deals do not work out. Let the voters decide.
Go to a primary. Why settle for anything less?

After all, isn't that what democracy is based on? A
government of the people, for the people and by the people. Hell,
I don't even like the national conventions. They, too, are usually
already decided ahead of time. But.. At least there are some

primaries. Even though all the states don't have a say on who the party candidate is. But... let's admit it, that's what gives these little political chairs the power that they do crave and love to wield. The only solution would be to go to a national primary day vote. That way all the states would hold their primary for the Presidential candidate the same day. Probably, that will never happen.

I hope that I have accurately reported what transpired. I also hope that I do not appear to be bitter because I am not. It really was a great learning experience and a lot of fun. Cindy and I found out just how many friends we have and the amount of respect they have for us. Publicly, I now thank each and everyone of you and ask God to bless you all.

Chapter 43

"Common Nesting"

Wyoming County historically has a much greater unemployment rate than the rest of the state. That makes economic development and job creations even more paramount to us. Keep in mind, that the County Economic Development Department was only created in 1987. Richard Tindell, was appointed as the very first Director.

Richard was under my Planning Committee at the time and I will testify that he and his very small staff did an excellent job. Richard not only had responsibility for economic development but he also was charged with Planning, Zoning and Agricultural Districts and even the County wide solid waste. He and Barb Shilling, the County Planner developed the first county wide garbage pick up that most municipalities including Java did NOT participate in.

Economic development is a very speculative and abstract issue. Most of the leads, prospects and even growth are highly confidential and Richard cannot nor should he, even share it with Supervisors. So... That also makes him and his department an easy target. What the hell has he done lately? That type of criticism. In October of 1996, the Wyoming County Farm Bureau actually had a Resolution prepared for their annual dinner meeting that read:

" *WHEREAS, the majority of our members feels that the County Department of Economic Development has not functioned according to its purpose, BE IT RESOLVED, that the Wyoming County Farm Bureau calls for its abolition.* "

There you go. On September 23, 1996 I received the invitation to attend this meeting at the Pike Fire Hall on October 16, 1996. Needless to say, this was like a shot heard around the world. None of the other Supervisors wanted to go. It was my responsibility. Richard, being the gentleman that he is, offered to attend with me. I said, no that I would suffer the slings and arrows of outrageous persecution. Jeff True, another gentleman, was the President of the Farm Bureau and Bonnie Smith was their office manager. They both afforded me the opportunity to actually see the responses they received from their members on the issue. I thanked them for that and still do.

I arrived at the Pike Fire Hall and went in with Senator Volker. Tom Reynolds could not be there but Warren Schmidt was his representative. During dinner, they both wished me luck . Senator Volker said his piece and Warren did likewise. They both thanked the group for the invitation and left me alone at the table.

The full Board of Supervisors has always met with the Farm Bureau every February to discuss current issues, so I was no stranger to most of them. After Jeff read the Resolution, he asked me for my comments.

I thanked them for my invitation and then said, sure, absolutely we can abolish economic development. But.. Let's think about it. Let's think about the signal that we are sending out. Let's think how the existing businesses, and the rest of the state will interpret it. Wyoming County will be saying, no thank you we do not need nor do we want any further development. In fact, to the existing businesses, we would be saying, hey people, you're on your own. We have plenty of jobs and furthermore, we have just the right tax base right now. Leave us alone. I also highlighted on some of the accomplishments and successes that Richard had achieved. I also pointed out all of his other duties. In the end, the Farm Bureau did the right and proper thing.

They passed an amended resolution that called for the Department to be aware of the importance of the agriculture community in the County.

There were good results from this whole thing. The County, the Business Development Corp., the Cooperative Extension and the Farm Bureau sat down at several meetings together and still do today. Everyone knows full well, what agriculture and in particular the dairy industry means to Wyoming County.

To get back to the BDC, the county was very fortunate to have true leaders like Peter Humphrey, Maggie Dadd, Tim Moag, Sam Gullo, Howard Payne, Brenda Copeland and many others in their ranks. The BDC was made up of local businesses and knew the importance of economic development not only for the County but for their future too.

As a result of those joint meetings, it was decided that the County department needed additional assistance. The county had one of the smallest development and planning staffs in the state. The department was also experiencing increasing demands for development and planning services. Richard simply did not have the time nor the resources for a real marketing effort. Many titles were thrown around. One of the first proposals was a development coordinator, that evolved into the Executive Director of the BDC. Among the duties were;

- Promoting and marketing the county as a location for new expanding businesses.
- Assist existing county businesses through retention efforts
- Coordinate and administer the affairs of the BDC
- Provide development assistance to the county department of Economic Development
- Be the liaison for groups such as the Farm Bureau and the Chambers of Commerce

Now, who the hell is going to pay for the salary? The BDC believed that the County and the County IDA (Industrial Development Agency) had a responsibility.

At one of the New York State Association of Counties (NYSAC), I had the pleasure of serving with Barb Monohan from Westchester County. We were both sitting on the Resolutions Committee. During a break, we talked about what was happening in our counties. I mentioned the controversy we were having with economic development. In Westchester, they had just privatized their department and contracted with what was known as the Westchester Association. Barbara was willing to schedule a meeting with all involved for Wyoming County to learn from their experience. Barbara was the Local Government Liaison under County Executive Andy O'Rourke.

Paul Agan, the Chairman of the Planning and Economic Development Committee, Kevin DeFebbo and myself traveled to White Plains to meet with Westchester County. It was a very successful and educating journey. We learned of some huge advantages of having a contract with an association to market the county. The cost was going to be about the same and might even be more. However; it was surely going to be more effective and be more competitive with other counties and other states. As an example, when Champion Products were pulling out of Perry, my first comment to Richard was get on a plane for North Carolina and do whatever you have to. Wine them, Dine them, who cares. We need them. Well, of course it could not be done. Overnight travel had to be approved by the Committee. No way is Wyoming County going to pay for a dinner in North Carolina.

It was putting the County at a disadvantage. Every time I see Barb Monohan, I thank her from my heart for the time she took out of her busy schedule to help a smaller rural county. It's people like her, that make you feel proud of government.

By the spring of 1997, the proposal from the BDC had been refined to accommodate all interested parties including the Farm Bureau, the County, the County IDA and the BDC. Now, how do we get the Board of Supervisors to approve a contract with the BDC for $55,000 a year to promote and market Wyoming County?

Kevin, Paul Agan, Anne Humphrey, Bob Bowles and Jim Schlick were supporting the concept. We were ready to introduce it at the July Board meeting but some questions and concerns had to be addressed. We wanted a multi year contract so that it would not put a new program in jeopardy. We wanted it to begin in July of 1997 and expire on 12/31/98. The estimated funding for Wyoming County was going to be $55,000 per year. Therefore; the 18 month contract was going to be in the neighborhood of $82,000. WOW ! Howard Payne was the President of the BDC. Richard Clapp was the Chairman of the IDA. Both were in favor of the agreement. In fact, Howard was willing to consider the position. Oh, Oh. When that word got out, there were several members of the Board who were not very receptive to it. On August 12, 1997, we were ready to present it to the Board. Our meeting was scheduled for 2:00 P.M. Around 1:00 P.M., the shit hit the fan. The Resolution was going to go down. It was going to be defeated because some did not want Howard to be the Executive Director. On the other hand, some members of the BDC and the IDA were offended and could not understand what business the Board of Supervisors had to do with it anyway. My Office for about two hours was like Grand Central Station except every discussion was behind closed doors. For the sake of protecting everyone, I will not mention names. The Board of Supervisors who were opposed to Howard, insisted that they would not vote for the contract unless it was assured that he would not be appointed. The BDC and the IDA had a real problem with this. If they were going to advertise, interview and select a director, they wanted the opportunity to appoint the best person for the job. Finally, I had an agreement from those Supervisors, that they would vote for the resolution if the BDC made a commitment that Howard would not be appointed.

The BDC compromised and conceded if they could appoint Howard as the interim Director.

That's how it all began. Wyoming County now had flexibility when it came to economic development. The BDC, eventually chose Jim Pierce as their first Executive Director. Jim came highly regarded and respected throughout the Southern Tier. He was a natural fit. I don't believe we could have done any better.

In the summer of 1998, Jim Pierce and I had a lunch meeting at the Charcoal Corral in Perry (Castile). We talked about how we might be able to improve our county image. We also talked about some of our problems. Our local businesses were also having difficulty in getting through some of the agency red tape. There was no clear road map on how to get around the maze of rules and regulations. If one wanted to expand, who were they to go to first? When does the IDA become involved? Can Job Development assist with their clients. Will the Business Education Council be an asset to them?

Now, if our local existing businesses were confused, can you imagine a business coming into Wyoming County with no background on government regulations? Jim asked me if I could imagine the benefits of a one stop business center? Imagine having the BDC, the Industrial Development Agency, the Business Education Council, the N.Y.S. Department of Labor, Work Force Development and even our own Economic Development Department under one roof, in one building?

This would provide the starting point for any existing business or potential new business to receive assistance and service from all. Now don't think this was a no brainer. Not by any means. Nothing in government is easy. I thought it was great idea. I can still remember Jim saying this is going to take a great deal of work and time.

Immediately upon arriving back at the office, I conferred with Kevin. What do you think Kevin? DeFebbo thought it was a great idea and it merited some investigation. First of all, could we get consensus on the Board and secondly, how will these agencies feel? I mean, remember the old turf wars? Also, where would this building be?

Anne Humphrey, the Chair of the Planning Committee was my first call. Anne thought it was a great idea and that Kevin and I should pursue it. I then called Marty Mucher from Community Action. He had just recently remodeled a building on Route 20A between Perry and Warsaw. The Community

Action Agency was occupying half of it and the other half was vacant. I ran the idea by him. Marty thought it was great and realized that if the county was involved there should be some financial benefits to his agency and a good chance for some grants for the renovation. He said that he would be more than happy to take the lead on planning, design and grant applications. Of course, the county would have to lease the space for a fair market value.

Richard Tindell was my next call. Richard loved the idea but was somewhat worried about the turf issue. Can we really convince the others that it is the right thing to do? Leave it up to us, I said. I thought we could.

I then sent out a letter inviting all of the officers and directors of the BDC, the BEC, the IDA, Tourism and Workforce Development to attend a meeting to discuss the concept. There was a lot of apprehension and questions. Was the county trying to abolish these agencies? Of course not. Why were we only looking at site on Route 20A? As far as site selection goes, we really had no other choice. What could be bad about the location on the major highway running through Wyoming County between two of the largest towns? It also had a huge advantage by being owned by a non-profit community agency. Grants and other funding was still available. I think those in attendance were aware of the potential benefits. It was a good deal for the BDC. After all, they were in cramped quarters in downtown Perry. The economic development department was on Allen Street in Warsaw. The BEC usually ended up wherever they could and they had never been treated as a true player in the whole process. The IDA would have a class facility and be next to the BDC, BEC and the county department. Tourism was the only agency that we could not accommodate due to space restrictions. However, Diane Johnson did endorse the idea and made a commitment to attend any and all necessary meetings. The consensus was to proceed but they wanted to be involved with the design and planning phase.

Kevin, Anne and I presented it to the Planning Committee. All members and in fact the entire Board of Supervisors thought it was great idea. It was going to be the first one stop business center in the state. I contacted Dale Volker for possible funding. I also wrote to my good friend, Tom Mazerbo from the Rural Development Agency and indicated the intention of the county to lease space from Community Action.

This inter-agency committee then went to work. They finalized and approved the lease agreement, design plans and even the allocation of space. There was going to be common conference rooms, copy room and break rooms. There was going to be building ' staff meetings'. Everyone was truly excited. Marty Mucher received his grant, the county received a member item from Senator Volker and we were off and running.

The new Wyoming County Business Center on Route 20A is one of my proudest accomplishments. Accolades should go to Jim Pierce, Rich Tindell, Anne Humphrey, Jon Cooper from Wyoming County Bank and of course Marty Mucher and Kevin DeFebbo who all made it a reality.

One final testament to how successful the arrangements between the county and the BDC. Early in February of 1999, Jim and Richard telephoned me and asked if Doug Berwanger and myself could attend a meeting in Orchard Park with Taylor-Pohlman, a light manufacturing company. Taylor-Pohlman was looking to relocate from Orchard Park and they were looking at property in Arcade. I accepted for both of us. The meeting was held in Orchard Park on 2/11/99. Several sites in Erie County and one in the south were also being considered in addition to Arcade. Wyoming county had one advantage because of the willingness of the Arcade Town Supervisor and the Chairman of the County Board to meet with them. Doug and I sent a message that Wyoming County and the Town of Arcade was committed to this project and we would do everything possible to secure 175 jobs for our residents. The meeting and its discussions were all confidential. No one knew that the meeting ever took place. If we broke that confidentiality, all bets were off. Jim and Richard were the victors and Taylor-Pohlman is now operating in Arcade.

Many experts on democracy have stated that it takes one of two things to occur in order to get something done. Action by strong leadership or action by crisis. I'd like to think that Wyoming County has good leaders who are trying to be even better.

God only knows how many times and how many meetings Jim and Richard have attended or tried to set up for the good of Wyoming County. Keep up the good work and thanks for being there!

Chapter 44

"Public Service or Profit from the Public"

The volunteers in the fire service and emergency rescue squads receive no pay and no benefits. They are required by law, to successfully complete training and other educational requirements. The Red Cross volunteers receive no pay and are also required to complete training. Girl Scout leaders, Boy Scouts leaders, 4H Leaders, Little League Coaches, Senior Volunteers and thousands of others who willing give their time, receive no pay and no benefits.

Local government officials receive a modest salary. Believe me, I know of no local official who is raising a family or supporting oneself on the salary. However; local government salaries are meant to hopefully reimburse the official for the time that they had to take off from their regular job. I believe that's what it is meant for. How could we expect, anyone to spend days away from their job or a potential job for no compensation? No argument. I think we all want the very best leaders for our towns and villages and even our legislative representatives. But, where do we draw the line? How much is too much?

Locally again, I can tell you that NO ONE in towns, villages or counties are getting rich by being elected officials. Maybe it's a different story in the bigger counties or cities, but not in rural New York State. In fact, I will go so far to state that in Wyoming County, a good, conscientious Town Supervisor is not even making minimum wage. They do it because they love their communities and they love their positions. Many times, Jim Schlick, Larry Nugent, Hank Bush and myself, (while working on the Railroad) had to take time off from regular jobs and lose vacation or personal days. But, then that was our choice to run for office.

I was always proud of local officials and supervisors for their commitment to public service. There are always a few that want raises every year, but that's human nature.

Does anyone deserve a pension from public service? I think not. We all know that a congressman only needs one term (2 lousy years) and they earn a federal pension based on some $135,000 per year. Good God! I hate to even think what that costs us each year. But should a local part time official receive a pension from the taxpayers?

In the 1960's, the New York State Retirement System allowed all municipalities to join their system. Many localities opted into the program. It gave their full time employees the benefit of a good retirement at no cost to the employee. Anyone who had been in the employ of that locality did not have to pay a percentage. They were considered a Tier I employee. Now, all new employees contribute to the retirement system.

Vince George was elected Town Supervisor in 1967. Prior to 1968, he was a councilman. In October and November of 1968, the Java Town Board indicated their willingness and desire to participate in the New York State Retirement System. Vince George enrolled in the State Retirement System in 1976.

In 1995, the Town of Java received a claim from the N.Y.S. Retirement System that Vince was claiming retroactive membership back to 1966 because he was not aware of the Retirement System. Wyoming County also received a claim. The Town and County sent an affidavit to the Retirement System that stated Vince was the Chief Elected Officer and should have been knowledgeable.

The State Retirement System then directed me to attend a hearing on the matter in June of 1998, in Rochester. I had no idea what I was getting into. When I entered the room, there was the hearing officer, Mylo Eytina, a stenographer, Vince George and his attorney, Mario Pirrello.

Now, when I had called about the hearing, I was told that I really did not need to bring an attorney to represent the town. But, once they began I knew that I had better have counsel. The hearing was adjourned to allow me time to meet with the Town Board to see if they wanted to go the expense of an attorney or to just settle.

After talking with representatives from the State Retirement System, I learned that if retroactive membership was granted, the Town of Java would be forced to pay back about $30,000 to the State Retirement System. Jeeeze, how much was this worth to old Vince? It did not matter. We could not make any settlements on our own. The Board unanimously agreed to hire Eric Dadd to represent the town in this matter. Java could not afford to pay $30,000. I should tell you that Java was not alone.

Small towns and villages across the state were being forced to pay this kind of lump sum retroactive payment. There was another town in Wyoming County that had to pay over $50,000. There was a town in the Catskills that had been ordered to pay over $200,000. In late 1998, the Town Board also passed a resolution that I presented to the Association of Towns that demanded that the state at least share in this financial responsibility.

The new hearing was scheduled for January 13, 1999. Eric had decided to ride with me. Of course it was one of the worst days of winter. I arrived at Eric's office in Attica in a blinding snow storm. Eric called and they said that yes, the hearing officer was flying in from Albany and the meeting was on. Off we went. It was terrible. All I could think of was, Jesus if I get in an accident and Eric gets hurt, my ass is done. The only thing we had in our favor was that nobody and I mean nobody was traveling faster than 30 miles per hour. The trip to Rochester took well over two hours, pushing snow all the way. Then the parking lots were full of cars and full of snow. A parking attendant waved me into one very small place. I didn't think I could squeeze into the spot. It was so slippery that when I put the brakes on, I slid right into the narrow fit. With that, Eric said, " that was really some aggressive driving, Tom". Leave it to Eric. Most guys would have said, Holy Shit or Goddam, but not Eric. You have to love him. We all do.

So, we got there. The hearing officer had been delayed at the airport. No shit. In walked Vince George and his attorney Mario Pirrello and who the hell was behind them? Jim Foley and Jim Hardie. Foley was scheduled to be a witness for Vince. Jim Hardie was along for the ride. Foley and Hardie were on the way to the Adirondacks for snowmobiling. They could have done that on the streets of downtown Rochester. Anyway, Jim Hardie is a class A gentleman. They don't come any better. Jim and his wife Betty are true friends and a pleasure to be with.

I was a little surprised to learn that Foley was a witness. I wondered where the connection was. Foley and Vince were both on the Board of Supervisors at the same time but that was about it. The irony of the Foley card, was that he always touted himself as an ultra conservative. The government should not give any pay increases or additional benefits to anyone. And.. here he is testifying that Vince George deserves more in retirement and the taxpayers of Java should pay for it. Hypocrisy?

The Honorable Robert Wagner opened the Hearing at 11:07 A.M. (It was scheduled for 9 AM) and stated that " At the present time, the city of Rochester is in a heavy snowstorm. All traffic has been delayed." Mr. Eytina arrived during the first part of the hearing.

I am not going to bore you with the testimony. Vince's argument if any, was that he was claiming he had no knowledge of the retirement system prior to 1976. Java and Wyoming County had other evidence. There were the Town Board Minutes that indicated two separate resolutions to join the system in 1968 while he was Supervisor. As Chairman of the County Operations in Committee in Warsaw, he introduced a resolution to join the system, in 1973. Vince admitted to both. Next, enter Foley. Eric asked Foley if he had an opportunity to review Vince's application back in 1976? Foley stated " No." Eric said, " So, you have no idea what he put on his application?" Foley again said, "No".

On August 18, 1999, H. Carl McCall issued a Findings of Fact and Conclusions of Law. It stated " The applicant has failed to carry his burden of proof. As Supervisor of the Town of Java, he participated in the adoption of a Resolution which clearly stated the right to join the New York State Retirement System. It would have been his duty as Supervisor to make the appropriate information concerning the retirement System available to any employee or officer of the Town. Similarly, as a member of the Wyoming County Board of Supervisors, the applicant was Chairman of the County Officer's Committee and participated in the County procedure with regard to the retirement System. " " It is hereby determined and directed from the credible evidence that the application of Vincent B. George for retroactive Membership Pursuant to Section 803 of the Retirement and Social Security Law is Denied. "

Now, Vince took this very personally. It was not personal by any means. I don't care who the individual or whatever the reason, I would always, at all costs, try to avoid paying an additional $30,000 of tax money that was not warranted. Can you imagine the cost of this fiasco? What if Eric or I had been injured in an accident in the snowstorm? What if any of the individuals were? Was it really necessary? You know, the Retirement System never told me what it would have meant to Vince in additional dollars for his pension.

Why couldn't he be happy with the pension that he was receiving? Why do some always try and squeeze more dollars from the taxpayer? What if all volunteers felt the same way? It would be a pretty sad world, wouldn't it, if everyone had to get paid for everything they do?

Chapter 45

"Smoke 'em if You Got 'em"

I believe that in 1995, the state of Mississippi was the first to file a lawsuit against the tobacco companies to recover their share of costs for medicaid that was paid by tax dollars to treat smokers and smoke related illnesses . That's pretty serious stuff. Later, Dennis Vacco, the State Attorney General also filed suit on behalf of the State of New York and all of its counties.

The national settlement was in the area of $206 billion dollars. In New York, the settlement was $24 billion in direct cash payments from tobacco companies to the state and counties.

I received a letter from Vacco and a fax from the Association of Counties on 11/24/98 that gave Wyoming County and all other counties until 12/4/98 to opt in or out of the settlement. Obviously, a county would only opt out if it thought they deserved more. Wyoming County elected to be included and we stood to receive $20.2 million dollars over 25 years.

That is what you call a ' true windfall'. The State originally wanted to receive all the money and they would then ' disperse' it to the counties. Yeah, right. The N.Y. State Association of Counties fought long and hard for the counties to receive it directly. They won. In large part by Steve Acquario of NYSAC. Steve is one of those relentless individuals who works on tirelessly. Steve and Ken Crannell of the NYSAC staff are always looking out for the best interest of the counties.

My good friend John Sackett from Genesee County and others were a bit concerned. Sure. Take the money but is it really government's responsibility to sue private business? Where could this precedent take us? Why not sue the liquor industry? The automobile industry? Hey, how about the gun and ammunition companies?

No one is going to argue about smoking. Sure, smoking is bad for your health. But, isn't there a point when the government should not be messing with our individual rights? For example, many counties have passed legislation prohibiting smoking in public places including restaurants, bars, bowling alleys etc. I agree that there should be no smoking in public places like stores, sports arenas, libraries, public buildings, but that's about it. In

Wyoming County, we have many small restaurants. Let the owners of these establishment decide whether they want smoking or not. The county government should not decide an issue that could have a huge impact on their business. If they decide to allow smoking and lose customers because of it, I am quite sure that they will change their policy. Customers too, will have a choice whether to frequent the establishment or not.

Where do we stop? What legislator or worse, what bureaucrat, has the right to tell us what we can do with our own free time if it does not offend anyone else? And, in addition to the above, can you imagine politics without cigars in the back room? I've already mentioned this a few times already.

Smoke 'em if you got 'em.

Chapter 46

Better Roads Program

In the summer of 1998, the Board of Supervisors also made a commitment to implement a better roads program for the county. Back in the 1930's and the 1940's most of the county roads were built under a federal program called, " Farm to Market ". Many of our county roads had not been rebuilt since. In 1998, the federal government felt that it was more important to buy $250,000 toilet seats, fund studies on the butterfly, give aid to small foreign countries that may not be in existence next week instead of giving it back to hard working Americans.

Gary Weidman was the County Highway Superintendent and had been for many years. Gary knew how to do more with less. Some of our roads were deteriorating badly. I asked Gary to prioritize them and give us an estimate. Gary, never had enough money annually in his budget to rebuild roads on a regular schedule. In fact, over the last 20 years or more, his budget was historically cut, mainly because it was the easiest to cut.

Gary did an excellent job prioritizing and he presented his estimate to the full Board of Supervisors in the summer of 1998, for their consideration and possible action. All in favor. We also realized that once we began, there was no turning back. I, too, had done some research and learned that most counties actually bond or borrow money for their major road projects. It simply is too costly to do it any other way. But, what do we do now that we are in such a hole? We decided to start with a million dollars for 1999. We also realized that we would be receiving the tobacco money. Perhaps that could fund a road or two.

Politics really stayed out of the priority list and the schedule. We were all upbeat. We were confident that the program was going full steam ahead. Wethersfield Road was scheduled for 1999. Instead of $1.5 million, it came in at $3 million. Oh.Oh.. Many on the Board got nervous and left poor Gary dangling out on the limb. I think the whole project went into the crapper never to be seen again.

The County had two choices. Earmark some of the tobacco money for highway improvement or take out a thirty year loan for the highway project. The average tax payer doesn't get much for their money. They want good law enforcement, good fire protection and good roads. And in that order, too.

Chapter 47

"The Doug Flutie Analogy"

On January 4, 1999 (My mother's birthday) I was unanimously elected to my fourth term as Chairman of the Board of Supervisors.

During my acceptance speech, I mentioned that the County had adopted a new slogan, " To provide the best possible service for the lowest possible cost." I also said that Wyoming County is recognized as a leader in the state, not just among rural counties, but the entire state. "Our number one priority for the state is reform of the Medicaid Program and to accept its obligation to the taxpayers of Wyoming County. Just the medical assistance for our county department of social services is about 2.6 million in tax levy. That equates to over one third of Wyoming County's property tax; this is totally unacceptable".

At the conclusion of my speech, I apparently offended Geraldine Luce by stating, " I am also here to tell you right here and right now that this board operates and governs as a team. It is by far the best that I have seen and this team is made up of all Doug Fluties."

Geraldine wrote a letter to the editor of the Batavia Daily News whining about the little Doug Fluties and that maybe I should have described the Board members as those little dogs that sit on the back shelf of your car, heads bobbing up and down in agreement.

Come on, Geraldine, quit your whining. Does every one have to fight in order to do a good job in your eyes? If she had read it and comprehended what she read she would have understood. Maybe she didn't know who the hell Doug Flutie was. Maybe she thought he was a bureaucrat from Perry. I don't know.

I was trying to say that the Board of Supervisors were finally accomplishing a great deal of good for all of Wyoming County. They were able to do this, by working as a unit or as a team. They had one goal. To make Wyoming County a better place.

Hey, Geraldine, let me tell you what the Board did in 1998. They dealt with three natural disasters. They handled the Samantha ordeal. They created a committee that investigated and eventually achieved centralization of our Business

Development, Economic Development, Business Education Council and even the Workforce Development Agency under one roof. They created a Transition Team made up of the Health Department, Office of the Aging and Social Services that enabled the County to provide long term health care more efficient and at lower costs to the taxpayers. The Board's first priority was the tax rate and stabilizing it. They built a beautiful new courthouse, began an aggressive road improvement program, began plans for the rehab of the old courthouse and improved and enhanced many of the programs that so many rely on. That Board was not content with business as usual because that's the way we've always done it. And they did all this without a tax increase. Call them what you want, but I don't think you could even sharpen their pencils.

And, we couldn't have accomplished all this if we were constantly bickering.

Maybe instead of calling them Doug Fluties, I should have said:

THEY ARE THE EPITOME OF WHAT
GOOD GOVERNMENT IS ALL ABOUT:
Good people getting good things done in spite of criticism
from people who haven't got a clue how it all gets done.

Chapter 48

"We're Mad as Hell and We're Not Going to Take it Anymore"

1999 started off with the State hammering the counties again. What happened to this great partnership? It all fell apart with the political games that are played in Albany.

The Democrats and Republicans are so busy fighting each other that little, and I mean very little, is accomplished in Albany. There is certain legislation aside from the state budget that MUST be passed by the boys and girls in the Assembly and Senate.

Hypocrisy is rampant. Remember, when I said that sometimes the state would require the counties, towns or villages to take action and give us only a few days notice? Well, the federal government also requires the states to take certain action. The Feds usually give the states a year or so. It doesn't matter how long they give. The state will wait til the eleventh hour or beyond.

In 1997, the Adoption and Safe Families Act was passed by congress and signed by President Clinton. As part of the sweeping welfare reform process, the Act was intended to reduce time spent in foster care and make the child's safety and health the number one priority. It assured the children of their rights and promoted permanency for the children by placing stricter regulations and requirements that focus on reunification and adoption rather than temporary placement. It also eliminated parents rights for some convicted felons including sexual abuse, neglect and abandonment. The Act required that all states adopt this law by 1/1/99 or face the loss of federal funding for this program.

As of 1/1/99, the ONLY state in the nation that had not adopted the Act was New York. Now in dollars that meant that New York State was losing $42 million per month. That's $1.4 million per day. It meant $52,000 in revenue loss for Wyoming County each month.

Jeannette Wallace was the Wyoming County Commissioner of Social Services. Jeannette not only knew her job inside and out, but she also had great contacts in Albany, Washington and other state associations. Jeannette kept Kevin, Paul Agan and myself up to date on the issue.

This was a critical issue to the entire state, not just Wyoming County. We were receiving faxes daily from NYSAC, other counties and the New York Public Welfare Association. I think I talked to Ken Crannell from NYSAC on a daily basis. Bob Gregory, the Director of NYSAC was so concerned that he made it the number one priority at the winter conference in January. We were all making calls and writing letters.

Why couldn't we get Albany to do something? Well.. the Senate passed their version of the Act. Republicans were in the majority of the senate. That meant that Sheldon Silver and the Democrats in the Assembly could not dream of passing a like version. They had to re-write the Act. Games and more gamesmanship !!

I wrote Assemblyman Burling a letter on 1/26/99 and stated:

" New York State's lack of compliance with ASFA (Adoption and Safe Families Act) places an under-funded system at further risk. I am also discouraged that the counties of New York, through no fault of their own, now face tremendous financial losses with virtually no sign from Albany that legislation is forthcoming. The counties cannot afford to be penalized by inaction in Albany. "

As a direct result of the outcry from all the Commissioners, county chairs, legislators and NYSAC, the state finally adopted the Act on February 11, 1999. That did not settle all our problems. Wyoming County still lost the $52,000 from January. Nice! All of Albany should be proud of their actions or inaction. Wyoming County could not afford to subsidize the State through no fault of our own because of their lack of cooperation.

Another example of the state's total disregard and disrespect for the counties came on 1/1/99 when all of the state's full time District Attorney's received a $20,800 raise ! Did they consult with us? Nope. Were they going to pay the additional money? Nope. Of course not. The Board voted 14 - 2 to have me send a message to the state complaining about this and other unfunded mandates. This was fairly easy. Through the efforts of Senator Dale Volker, the state agreed to increase its reimbursement by $20,800. Finally. Thank you, Dale.

Medicaid Cost Containment was another issue that the state failed on. That was going to amount to about $900,000 loss of revenue. The state was also being penalized by the federal government for lack of maintenance of effort to about $100,000 for Wyoming County. The ASFA failure resulted in the county losing $70,000.

At the July, 1999 Finance Committee Meeting, Wyoming County fired the shot heard around the state of New York. The Finance Committee proposed a new county law that would make it a criminal act, a misdemeanor, for state and federal officials to take action or inaction that cost Wyoming County money. The Committee voted to send a draft of the local law to the full Board of Supervisors.

LOCAL LAW INTRODUCTORY NO. B, YEAR 1999

Section 1: Purpose and Intent

The County of Wyoming, through its County Board of Supervisors, declares that it is imperative for the security and well being of all its residents to prohibit any further deterioration of the County's financial condition, tax levy, or other fees. Property Tax as a whole throughout New York State is not only excessive but it is also the most regressive tax that is imposed. New York State and the New York State Legislature by not complying with its own laws is hereby compelling Wyoming County to adopt this local law.

Section 2: Prohibited Acts

No State or Federal government, government agency, Representative or employee of any State or Federal Government shall have the right to either by their action or inaction, affect the financial condition of Wyoming County. Wyoming County will forever be held harmless from State and Federal mandates, rules, regulations, and other irresponsible actions of agents or representatives of such governments, that affects the County's financial condition.

Each violation would be punishable by imprisonment and/or a fine of not more than $1,000 and not more than 1,000 hours of community service.

Man, oh man, did we get reaction. Other counties loved it. Several adopted resolutions supporting our actions. I received faxes from all over. The most amusing was from Gerald Simons, Chairman of Columbia County Board of Supervisors. His was addressed to Tom Moran, alias, Robin Hood. Gerry went on and stated, " Recruitment is currently underway and volunteers have come forward for the position of Little John and the Merrymen. "

The Batavia Daily News in an Editorial of 7/15/99 wrote:

" A lot of people have been saying it's a crime that the state budget is three months late and counting. Wyoming County supervisors want to make it just that.

Imagine - Governor Pataki mowing the lawn at the Wyoming County Courthouse... Assembly Majority Speaker Sheldon Silver raking the clippings... Senate Majority Leader Joseph Bruno weeding the flower beds. Assemblyman Daniel Burling cleaning out the storm sewers. President Clinton cleaning the restrooms (under close supervision, of course)."

Niagara County under the leadership of Gerry Meal, the Chairman, also introduced the Local Law. Allegany County with John Walchli and Ed Burdick did the same. Steuben County had a similar resolution. The ball was beginning to roll.

In the Niagara Falls Gazette of 8/1/99, I was quoted as saying, " We are not passing this to humiliate them. We are passing it to send a message loud and clear to Albany. People are fed up and don't want to hear the blame being put on others. They (legislators) need to take responsibility for their actions."

Bob Bowles, the Chairman of the Finance Committee, compared it to the Boston Tea Party of 200 years ago and said, <u>" when we were the colonies and England wasn't listening to us "</u>. " I think we're as frustrated as those people dumping tea in the harbor ", Bob said. In the Batavia Daily editorial of 7/15/99, Bob was quoted as saying, " It's like drawing a line in the sand ". Bob was great. It took a courageous Chair of Finance to introduce a Local Law like that.

The Daily did end their article with, " The state gets away with far too much. It's good to see a county take a leadership role in making Albany more accountable. .. A little community service wouldn't hurt these guys."

How was the rest of the reaction? Tom Reynolds and Dale Volker were smart enough to know what we were doing. We had no intention of arresting anyone. We were frustrated, outraged, disgusted and angry at the whole system. Tom and Dale joked about it each time that I saw them. Senator Chuck Shumer just ignored it, on his summer of 1999, tour through

Perry. I think even Burling realized it was not a personal attack on anyone individual. The most absurd reaction came from two representatives in the southern tier. In the 8/2/99 edition of the Olean Times Herald, under the title, " McGee not amused...". " I think it's a waste of taxpayers' money, Senator McGee said Thursday." Excuse me, lady? You have the audacity to talk about wasting money, when you were DIRECTLY responsible for losing $42 MILLION PER MONTH TO THE TAXPAYERS OF NEW YORK STATE. Maybe you'd better stay out of Albany more. Get on the streets of Olean and listen to people, for God's sake. Oh yeah, Assemblywoman Cathy Young stated the law was targeting the wrong people. Young thought just Sheldon Silver should be targeted. Yeah, right spoken like a young assembly member. Blame it on the other party.

Anyway.............the Budget was adopted in early August some, four months late, so the Law was now really meaningless.

We held a Public Hearing at our annual Fair meeting. No action was taken and the law was tabled. But, we were ready to resurrect it at any time.

Chapter 49

The Beginning of the End

All municipalities in the State are audited every two or three years. The Town of Java was audited in late spring of 1999. The audit report was released on 7/16/99. The report is mailed to the Supervisor, Town Clerk and the Town's Official Newspaper (The Arcade Herald).

Sometime between July 16 and our Town Board meeting on August 10th, lies were told to the residents of Java. Keep in mind that only three copies existed at that time. I went to one of our local businesses in Town for personal reasons. The individual mentioned that he had heard a rumor that I had embezzled $40,000. Not to worry, it's not true. Forget about it. That night, a very good friend of mine called and repeated the rumor. He told me who he had heard it from. Now it was beginning to snow ball and I did not like it.

At the August 10th Board Meeting, I made a statement. The Arcade Herald of 8/19/99 reported it this way: " The action in question regarded Moran's accusation of an unnamed town official. He said, ' This official actually told people that there was $40,000 missing from town funds, allegedly uncovered as a result of a recent audit of the town's books. The examination by the New York State's Comptroller's Office covered the period from 1/1/97 through 12/4/98 with the report dated 7/16/99."

" The comptroller's office report states that, ' Total general fund cash was understated by $40,782 as a result of inadvertently reporting the beginning balance of the money market account instead of the ending balance, and not adjusting the amount reported for outstanding checks in the general account'. Moran said, ' In other words, it was an entry error in the books'. He additionally stated that, ' Nowhere, I repeat nowhere, does the report state that there is any money missing or even misappropriated.' According to Moran, this statement was verified by David Kelly of the Buffalo Office of the State Comptroller, who Moran described as being miffed that the individual could not read and understand the wording of the report. Mr. Kelly went further and stated, ' There was absolutely no indication that any money was missing.' Moran declared that he can accept criticism for any wrongdoing but outright lies and rumor spreading, I cannot and will not accept any longer. "

" Following the meeting, the board went into executive session to discuss what Moran described as a personnel matter. Town Clerk Janet Zielinski objected loudly to being excluded from the session, alleging the action was ' illegal' and repeatedly calling Moran ' ignorant'. Moran asked her to please quiet down as members of the board could not hear each other in the adjoining room, which prompted another loud outburst from Zielinski, which included more name calling and threats to contact a lawyer ".

Now, the above is in the Arcade Herald of 8/19/99 and written by Merilu O'Dell. Having been present at that meeting, I can tell you that Merilu O'Dell was very kind to Janet Zielinski. I only wish that it had been televised. It would have made the Clarence Thomas hearings look like Sesame Street.

Java had also just finished the update on the assessment of property. Keith Kersch and some others were whining about their assessments. The Town Board did not make the judgments nor could the Town Board change any assessments. The Arcade Herald quoted Kersch as saying, " Many older people are afraid to go to a review hearing because they are afraid to get upset, so they just pay their bills " . At that same meeting in July of 1999, Kersch owner of Kersch's Collision, expressed concern over bulldozing work being done on a Minkel Road property(Hillcrest collision). Kersch was quoted as saying, " My concerns are that the property owner is utilizing this for commercial use ".

So, we now had riled up the property owners on Minkel Road who had always been opposed to Hillcrest Collision by the owner of Kersch's Collision. Kersch was actively going around Town mounting opposition to the update of assessments. One final word about assessments. As I've said before, if a resident believes that their assessment is too high, they first go to the Assessor. If they are not satisfied, they may then go to the Board of Review. If still, not satisfied, they may go to small claims court. And, if they still are not satisfied, they can take the town to court. The Town Supervisor and the Town Board have no authority to change assessments.

We also had fuel for the ever burning rumor fires. And by God, they were burning and the church was still packed with a few good old catholics who were praising the Lord and still bearing false witness. I'll bet God has a special place for hypocrites - it's called Hell!

Chapter 50

Da Bear

In May of 1999, I went bear hunting in New Brunswick for the first time in my life. Now what the hell does hunting have to do with politics? Well, I think it's all relative. It should give the reader a picture of who you are reading about and who I am writing about.

My uncle Fred Mosher, lives in western New Jersey near the Pennsylvania border in Washington, N.J. Fred owns and operates a sporting goods store in addition to being a full time architect/engineer. My Uncle Fred is my mother's brother and is only five years older than I am. Fred called me in late 1998 and asked if I'd like to go. Why not?

The trip was going to cost somewhere around $600. There was a group of eight hunters including myself. We were going by car from New Jersey.

Prior to my departure, I was telling everyone about the trip. I was getting pretty excited. I had never been on a guided hunt before. At lunch, one day, I was telling Sheriff Capwell, Ron Ely and Tom Reynolds about the trip. Cappy asked what type of gun was I going to use. I explained to him that I intended to use a Winchester 30/30 lever action. The gun had been my grandfather's and my father's and now I was going to shoot a bear with it. Cappy said, " you're nuts. You better use a bigger gun. Bears are tough. "

Suzie Aldinger, Melane Spink, Janet Coveny and the rest of the office just thought it was another crazy idea. They simply could not understand how I of all people, was going to sit in a tree stand for eight hours with nothing to do. Even Cindy was somewhat worried.

Fred told me what I needed. I would need enough clothes for summer, winter or fall. I would need toilet paper, bug spray, matches, netting for bugs, flashlights with extra batteries and of course enough snacks to ease the boredom. Fred also said to bring cigarettes for treats for the guides.

When I left the house for New Jersey, Cindy said, " Now be careful, you know you really can't run as fast as you think you can." I wasn't sure what that meant.

I arrived at Fred's house the day before we were to leave for Kedgwick, New Brunswick. The next day we left at about 6:00 P.M. Accompanying us were Rick Dotzenrod, the gunsmith from Fred's store, his son, RA, Mike Aneskewich, Jr., a New Jersey State Trooper, Bob Kennedy and his two friends, Glenn and Henry.

We drove all night long and arrived at the L.L. Bean's store in Maine sometime in the early morning hours. Shopping for more crap. There was free coffee but they were out of donuts. We arrived in Kedgwick about 1 or 2 P.M. I rode in Fred's vehicle with Trooper Mike. All the way, Mike and Fred were telling me about Kedgwick, the hunting terrain and of course the guides. I had no idea what to expect.

Upon arrival at our lodging place, ' Mom's Bed and Breakfast', I was pleasantly surprised. It was like having two apartments. One upstairs and one down. Each had its own bathroom, kitchen and living area. Fred, Mike, Rick, RA and I stayed upstairs. Bob and his two buddies were downstairs. Bob Kennedy was the group leader and he ran a tight ship. All hunters had to do what Bob wanted to do. If Bob wanted to eat breakfast at 9:00 A.M., that's what we did. If Bob wanted to go to the hardware store (a highlight in Kedgwick), that's what we did.

Monday, was the first day of the hunt. The starting point of the hunt was at the guides' house which was about 5 miles from where we were staying. The boss of the guides and the owner of the Lucky Bear Guide Service, was Real(being French, it is pronounced Reeee - al) Talbot. Why he called it the Lucky Bear, I have no idea. All of the guides were French/Canadian with a huge emphasis on French. They all smoked like chimneys. I mean one cigarette after the other. We usually arrived at Real's about 2:00 P.M. and you hunt until dark which is about 9:45 P.M. up there. There was one guide for two hunters. The system was that the guide would drive to some location, then walk you in, leave you and pick you up later. Simple, huh?

My guide was Dennis. Dennis could speak very good English compared to the others. However, they all had heavy French accents which I will attempt to spell the way the words sounded. We got into Dennis' ole Toyota pick up truck and off we went. We drove forever. There is nothing out there, trust me. I was the first to be dropped off. Dennis took all my stuff and I only had the gun. We walked about two miles into the woods farther.

They all knew that I had a bad left shoulder, so it must be an easy tree stand to climb for me. Sure enough, it was. I climbed up, and Dennis carried the bucket with all my necessities and my gun. Dennis says, " I peek you up at about 9:45 P.M. ". " OK, don't forget", I cautioned.

When Dennis walked out that trail, I probably felt like I did when my mother left me at kindergarten the first day of school. What the hell was I doing here? To describe the surroundings, all you have to think of is the deepest, thickest woods that you have ever seen. Got it? These woods were even thicker.

All you hear is the damn birds chirping, chirping and chirping. I had brought a transistor radio with me with ear phones. It didn't matter, there was no reception. Just about dusk, I got the begeeze scared out of me. A moose came running full speed under my tree. Jesus Christ, what the hell am I doing here, I asked myself. All of a sudden, out of nowhere, appeared a bear. HOLY SHIT ! It's a bear. I brought my rifle up, aimed and shot him. The old bear was knocked down immediately. Then, he raised up on two legs and gave out a huge GRRRROOOOWWWWLLL. Then he sauntered off to die, I thought.

I couldn't believe it. The first day, and I shot a bear. I had my cell phone with me. I tried to call Cindy to tell her what I had just accomplished. Yeah right, no cell phone is going to work in the woods up in New Brunswick. The minutes went by and then the hours.

It got darker than dark. Where the hell was Dennis. There I was sitting in a tree in the middle of bear woods, 1200 miles from home and was waiting for some guy that I just met to pick me up and save my sorry ass. On top of that, my bear was laying over there somewhere either dead or wounded.

When 11:00 P.M. came and went, I didn't know what to do. Maybe he forgot where he dropped me off. We were hunting in a million acre plus area. In fact, we were never closer than one mile from each other. One time I was 25 miles from the nearest hunter. My imagination was beginning to go wild. Where the hell was he?

Finally, at about quarter to midnight, I heard the truck and a few minutes later, I see a flashlight coming down the path. God Bless You, Dennis. I immediately told him about my bear. " Oui, Oui, you shoot da bear, you shoot da big bear, huh? " You bet your ass, I shot him. Dennis goes over to the point where I said the bear was. Yup, he found blood and some small trees that the bear knocked over. Dennis said that we would come back in the morning when it was daylight with some other guys. That night, back at our place, I repeated my story about the kill so many times that I eventually put myself to sleep, then it was daylight and time to get up and get my bear.

We arrived at Real's. Real said the game plan was that Dennis and another guide, Pee Wee, Rick, the gunsmith and myself were going to track this bear down. Back to the scene of the kill, we went. Pee Wee is short, slender and muscular. He immediately took off running. You'd think he knew exactly where the bear ran. He was an excellent tracker. Anyway, Dennis, Rick and I were wandering around looking for blood or any other sign. We had lost Pee Wee and couldn't hear him yelling any longer. I looked at Dennis and he was looking up at the tree line. I said to Rick, " I think the son of a bitch is lost ". Dennis came over to us a few minutes later and asked if either one of us had a compass. I screamed back, " Why the hell would we have a compass. We've got you. You're suppose to be a professional guide." Well, he did get us back to the truck. Pee Wee was waiting there and said, " Da bear, he is gone". Sheriff Capwell was right. The 30/ 30 just did not kill him. He kept going.

I was thoroughly depressed. I had my chance and blew it. Because of all the tramping around, I had to go to a new site for the hunt. Real took me to this new tree stand. It looked a little shaky and it looked like I would have to use my left shoulder, which I just could not do. I told Real that I would try. I climbed up to about the third rung on the ladder. The goddam rung broke. I wasn't very far up, so I didn't get hurt. Real says, " I feeex ". He reached into his pocket, pulled out some twine, tied the rung back and said, " You walk on thees side. " OK , Real, buddy, I'll try again. When I got up to the platform, I could see there was no way that I could pull myself up. I looked down and told Real, no good. Real said, " I poosh you up". Bullshit, Real, this stand is just not going to work with my shoulder. "OK,OK, I take you to da cabeen". Jesus Christ , Real, I said, you should have taken me to the cabin right away, this will be great!!!

Off we go. To the "cabeen." We drove for about 30 minutes, got out of the truck and walked to the cabin, that I couldn't wait to see. The cabin was a small wooden box the size that a Lazy Boy Recliner would come in. It did have a makeshift roof and a tarp over it. Inside there was an old wooden kitchen chair that had the legs sawed off except for about three inches, that I was supposed to sit on. There was a small shooting hole out the front. It had a small opening in the back so you could crawl in. Now, this thing was on the ground. That's bear height. A big old bear could come over and slap that thing right over. He could open it up like a peanut and then eat the nut that was inside.

After a couple of hours, every bone in my body ached. I had cramps, itches. It was terrible. Then it started to rain. I should say it poured. I thought thank God, I do have a roof at least. Yeah, the roof leaked where there wasn't any. Then the sun came out and about 6 million mosquitoes came out of the ground. I couldn't stand it any longer. I had to get out. I did, and I never saw another bear again.

I had so much fun that I decided I was going back in 2000 and I was going to bring some friends, this time.

The 2000 hunting gang was made up of Mike Ash, from Strykersville, Tim Roll from Arcade, Chuck Snyder from East Aurora, and Ken Herman from Varysburg. Jim Schlick, a fellow supervisor, Kevin DeFebbo, the county administrator and Wally Herod made up the eight. Wally was Anne Herod's husband. Anne was the County Director of Probation. We held several meetings to discuss the bear hunt.

We were taking three vehicles. Jim, Ken and I were going together. Mike, Chuck and Tim in another vehicle. Kevin and Wally drove in Wally's truck. We had agreed to be at the Bed and Breakfast sometime around 2:00 P.M. On Sunday, June 4th. Jim, Ken and I left my house around 3:00 P.M. Saturday.

The trip is about 18 hours of driving time. We made plenty of stops for coffee and fresh air.

The scenery really got spectacular in Maine. We saw several moose and lots of woods and mountains. Each one of us was supposed to bring a case of beer. Beer is about $35 a case up there so we brought as much as we could get over the border. One case per man. Everyone did as they were told except Kevin. He brought a six pack. Said he didn't drink much. Who cares, how about the rest of us, Kevin?

Jim, Ken and I were the first ones to arrive. We were greeted by Diane who ran the Bed and Breakfast. I had been dealing all year long with Real and Diane for reservations, deposits etc. Diane told us we should stay downstairs. We were a little reluctant because we thought all the action was going to be upstairs. Diane begged us to look around. As soon as we saw the downstairs apartment, the three of us agreed that was going to be our home for the week. Because I was the group leader, I even had my own bedroom. Jim thought this was great because I snore and all he would have to do is close the bedroom door. Not so easy, Jim. There was a door but there was also an opening of about 4' by 8' where there probably was a window once. That opening was right above Jim's bed.

Mike, Tim and Chuck showed up next. The six of us were all unpacked and moved in. Diane wanted to know what time we wished to have dinner. At first we said five o'clock then we decided to make it six because Kevin and Wally still were not there.

We sat around all afternoon drinking beer and bull shitting. The rest of them were getting on Jim and I about politicians etc. It was good ribbing and they certainly did not offend us. That's for damned sure. We had been through a lot worse things in our campaigns.

Kevin called and said they were still in Maine. Go ahead and eat. We did and when were about done, Kevin and Wally pulled in. After dinner we drove over to allow the other seven to meet Real and the boys.

Jim told me later that he could not imagine what he was getting into. This year's guide roster was made up of Pee Wee, (Real's son), Maurice, Michelle (Michael), and Leo. Pee Wee was the brains of the outfit next to Real, of course. Maurice was a happy, go lucky guide who wanted to go to New York City to find a woman. Jim and I told him that he should go to Albany or Washington for that sort of thing. Maurice was the interpreter. He could speak and understand English very well. Maurice always either began each sentence or ended each sentence with " My Friend". Michelle was a volunteer fire fighter and seemed to be pretty active in the community. Michelle could speak English too. Leo could not speak or understand any English.

Real told us to be at his place at 2:00 PM the next day. Tim, Mike and Chuck were using bow and arrows and Real was not real excited about that. It was back to the B&B for more bullshit and more beer.

The next morning we got up, ate a Diane's great breakfast and waited for the hunt. Now, Tim, Mike and Chuck are serious and experienced hunters. They got their bows out and planned on shooting all morning. Kevin and Wally planned on taking a nap. Jim, Ken and I decided to drive around Kedgwick. We found a local bar in Town called Buck's. We didn't go in but figured we would sometime during the week.

After lunch, we all prepared for the big hunt. All of us except Jim were decked out in total camouflage. Jim had camo pants on but he also had a nice casual sweater on. Jim and I were probably the most nonchalant about "da bear hunt". Both of us showered and shaved everyday, with regular soap, deodorant and after shave. The others would never dream of using scented soaps and aftershave. Did they know something that we didn't?

We got to Real's and were split up into pairs. Pee Wee took Wally and myself to some remote area miles back. When Pee Wee walked me to my stand, I just could not believe it. It was gorgeous, comfortable and fantastic. My tree stand was like a little hut that was completely enclosed. It had pop out plexi glass windows. It even had a back door. I was not going to be bothered by bugs or anything else. I settled in for a long evening of watching the woods. I practiced raising my rifle out the window and became so proficient that I did not make a sound doing it. I played my little video golf game and was doing quite well. I was getting sleepy so I figured I better open one of the windows to let some fresh air in. Then there was more golf and snacks.

At about 9:15 P.M. something caught my eye coming from the right side. Holy Sheet, it was a huge bear. I watched him strutting side to side and finally he was in my range. I raised my gun quietly and looked through the scope. Shoot!!!!! I never adjusted my scope. All I could see was black. I eyeballed the bear again and thought I was aiming behind his shoulder. BANG!!

This bear never went down. This bear never made a sound. This bear just ran. I could not understand how I could miss him. I must have got him. But, I kept remembering last year's bear. Shit. The only thing to do now was wait for Pee Wee. He should have heard my shot.

At fifteen minutes to eleven, Pee Wee and Wally come walking down the trail to get me. " You shoot da big bear?" Pee Wee asks. Yup, sure did. Over there. Pee Wee went over and said " Oui, there is blood. We come back in the daylight." Shit, not another one.

Wally already had his bear in the truck. Congrats, Wally. When we got to Real's, you could see and feel the excitement.

Kevin had shot a little bear too. Jim had a 325 pounder in Maurice's truck. Tim Roll hit one with an arrow and he too had to wait for daylight.

That night back at the B&B, the beer really was coming fast. All the bear stories that we all had to hear. It was great. Where was he coming from? Did you hear him first or just see him? Jim Schlick's story was first. He told us that when Maurice dropped him off, he said, " About eight or eight-thirty, you shoot da bear ". Jim asked him why he was dropping him off so early, then. He figured he could stay in the truck until about quarter to eight. Jim told us that he shot his bear about 7:15 P.M. He hadn't even put his jacket on. He was still wearing his casual sweater. Jim was probably the best dressed bear hunter that New Brunswick had ever seen. Then Jim told us that he couldn't remember how to load his gun. Maurice had to load it for him. In his defense, Jim and I had bought the guns that spring. So, he really wasn't that familiar with it. You should have heard the rest of the guys. You mean you had to have the guide load your gun? You were sitting in the tree with a sweater on and no camo? Yup. Then it was my turn. Mike, Tim and Chuck got on my case. Moran, you mean to tell us that you were playing a video game just before you shot the bear. You didn't even have your scope focused? Yup. And.. For toppers, Kevin was listening to " Volare" on his headset.

Morning came pretty early. Everyone except Wally and Kevin were going to Real's to track my bear and Tim's. Pee Wee and Maurice were leading our party with Jim, Ken and myself. I laid back a little ways. I did not want to hear, " Da Bear's gone". Suddenly, Pee Wee was yelling for Maurice. He then began to yell at me, " You shoot da big bear, you shoot da grandfadder bear. " The bear was huge. It was a real struggle for Maurice and Pee Wee to carry him out on a stretcher. They threw him into the truck and we were headed for Real's. It was one of my best days.

Shortly after we got there, here comes Real with Tim's bear. We had shot five bears the first night. Real was so excited that he drove around showing my bear off. That's when I knew he was a big son of a bitch. We went to the lumber yard and then to the Ranger's office. The ranger estimated my bear at 400 pounds. The bear would have been about 600 pounds in the fall. The ranger measured the head. They measure a bear first between the ears and then from the middle of the ears to the end of his nose. The New Brunswick record was 22 inches. My bear measured 21 inches. Holy Sheet, my friend!!!

After you shoot a bear, you're all done hunting. The other three guys went back out hunting that afternoon. Jim, Kevin, Wally and I found Buck's. We went back to the B&B for a little nap and Jim and I went back to Buck's before we met the group coming back from hunting.

Tuesday night, Ken shot a bear. We were on a roll. Another good night of bear stories, bullshitting, beer and getting on everybody's ass. Wednesday, Kevin and Wally left. That afternoon, Tim, Mike and Chuck went out hunting. Tim was video taping Mike. Ken, Jim and I went out about 7PM for pizza. When we got back to the B&B, Chuck was already there. Chuck had shot a bear earlier with a bow. Unbelievable. We only had Mike to go.

The four of us went to Real's to meet Mike and Tim. Mike did see a mother bear with two cubs. Tim had it all on the video tape. Chuck also had taped his kill. We had a couple of beers at Real's and decided it was time to go to Buck's.

We were the hit of the night at Buck's. They all loved us. Buck even bought us several beers and shots. We stayed until closing. They must have taken 15 or 20 pictures of our group. They just loved ' da bear hunters'. Of course, Buck being the owner was concerned about our safety, so he asked me if we were alright to drive back to the B&B. I said of course, we had a designated driver. Who was that he asked? I pointed to Jim who was at the other end of the bar just ready to chug a shot of something. Buck and his patrons all shook hands with us and said to make sure to stop by before we left. We exchanged addresses for Christmas cards etc.

Instead of going to bed when we got back to the B&B, we had to have a few more beers because we were still thirsty, I guess. Anyway it was daylight when we hit the sack and Jim was up by 6:00 A.M. Ken, Jim and I talked about whether we should leave or not. At first, I suggested we stay one more day allowing for us to get some much needed rest. Jim said that I was crazy and if we stayed one more night, we'd probably be back down to Buck's anyway. Yeah, Jim you're right as usual.

The amazing thing about the trip was that Jim and I learned that there is life after politics. Aside from the teasing, we never thought about the past or its politics. Hell, as far as we knew, there weren't even any rumors about us up there. And no one was bitching.

The three of us left that afternoon. It was a terrible ride home. We were tired and hung over. By the time dark came, we were stopping at every rest area to wake up. We made a deal that two people should be awake at all times. We arrived back in Wyoming County, early Friday morning. What a trip, but one that I probably will do again. .

Chapter 51

It's Over

All the supervisors were up for re-election in 1999. In addition to those positions, Sheriff Capwell was retiring after many years of service to the county as was Jean Krotz, the County Clerk.

Ron Ely was the longest standing undersheriff in the State. Ron had been the undersheriff for the entire 28 years that Cappy was the Sheriff. How could anyone deny Ron his due? No one did. Ron easily won the endorsement from the Republicans and Democrats. All of Wyoming County was thankful for the dedication of Sheriff Capwell and the luxury of having a very capable new Sheriff in Ron Ely.

I cannot praise Sheriff Capwell, Ron Ely and the entire Wyoming County Sheriff's Department enough. They are a great group of highly trained professionals. I won't list them all here for the sake of their privacy and protection. I do know that some of them could use golf lessons as well as lessons in golf etiquette.

Allen Capwell was honored, and I mean honored, at a retirement dinner on December 4, 1999 at the North Java Fire Hall. Tickets were extremely hard to come by. Cappy was paid tribute by his fellow sheriff's, State Police, FBI, Governor, Senators, Assemblymen, Congressmen Reynolds and Paxon, village police chiefs, supervisors, former supervisors, employees, family and friends. If my memory serves me correctly, I believe there were also over 30 Sheriffs present.

I had the distinction of being selected as the Master of Ceremonies for the celebration. It truly was an honor and one that I will cherish forever. The Fire Hall was packed. Denise Stowell from the Sheriff's Office, Sue Aldinger, Melane Spink and of course Ron Ely were all instrumental in the planning of the event. Denise Stowell usually answers the telephone at the Sheriff's. Every call was answered like, " Good Morning, Sheriff's Office, Mrs. Stowell, how may I help you?" Many times I would call over there grumpy or upset about some little thing and after I talked to her, I forgot my little problems and had a great day! Well... the invitations went out and asked if any attendee wanted to speak. There must have been over 40 people who wanted to speak. It was up to the committee to pare that number down. They decided to have about 20 speakers with a three minute time limit. It was my job to keep them to the three minutes and have a line up for the speakers. We were so organized that the next speaker was standing up near the podium so we would not lose any time. Keep in mind, that Cappy was receiving awards and thanks from all over the state. I'll tell you, it was a great evening for a great man. To Sheriff Allen Capwell and his wife, Sally, I thank you and may your retirement be a long and blessed one.

In addition, Jean Krotz was also retiring as the County Clerk and that race was not quite as clear cut. In fact, it was a real disaster. Janet Coveny, the Deputy Clerk to the Board of Supervisors, Cheryl Mayer, the Purchasing Officer for the County, Ellen Grant, Mental Health Fiscal Officer, Mark Cali from Perry and Tammy Donahue, the Deputy Clerk, were all vying for the position.

What to do? Carole Butler, the Republican Chair, had no idea what to do. We all suggested having an early Republican committee endorsement meeting, thereby eliminating a primary. Nope. Instead, Butler never scheduled a full committee until the evening of May 6, 1999. That was the night of nights. A real "cluster", if you know what I mean. The plan was that each candidate would say a few words and then the committee members vote to endorse or not to endorse.

It was a multitude of mistakes and blunders. First, Carole Butler talked to each of the candidates behind closed doors. They all agreed that they wanted a primary. Well, if that was the case, there was no sense of having an endorsement vote. Butler never told the rest of the committee. Secondly, there was Gordon Brown. Gordon is a really nice guy, but because of Gordon's interpretation of the bylaws of the county committee, we had to have secret paper ballots based on the republican votes that were cast for Governor Pataki the last election. Sweet Jesus pray for us.

The committee itself was split between the candidates. They were all good and they all had their own merits for the position of County Clerk. Tammy should have been the favorite as she was the Deputy Clerk. However, remember what I said about the party Chairs a while ago. Tammy had also indicated that the Democrats were going to endorse her anyway. Ellen Grant had probably worked the hardest as a Republican committee person.

Ellen was actively involved in the Republican Women's Club and also volunteered to serve on the annual fundraising committee, every year. Janet had been the Deputy Clerk before she came to the Board of Supervisors. Cheryl was a young professional woman with lots of talent. Mark Cali was an articulate, intelligent young man who obviously could handle the job.

The committee asked Brown if we could just go to a primary. Brown said that it was HIS opinion that we as committee members had a responsibility to endorse a candidate. OK. Let the games begin. The games began alright, and never ended until close to midnight.

All of the candidates were excellent. The votes were finally cast and counted according to the Brown/Butler Rules, the winner was Cheryl. Fair enough, she was the endorsed candidate. Yeah, right. That was another joke. According to the American Heritage Dictionary, the word ' endorsed' is defined as: To give support and/or approval. Cheryl received NO support from Butler or the rest of the committee at any time. The committee was split that night and would continue to be divided until Primary Day, September 14, 1999.

That summer was grueling for those candidates. They were all over the place. They were at the County Fair, they were at the Firemen' Parades. They were at the barbecues. They all worked hard but none harder than Janet and Zeke Coveny.

Zeke actually went door to door throughout most of the county. Janet was campaigning every day, 24 hours a day. They both worked hard and by God, on Primary Day, Janet was the winner and would be on the ballot as the Republican Candidate against Tammy Donahue who was endorsed by the Democrats.

I have no idea when a Democrat last won a county wide election. It has to be well over 30 or 40 years, at least. Janet continued to work hard, anyway. She won the general election, handily. Congrats, Janet.

Now, the Supervisor races were different. The word was out that Java, Bennington, Castile, Perry and Attica were all being targeted by the Democrats. At every Republican committee meeting, we all emphasized this. Carole, our leader, was engrossed in the county wide races. We were on our own. Baffling but that's the way it was.

A very nice, young lady was my opponent, Angela Brunner from North Java. I knew I was carrying a lot of political baggage too. I cannot say a bad word about Angela's campaign. She was a lady and did only what she had to. Remember, I had the North Java Water District, the JAVA SIX, the Town Park fiasco, the infamous audit that some wanted to portray as my indictment of theft. I also had the assessment update, the zoning issue on Minkel Road and some " good friends " that were stabbing me in the back. I also had the outright liars and rumor mongers out there in full force. They just couldn't wait to ask someone, hey did you hear about Moran and then spew their lies. Then they would run down the road to church and <u>pretend that</u> <u>they were</u> <u>little holy saints</u>. Yeah, God remembers. And so do I . Here's a quote that I received in the mail from an anonymous supporter.

SLANDER

It all seems so harmless at first. We hear a bit of juicy gossip about someone from a "reliable source" and we pass it on, never asking ourselves:

Do I know it to be personally true?

What is my motive for spreading it?

What will the effect of the lie be on those being lied about?

How would it feel to change places?

Would I want someone to slander me and my family?

Forget that old adage that " there is always a little bit of truth in every rumor." That is simply a feeble attempt to justify what we know is untrue and unfair.

The truth of the matter is that gossip is wrong, and often just personally vicious or pathetically political.

For those of us that just forgot this lesson, all is forgiven.

For those of you who create slander to hurt others,

I'll be back to deal with you later,

Signed,

GOD

We also had "good" Republicans that were out there campaigning against me. It was quite obvious. I also had the disadvantage of being in office for fourteen years. That really is a long time. Sometimes I think that I had an expiration date of 12/31/99 stamped on my butt.

Anyway, besides the lies I was also being blamed for everything that ever went wrong in the county and some things that I had no control over. The Democrats had people going door to door and asking questions like, where was the tobacco money going? In reality, no one knew. The Board of Supervisors had not made any decision. Who was on the Town Park Committee? Man, look at the Town Board Minutes or come to a damn meeting. Why did Java go with an assessment update? The Town Board (Ron McCormick, Fran Brunner, Don Roche, John Meyer and myself) made that decision. Why was the Town's accounting now being done by a firm in Nunda? Because they were professional accountants and no one could accuse anyone of anything, that's why. That decision was also unanimous by the Town Board (Fran Brunner, Don Roche, John Meyer and Ron Falconer). We had never experienced this type of campaigning in Java. It was a clever maneuver and it did work. I guess if you pound and pound them with untruths, people finally listen.

NOVEMBER 2ND, as Carole Butler said at Republican Headquarters in Warsaw, " The people have spoken". Thanks, Carole, for the lethargic attitude!

Cindy and I went to North Java like we always did. I had lost at North Java and could not get through to Carl Heterbring to see how I did in Java Village and Strykersville. I went outside and decided to head to Sad Dog's to get the rest of the bad news. Carl was just pulling into the parking lot the same time as we were. Nope, I had lost down there, too. It was now over. The sons of bitches.

When we walked into Sad Dog's, we were greeted by about 75 supporters or more. The word got around fast and I was approached by most with hugs, kisses and apologies. I think some of them felt worse than I did. Then the door opened and I saw Jim Schlick and Don Joller walk in with huge smiles on their faces.

I said to someone, well, there's the new Chairman of the Board. Jim says, " I don't think so. They kicked my ass out in Bennington". Jesus Christ, what was happening? We called headquarters and found out that Bob Bowles was losing in Castile and it looked like Ron Herman in Wethersfield was going to need the absentee ballots to win. Attica and Perry were close but Paul Agan and Anne Humphrey were going to win their races. Doug Berwanger and Ron Ely arrived at the Dog's. Jim and Betty Hardie showed up too. What the hell happened?, they all asked.

I decided that it was time for me to speak to all those who were there.

I thanked all of them for their wonderful support over the years. Donna and Jay Schofield, Carl and Debi Heterbring, Ron and Laurie Falconer, Mark and Becky Hopkins, Mike and Debbie Zielinski, Janet and Steve Beechler and many many others. I mentioned that we should not forget what we accomplished in the Town and the County. I said that we should all be proud. Java was represented even on the state level by my being elected as a Vice President of the N.Y.S. Association of Towns, on the Board of Governor's for NYMIR. I represented Java as the Chairman of the Board in the County. It was a great ride and all good things have to come to an end sooner or later. I promised them that I would assist Angela in anyway that I could. I thanked them for coming and went immediately to the bar to drown my sorrows.

We all proceeded to get hammered. That's the nice thing about having a tavern as your campaign headquarters. Could you imagine if we all had headquarters in Lawyer's Offices or Carole Butler's house? The day before the election, Ray Barber, the County and Town Historian had given me an excerpt from the 1855 edition of " Powers and Duties of Town Supervisors". Section 4 stated:

" The Town Supervisor shall have the power to grant licenses to keepers of Inns and taverns to sell strong and spirituous liquors and wines to be drank in their houses but not to be drank in their shops, outhouses, yards or gardens". Section 7 further states: " the applicant will not allow the Tavern to become disorderly or suffer any cockfighting, gaming or playing with cards or dice, or keep any billiard table within the Tavern or in any outhouse, yard or garden."

I guess it was a fitting piece of information for that evening. I could never imagine, God forbid, walking into the Sad Dog Saloon without seeing a euchre game going on. That morning I wondered if the State legislature ever amended or repealed the Law. I certainly hope so, but, hey with the N.Y.S. Legislature, anything's possible. And what's the deal with the outhouses? Can you see a euchre game or pool table in an outhouse? Apparently, they were doing just that somewhere in this state. I say that because at least nowadays, no action is taken in Albany unless it's considered a reaction. Oh well I'll let the outhouse police worry about this one.

The next day, I phoned Angela to congratulate her and offer my assistance to her. Later, in December she came to my house and we spent the morning going over files, correspondence and the books. I told her that she could call at anytime. I also told her that I thought she was going to learn that I was a better supervisor than some people thought.

The county was more stunned than you can imagine. It was like another disaster. Bob Bowles was defeated in Castile and Ron Herman squeaked out his victory with the absentees. The Board of Supervisors were losing me as their Chairman, Bob Bowles as the Vice Chair, Jim Schlick as the Chair of Public Safety, in addition to Earl Dominesey, Larry Nugent and the vacancy created by Dwight Gillette's death earlier in the year.

Those remaining Republicans decided to have an emergency meeting with the new Republicans coming in. What happened? Was it as clear as Carole Butler thought? Was there anything we could have done or should we have done something differently? The consensus was that we better gear up for the 2001 elections or the County Board of Supervisors was going to be in the control of the Democrats. Those in the room were furious at the County Republican committee. They felt that they should have done more. They designated Jim and myself to go and spread the message to the executive committee. That was a mistake. Jim and I both knew that we would be tap dancing down "jack ass alley." Carole did not want to hear it. She felt good that we won the sheriff and the clerk's race. She was happy with the Republican glass being 1/4 full. She seemed to be the best thing that ever happened to the Democrats. In 1999, the Democratic donkey took a huge bite out of the Republican elephant's hide. There was Republican blood everywhere. Charlotte Smallwood-Cook, Maggie Dadd, Terry Murphy and Bill Bryuere would have all been mortified. They were all strong and effective Republican Chairs. They were Republicans through and through. I am quite sure it would never have happened under their able watch. And... Butler, at that executive meeting, pointed out that the Board of Supervisors was under the control of the Democrats in the 1950's, so big deal. Does that mean what goes around, comes around? She really believed that her and her followers were doing a good job. Get a grip, she must have been having delusions and she should have quit following those other county Chairs so closely that she couldn't smell the roses or the coffee, if you get my drift.

Jim and I also mentioned that the remaining Republican supervisors thought more emphasis and more money should be directed to the supervisor's races. All over the county, the Democrats were raising money from people that normally did not contribute. Hank Bush donated. Dick Reisdorf contributed to the Democrats. It used to be unheard of for a local businessman to donate to the Democrats. They always knew that control of the Board would always be by the Republicans. Not anymore. That's good news if you are a Democrat or a Democrat dressed in Republican clothing.

Even though we had two months as lame duck supervisors, we knew we were all going to miss each other.

Chapter 52

"Networking"

God works in mysterious ways and did when He sent Mrs Kulander as my third grade teacher and she pegged me as a "social butterfly ". She was absolutely right. I love people. I love to be with people. I love to talk to people. I guess that's why I did have success in the networking business.

At the N.Y.S. Association of Counties or the Association of Towns, I simply can't sit quietly. I would always strike up a conversation with someone. And always, you learn from others and their experiences.

I remember at one of the NYSAC conferences, Bob Bowles, Kevin DeFebbo, Sue Aldinger, Norm Effman and I were all eating breakfast. As people would walk by, they would say, " Hey, Tommy", "Good morning Tom" " How ya doin' Tom?" Bob finally said, "Jesus Tom, do you know everyone in the place?"

And after the sessions, I could always be found at the bar. They knew it and they would find me. Wyoming County became friends with other counties from all over the state as a result.

Kevin and I were invited to speak to other counties. Two speaking occasions that I will never forget were Schuyler County and Otsego County. On 12/8/98, Schuyler County Legislature Chair, Patricia Hastings asked us to come to Watkins Glen to give our views of having a County Administrator. I opened my statement by stating, " We, the Board of Supervisors, issue policy and procedures. We do not micro manage. County government is big business that requires someone to be on the scene daily. If the electorate wants <u>part-time lawmakers</u> elected in popularity contests, they cannot be expected to know how or have the time to give county government the best management. "

Kevin explained his daily routines. Kevin said his job was to implement the policy and procedures of the Board. Then we opened it up to questions. There were a lot of negative people in the audience. They did not want Schuyler County to have a County Administrator. One resident even looked at Kevin and I said, " We should not compare ourselves to Wyoming County, they're too big for us". Are you kidding?, we said. We've been called a lot of things, but NEVER big. Then Paul Fitzsimmons stood up and accused us of coming to Watkins Glen for a free lunch. My first thought was that I had somehow been zapped back to the North Java Water District. This guy could have been a Water Commissioner. I said, Yeah, right, we drove over 90 minutes so we could get a free lunch. My goodness, Paul, get a grip. Guess what? Paul Fitzsimmons followed us to the car still arguing about the pros and cons of a county administrator. By the way, early in 2000, Schuyler did hire a County Administrator and, no, it wasn't Paul Fitzsimmons.

One of my favorite trips was to Oneonta in October of 1999. Georgia Schadt, the President of the Otsego County League of Women Voters invited Kevin and I to be the keynote speakers for their meeting on the nineteenth in Oneonta.

The only way to get to Oneonta is to drive through Cooperstown. Cooperstown is where the Baseball Hall of Fame is located and one of my favorite places to visit. October is baseball month with the playoffs and the world series. Kevin and I both had horrible colds. I mean horrible. We were on prescribed medication, tissues, aspirin and cough drops. We arrived at the hotel a few hours before the dinner, so we took a nap to see if we got any better. It didn't happen.

Even though we were both sicker than dogs, we were great. Kevin and I do seem to bring out the best in each other. We're both very competitive and we insist on outdoing each other. We talked about the merits of Wyoming County Government. This was really a tribute to the Board of Supervisors to have the County recognized as a true leader and trend setter in New York State. We had a question and answer session and all went fine. In fact, Georgia wrote a letter later and thanked us and said that all the members and the board found our talk very informative and that they would invite us back. We went back to the motel and had ONE beer at the bar while watching the Mets and Atlanta play in the playoffs. That's how sick we were.

The next day, on the way back to Warsaw, we stopped at Cooperstown. Kevin had never been there. Cooperstown will always awe me. I love baseball and there's such a tremendous feeling around Cooperstown. Imagine the history and those that walked the very streets that Kevin and I walked. Babe Ruth, Mickey Mantle, Willie Mays and even Willie Stargell for Kevin as a Pirate fan. Once I was in Cooperstown and one of the Sports Shops had a sign that Clete Boyer, a New York Yankee in the 1960's was going to be signing autographs the next day. I asked the owner if she knew of the other Boyer brothers. Nope, who were they? I told her Cloyd and Ken. Ken was probably better than either Clete or Cloyd. Ken played for the Cardinals.

There we were on the streets of Cooperstown and my cell phone rang. It was Suzanne West. Suzanne was very concerned about her election in Orangeville. It seemed that Geraldine and Ray Luce and some others were working against her. I bid her welcome to the club. Suzanne wanted to know what I thought she should do about the rumors and lies. I said you just have to ignore them. You cannot deny and defend yourself everyday. Suzanne won but at what cost? By that I mean, yes, she was still on the Board, but then it gets worse. Suzanne always tried to do what was best for the Town and the County. Why criticize someone like that? Eventually, we won't have anyone willing to run for office. Thanks to all those small people who lie big.

Rumor mongers are agents of the dark side or the underbelly of networking. I prefer to be positive so that brings us back to networking. NYSAC was probably the best forum for examples of this and also as a stage for prototypes for all types of different county issues and possible procedures.

I won't begin to document the great and also learning experiences I had at these conferences. I met some really great people that all genuinely cared for their constituents. These conferences were dedicated and focused on the hot issues of the day: welfare reform, pre school handicap program, courthouse mandates, tobacco settlement money, highways etc.

The discussions were led by the NYSAC staff, Bob Gregory, Steve Aquario, Ken Crannell and who could ever forget our very own Matt Lauer. Matt's real name was Millea, but I affectionately called him Matt Lauer because all of the women just loved Matt. They were all informed and just great people. These same sessions then spilled over into the lobby and eventually the bar for further conversations.

I mentioned John Zagame, the previous director, earlier in the book. I should also mention Bob Gaffney and Art Shafer, former Presidents. Bill Jones from Suffolk County. George Canon, Jean Raymond, Dale French, Don Ninestine, Ed Burdick, Dennis Pelletier, Jimmy Keane, Sean O'Connor, Gerry Meal. Clyde Burmeister, John Walchli and I could go on and on. I consider them all very good friends.

Real friends are often in short supply, so when Christmas rolls around you like to celebrate with them. The Supervisor's

Christmas Party had been going on for years. I went to my first one back around 1988 . George LaWall and his wife Jean talked Cindy and I into going. It was at the Glen Rock Restaurant. I was working on the railroad and had to use a vacation day to attend this gala. We finished our dinner and I noticed that everyone had left the back room. I told George that we probably should head for the bar , everyone must be there. NOPE. They were gone. The party was over about 8:00 P.M. We were back in Java by 9:00 P.M. and I had wasted a vacation day. I never showed up again until 1995. The following year, I was the Chair and I was put in charge of the entertainment committee for the party. I convinced Kevin that we could play Santa Claus and his helper. Of course, Kevin was going to be the little elf. It was a total surprise and you should have seen some faces when they saw their Chairman and County Administrator walk in as Santa and an elf. We repeated our performance in 1997. In 1998, we wanted a new idea.

One of my favorite movies was " The Blues Brothers " with Dan Akroyd and John Belushi. Kevin and I decided that we could lip sync and dance six songs or so. We put hours of practice in at work and at home. We had props like a toy saxophone, bull whip and dark sunglasses. We were dressed in black suits, white shirts with narrow black ties and of course the infamous white socks. Not the dirty ones, though.

If you thought we surprised everyone by being Santa, they had no idea what we were doing in 1998. They loved us. They loved us so much that they told Bob Gregory and the rest of the NYSAC staff. Steve Aquario, Ken Crannell and Matt Millea arranged our booking at the Desmond Hotel in Albany, for the 1999 Winter Conference of NYSAC. It was on a Monday night and there was a disc jockey playing a sound system. Steve gave him our tapes and we waited for the big moment.

The lounge at the Desmond sits about two steps down from the bar. So the dance floor is almost a pit compared to the bar. It is extremely dark. Kevin and I were sitting in the lobby until Steve or Ken would give us the sign. It was about 11:00 P.M. when we entered. There was probably 150 people or more. Of course they were all in the right mood by then. The DJ announced that NYSAC had a special treat and the Blue Brothers were here. Let's hear it for the Blues Brothers.

Kevin and I came running in, down the steps to the dance floor and right to the microphones. The crowd was going bananas. They loved us. We couldn't see real well, all I could see was silhouettes of bodies. We lip synced and danced about six songs and of course had an encore with "Soul Man" as the finale. Many people thought that we were the hotel entertainment. They all flipped when they found out who we were. It was great. To this day, I still have people come up to me thanking me for providing the entertainment that night.

The 1999 NYSAC fall conference was held in Lake Placid. That is truly one of the most beautiful places in all of New York and probably the world. Bob Bowles, Sue Aldinger, Earl Dominesey and Anne Herod were all among the contingent from Wyoming County. NYSAC also elects their officers in the fall. John Walchli from Allegany County was running for 2nd Vice President. The Western New York Intercounty Association was supporting John.

Tom Tranter, the County Executive from Chemung was also running. There were many in NYSAC that thought the County Execs were taking the organization over. After all, they represented the counties with the highest populations. The County Administrators were being ignored for the most part. There were 18 county executives in the state at that time. County executives are for the most part elected and from the larger counties. There were 27 county administrators in 1999 and they were all appointed.

I was actively campaigning for John. So were Don Ninestine and Dennis Pelletier. We even had signs made up for John. I converted my room into campaign headquarters and a hospitality room.

Forty-eight hours before the nominations and elections, high pressure politics was running rampant through the streets of Lake Placid. I was across the street from the Holiday where we were staying, when Bob Gregory came over and asked if he could see me outside. Lake Placid in September of 1999 was a very chilly place. The temperature had to be in the low forties or colder. Bob explained to me that NYSAC discourages floor fights and elections for its officers. We should decide this thing beforehand. What will it take for John to withdraw? I don't know, I'll have to talk to him. Now, I could understand the reasoning.

Sunday morning, I met with John Walchli first and asked him what he thought. John was a little disappointed but for the good of NYSAC, he would entertain a compromise. Then John and I talked to Don Ninestine from Ontario County. At least western New York was going to have a say on who was going to be the 2nd vice president of NYSAC.

As the day progressed things got tenser. It was power politics and I was loving every minute of it. George Canon ran into me in the lobby. " Hey, Tommy, you better do something. You're in charge of this thing and you better broker a good deal for everyone." Holy shit, why me?

That night, after dinner, we all went to the hospitality chalet across the courtyard from the hotel. Art Shafer, Jean Raymond, Bob Gregory and Tom Tranter were all there. Walchli was in his room already. One by one they took me outside in the 40 degree temperature. I was shivering uncontrollably by now. I understood exactly where they were coming from and they understood our concerns.

I would go back and forth inside and outside trying to cut a deal and stay warm at the same time. After hours we had a tentative agreement. Now, it was my job to call John, wake him up, ask him to come outside the chalet with me and agree to the deal.

John, being the gentlemen asked me to give him five minutes. John and I now went outside to freeze a little more. " OK, John, they have the votes anyway. They will appoint you as Chairman of the Government Relations Committee, they will also agree to have a representative from the County Administrators Association on the Board. They will in no way hold this against you. John, you will be nominated and then you will respectfully decline and throw your support to Tom Tranter." Now don't think this was a huge surprise to John. I mean, we had been talking all week end and also adding votes up. There was no way that John was going to win. All he would have done was make it a messy affair and maybe even divided NYSAC. NYSAC is too valuable of an organization to the counties, to allow that to happen. Without NYSAC, the counties would have no presence in Albany. In addition to the presence and lobbying effort on behalf of the counties, NYSAC provides important education and training that is so vital to all county legislators and county department representatives.

John wanted to sleep on it but thought he could agree for the sake of NYSAC. Immediately after he left, I had to go back outside and tell the others that I thought we had a deal. They wanted the deal right there but I told them that my grandfather used to always say that people in hell wanted ice water too. You'll have to wait till morning.

John wavered a little but eventually he agreed. Not all of his supporters were happy. But again, Eric Dadd always said if you reach an agreement and no one is real happy about it, IT IS A GOOD AND FAIR DEAL. Ironically, Tranter was elected by acclamation and resigned less than six months later. Oh well. It was still a great experience and I thank all concerned for their patience. I think Bob Bowles was getting a little worried about where I was all week end.

I cannot overstate the importance of NYSAC, the Association of Towns, and other similar groups. Through it, I was able to meet and become friends with the true leaders of the state. If you think the political party leaders are leaders, you're crazy. It's the people that attended NYSAC in Lake Placid. They are the leaders. They cared enough about their organization and its future, to brave the elements, forego dinner and drinks and even spend time away from their county and their spouses. Via con Dios to my friends at NYSAC.

Chapter 53

The Farewell Tour

The week or two right after my election loss was the hardest. I felt hurt, betrayed and generally just defeated and depressed. When that wore off, I felt a whole lot better. It was not the end of the world. Fourteen years is a long time. My good friend, Dave Hackett told me one day that he found out why I lost. I asked him to explain. Dave said, " You lost because of illness and fatigue. Yup, the voters got sick and tired of you. " I've used that line many times since. I was not going to let myself dwell on the loss. There were many proud accomplishments and many more proud moments. I was determined not to go with a sour grapes attitude.

Bobby Knight former basketball coach at Indiana University once said that he'd like to be buried upside down so everyone could kiss his ass. I didn't want that. I decided that I would leave office the way I came in. As close to the gentlemen that Tom Moran can be.

My first formal farewell was the Java Town Board Meeting on December 14, 1999. After the monthly business I made this statement:

" I would like to take a few minutes to express my pride, gratitude and appreciation to the people of the Town of Java.

I have been your supervisor for the past fourteen years. Yes... that is a long time but together we accomplished a great deal.

To name a few..

-We adopted and passed a Master Plan and Zoning Ordinance

- We are now on a regular schedule of replacing and updating our highway equipment

- We have developed a new Town Park of about 35 acres through donations and volunteer work that I would be remiss if I did not thank Kathy Wilson, the Java Strykersville Kiwanis, Ron George, the National Guard, Bob Kibler, Tom Reynolds and of course the Park Committee and many others.

- We instituted a transfer station that cannot be matched in western New York. Many said it's never going to work. The usage continues to grow each year. The major reason is that the employees are truly dedicated to the operation. Dennis McCutcheon and Brenda George

along with all the others that work or have worked there, I say thank you. (Deb Zielinski and Ray Wilson, too)

- The Town has a Youth Program that we should all be proud of. Again through the efforts of Sue Stephan, Sheri Stemper and Anne Price. The budget is about what it was 14 years ago.

- We have a Sheriff's Substation at the Transfer site that affords all of us a little better police protection. Java was the first town to establish the position of Town Prosecutor. When the Prosecutor was eliminated, we lost revenue. This year already, we have received over $8,000 more than last year. And... it eliminates the conflict and possible conflict for our Justices and actually expedites our system.

- We have taken bold steps over the past few years. We were one of the first towns to sign on with the Municipal Insurance Program (NYMIR) that saved us thousands of dollars. We have held the county and the state accountable for their actions. Once, we were even criticized about being " too hard " on then Governor Cuomo.

- Financially, this town could not be in better shape. We have controlled spending throughout the years. In fact, over the past eight years, the entire tax levy has only been raised about 7%. That's less than a 1% annual increase. Further good news is that we have accumulated over $200,000 in reserves through good fiscal management.

- In closing, there still is work to be done. The water district project is about 95% complete but there still are decisions that have to be made. It's unfortunate that the project took so long.

- I wish Angela, and the new Town Board members, Doug George and Jeff Gerde the very best. I offer any assistance that you may need, to simply call on me. I am sure that you will all do your very best for the Town of Java.

- Again, I thank each and everyone of you for this tremendous opportunity and especially thank my family, Cindy and the kids who loved me through the good and the trying times.

- God Bless you all and Merry Christmas."

It was a very emotional night for me. I was especially pleased to read the Batavia Daily News' account of the meeting on 12/15/99, written by Johanna Braciak:
" Thomas Moran bid farewell to the Java Town Board, ending more than a decade of service, as supervisor. Rather than dwell on his loss in November, Moran used his speech to note the many things he and the board have accomplished during his tenure".

Leaving the Java Town Board was a hell of a lot easier than leaving the County Board of Supervisors. Java was where all the political heart aches were. Java was where the complaints, rumors, lies and some mean spirited people were. So, in a way, it was a relief to have that cross taken off my shoulders and the bulls' eye off my back.

The last Board of Supervisors' Christmas Party under my leadership was scheduled for December 11, 1999 at the Moose Club in Warsaw. Clint and Marge (God love her) Cleveland were the point people at the Moose. They both did a splendid job.

The hall was decorated just beautifully for Christmas. The atmosphere could not have been any better, because it was going to be the LAST performance of the Blues Brothers.

Sue Aldinger and Melane Spink had done up a poster on the computer complete with a picture from the year before. The title of the poster and the theme of the party was " A Farewell to Ellwood (me)" One night only.

I must say that Kevin and I were at our best. Some of the Department Heads had a special surprise for me. Jeannette Wallace, Anne Herod, Sheila Gerasimchik, Sue Ventresca and Patti Hughes all came dancing out like the Supremes or the Ronettes. Jeannette was the lead singer in " R-E-S-P-E-C-T". It was great. I don't think it had any hidden meaning, though. The last song of the night was " I did it my way" by either Frank Sinatra or Elvis, I don't remember which. Anyway, Cindy and I were dancing inside a circle made up of everyone that was still left standing. They all had their arms around each other. You'd think it was my funeral. There were quite a few teary eyes including Cindy's. It was another special night for Cindy and me. I love you guys. And you know who you are.

Warsaw was different. I had many close friendships with employees, department heads, and especially my colleagues. That last meeting was my most difficult. I think what made it easier was that the offices had to be temporarily relocated to Buffalo Street. The old courthouse was being renovated and all the occupants had to be moved. Fortunately, I never really anchored myself in those headquarters. When we moved from the courthouse, I simply took all my personal items home. I had a box or two of memorabilia that I had accumulated over the years. I had autographed pictures of Governor Pataki, Tom Reynolds, Bill Paxon, Dale Volker, Newt Gingrich, Al D'Amato,

Rick Lazio and even Chuck Shumer. I had a plaque that Sue Aldinger made for me that stated " Irish Diplomacy was a way to tell someone to go to hell and have them look forward to trip." I brought home two baseballs that I threw out for the ceremonial first pitch at a Rochester Red Wing game and one for the Junior College World Series in Batavia. I had a St. Louis Post Dispatch newspaper headline printed the day after Mark McGwire hit his 70th home run in 1998, that was given to me by Kevin DeFebbo. I had my political posters from Marty Mucher and many other items that I will cherish forever.

December 16th was also going to be the last Board meeting in the old courthouse. It was also going to be the last meeting of the 1900's. It surely was historic in more ways than one.

In one way, I was looking forward to it and another way, I was dreading it. I intended to recognize many people at the meeting, so I was anxious. There was also fear on my part. What if I broke down during my speech? I warned Kevin, Sue, Melane and others not to show any emotion. If they started bawling, I probably would too.

When I entered the Chambers to sit at the Chairman's desk for the last time, I looked up to see almost every department head in attendance. The sheriff and sheriff-elect was there. So were other deputies. Many employees were there. It was the largest crowd that we had in some time. I knew that they were there for me. They were not there to make sure that I really was leaving. They came out of respect to me and I'll never forget it.

At the end of the meeting, I gave my parting remarks:

" I would like to take this opportunity before we adjourn into the next millennium to make a few comments.

First, I cannot explain in words how honored and proud I have been to serve as your Chairman for the past four years.

I am not going to give a litany of our accomplishments, though there were many. Instead, I am going to seize the moment and recognize some people that are more than deserving. These are people that have touched my life and have made a difference. I would be remiss if I did not mention several people that had a huge influence on me. I was tutored by some of the best supervisors this county has ever seen. I thank Gus Petrie from Attica, Ken Lowe from Covington, Ross Roberts from Perry and of course Howard Payne from Arcade. These gentlemen will always be near and dear to my heart.

- *Doug Berwanger: Doug has only been on the board for four years but you wouldn't know it. When Doug came on, the Board was divided about whether to build a courthouse or not. I made Doug the Chair and boy did he run with it. I believe almost every major decision after that was unanimous. He's open minded, willing to learn and has earned the title of a leader. At times, I saw the frustration in Doug of having to deal with mandates and edicts from the State. I saw his bewilderment when another supervisor suggested the sheriff buy Ford Escorts for patrol cars. But.. he convinced him otherwise by asking a simple question, "What if the deputy had a prisoner the size of me and he tried to get me in the back of an escort?" Doug, you were a welcome addition to the board and a breath of fresh air. The new board will depend and look to Doug for his leadership and guidance and I know that Doug will be a huge success. God Bless You, Doug.*

- *Paul Agan: Paul has come a long way from climbing on the hospital roof to make sure they really needed a new one. He has been the Chairman of Human Services during a very trying time. He and his committee have endured the fiscal storm coming from Albany and reinvented ways to serve those in need. Social Services, Health, Mental Health, and the OFA to name some, come under his committee. Perhaps, someday we can go on another 10 hour ride with the buzzer going all the way.*

- *Jim Schlick: Wow, Jim this Board is probably going to miss you most. I'm not going to tell any of the stories here today, because there are just too many. Many times I would be extremely worried and unsure of some issues and Jim would always say, " We'll be alright". He was usually right except once on a trip, when he had control of my EZ Pass. He told me we'd be alright and ten days later I received a violation notice and a $50 fine. He was probably at his best in Public Safety and Finance. He's always, and I mean always, been a fiscal conservative. He actually practices it in his own life but you have to love him.*

- *Bob Bowles: Mr. Finance, Mr. Hospital, Mr. Glow. But we probably should also call him Paul Revere or Patrick Henry. No matter what assignment or committee I gave him, he was always the lead man. At times, I felt guilty giving him any more assignments but he wanted to do his best. And he did. I'll never forget the first trip we made to Albany to sue the State along with NYSAC, over the back payments for our Pre School Program. That lawsuit and the subsequent reforms to a program out of control, came from one man. Bob Bowles in committee said, " We're not paying our share until the State fulfills their responsibility." Bob... that was another one of your shots heard around the State.*

- *Bill Guthrie: I really never got to know you. But, I believe that you were like the rest of the supervisors and tried to represent Covington the very best that you could.*

- *Madonna Barber: I always admired her for being able to juggle this job along with that of a mother of two young children. But maybe your talents as a mother actually helped the board. Many times, some of us would be in heated debate and suddenly you heard Madonna, quietly state that maybe there is another way to go about this. Thank you for that Madonna.*

- *Hank Bush : Hank and I have had many lunches together and we always took turns buying. Hank was also involved in many projects. Probably the biggest was the Amoco Project. Hank was the leader and coordinator for all the agencies, interested parties and the county. How many hours did you put in because you knew it was good for the entire community. We always got along and that was probably because we had similar interests and hobbies.*

- *Larry Nugent: I sat next to Larry for several years before I became Chairman. You supervisors know how that is. Larry was like Madonna, but he was juggling a full time career with this job. I don't know how you did. I used to work nights on the railroad and then come down here. I know what it took.*

- *Arnold Cox: Arnold probably gave me hell more than any other supervisor. It was always little zingers. But Arnold also cared enough that whenever he was in the building, he'd poke his head in my office and ask how ya doin'.*

- *Suzanne West: Suzanne is practical, hard working, common sense. She can really let somebody have it. Ask me. I know first hand. She knows when to work but she also knows when a good laugh is needed. She is also caring and compassionate. She may not want everyone to know that but now you do. I know that I'll miss her and her great laugh.*

- *Anne Humphrey: Oh Boy... Anne and I are products of the 1960's. At times that was our only common link. Over the years I have really come to admire, respect and truly appreciate Anne. One of my proudest moments came when she and Anne Herod presented me with my degree in feminist studies from the women of Wyoming County. That wasn't a joke was it, Anne? I don't believe anyone on the board had a bigger impact on me than Anne. Periodically, she'd come to my office and have discussions and convince me to see her point of view. And usually I did. Anne will also be looked to for leadership and guidance and I know that she will provide that to the Board. Best wishes Anne.*

- *Earl Dominesey: from neighboring Sheldon. I can describe Earl in one word. A Gentleman.. In many ways, he's the cream of the crop. Earl has known for the last five months that he won't be here next year and I don't believe that he has missed one meeting. And Earl always did his homework and researched issues on his own. His votes were all educated and informed. And personally, I look at Earl as a good friend and neighbor.*

- *Howard Miller: Our military man on the Board. Howard brought a real sense of humor to us all. In the thick of things, here's Howard with a smart comment. I also had the pleasure of serving with him on the Genesee Finger Lakes Planning Council and got to know Howard, the man. Like his colleagues, Howard is doing the very best for all the residents of the county.*

- *Ron Herman: At my first meeting, 14 years ago, Ron held up a pair of work gloves. It seems the month before that the Sheriff's Department bought winter gloves for the deputies and Ron thought they paid too much for them. So.. He said he stopped on the way to the meeting and noticed a farmer in the field that had old ratty gloves on. After 14 years, I still can't believe you left that farmer without any gloves that day and did you ever give them back? Ron is the senior member of the Board and has yielded his right to adjourn, today to Jim Schlick.*

- *Sue Aldinger, Melane Spink, Janet Coveny, Cheryl Mayer, Kathy Schwab.. What would I be without you guys? They are the office staff and believe me without the staff, the Chairman and this Board cannot function. I thank each and everyone of you. They had to deal with me on a daily basis. And I know that wasn't easy. Janet, the very best in your new position as County Clerk. Suzie put up with me quite well. Usually, she just ignored me. Suzie too is very conservative with taxpayer dollars. When my stapler broke, she immediately went to the dollar store for a replacement. She is not only the Clerk to the Board, she is our personal secretary, confidante and at times, she needs to be our mother and caretaker. But above all, she is an honest, trustworthy, dedicated and loyal person. It has been more than a pleasure to work with you, Suzie.*

- *Kevin DeFebbo: How do I begin. Over the last four years, we have truly become a unit, a team. I don't mean the Blues Brothers either. I don't even want to begin to mention some of his accomplishments, there are too many. Besides running the day to day government, the Board would decide to set new policy or a task whether it be research or actually devising a plan, and then we would give it to*

Kevin. Kevin did it. No questions and we knew that it was going to be completed the right way. Kevin once told me to be less strident and more magnanimous. We shared all major issues and crises in the county with each other. AS you all know, we became good friends and I don't think anyone could ask more from a County Administrator. This county is very fortunate to have an Administrator the caliber of Kevin.

Four years ago, I asked this Board for the cooperation that they gave Howard Payne. I got more than I ever asked for. This Board truly became a cohesive unit and not only worked together but actually became a close knit group, almost our own little family. We did not have the infighting that so many counties have. Heck, we were even criticized for getting along too well. Baloney! The better a Board can get along, the better it works and the more productive it becomes. Sorry, Geraldine. Wyoming County has been raised to another plateau by this Board. These ladies and gentlemen are the very best and I thank them for making my job so much easier and a real pleasure. I also have said many times, that even on the worst day, this is a fun job.

In departing, I thank each and everyone of you for the privilege of serving as your Chairman. I hope that I have represented you well and would like to wish the new Board the very best in the coming year.

I wish you all a very Merry Christmas and a Happy New Year!

My good friend Earl Dominesey insisted that we invite the 1999 Board of Supervisors to the Vets' Club in Warsaw after the meeting. Earl and others arranged to have pizza, wings, etc. at the Club for all to enjoy while they were saying their good byes. I thought it was a great idea. It was. Many people came to say their good byes to the six of us who were leaving. Even though it was another one of those terrible days in December in Wyoming County. We were having one hell of a snow storm. The political storms were also over and everyone made it " home " to civilian life, safely, including me.

Chapter 54

Revelations

So, what's it all about? Was it worth it? Knowing the ending, would I do it again? Should everyone take a stab at it? I think I saw the following on a talk show once. The top five famous last words:

1- Let's see if it's loaded
2- Gimme a match, I think my gas tank is empty
3- If you knew anything; you wouldn't be a traffic cop
4- Gosh, Honey, these biscuits are tough
5- Sure I was out with your wife, what about it

I would not trade any of my experiences. It was more than worth it. Even knowing and tasting defeat, it was still more than worth it. Being directly involved in the decision making process of local government was one of the best educations that one can receive. What I mean is that when I first entered the political arena, I had fears and also mistrust of government. I guess that's the American way.

However, after you meet and work with fellow electeds, government department heads and government employees, you see the other side. Believe it or not, they are just like you and me. They really care for the people they serve. They are doing the very best that they can.

I've probably written about hundreds of politicians throughout this book and what, have I said maybe two were not quite up to snuff? That's pretty good odds. Remember, I am talking about your local government leaders. Not State or Federal. Forget about them, once they arrive in Albany or Washington. That ball game is too big and chances are that by then, they are either totally bull shitted or are well on their way. It's sort of like the all star minor league baseball player who gives it his all for about $25,000 a year. He becomes a major leaguer for over $25 million and doesn't have time to sign autographs for kids anymore. Enough said.

Many experts have always said that local government is the closest to the people. How right they are. That's a good thing. The local town official receives telephone calls from residents concerned about everything from the national defense to the dog next door that won't quit barking. I always enjoyed those calls. I mean the calls from legitimate people, not the whiners. I always enjoyed talking to someone about Albany or Washington politics. Even though it wasn't my area of expertise, I could still enjoy it. I can only recall hanging up on one person. I hung up on the son of a bitch because he wouldn't listen. He just kept ranting and raving over the same old bull shit. I could list his name here because I'm sure he can't read, but I won't.

My biggest concern and worry is the thing that Spiro Agnew warned us about 30 years ago. The silent majority. I worry about the silent majority's opposite: ' The Loud Minority'! It seems that government at every level listens and responds to the loud minority. It's amazing but true.

Even at the Town level, if six residents show up at a Board Meeting complaining about the condition of their road, you can bet that action will take place. That's sad. It goes back to the bull shit editorials, you read in the paper on a regular basis. How about the thousands of people out there who don't write? They are too busy with their own lives, jobs and families. They HAVE A LIFE. I wonder if the newspapers would print them if everyone got together and wrote a letter to the editor stating what a great job local government was doing. I THINK NOT.

Mayor Jimmy Griffin of Buffalo said in 1983, " I guess athletes are like politicians in that we all have our Monday morning quarterbacks. It's the easiest thing in the world to be, because it's very easy to snipe and ridicule after the fact." Now, there was another good politician and local government leader.

So.. Why do we listen to the loud minority? I really can't say. Maybe, the silent majority has to be heard from. Maybe we continue to hope that they will rise up and shout down the loud mouths. That's what I hope will happen someday.

But it really doesn't get any better than this. Only in America, can a guy like me be elected as Town Supervisor for fourteen years, Chairman of the Wyoming County Board of Supervisors for four years and do it the way I wanted to. It was a great ride. I only hope that I have recognized, and now, you the reader, recognizes the dedication, value and good fortune of having true leaders who I have mentioned in this book. My fellow supervisors and others, made my job so much easier. I could compare it to President Reagan. Reagan may not have been the most intelligent President, but by God, he was smart enough to surround himself with professional experts. Jimmy Carter on the other hand, surrounded himself with his Georgia buddies and only served one term. I believe that I was lucky like Reagan. I had great supervisors that tutored me, I had great Chairmen before me who led the way and most of all, I had the very best Town Supervisors on the Board while I was Chairman. Except maybe one. And he knows who he is.

I would urge everyone to consider running for local office whether it be Council Member, Clerk, Highway Superintendent or Town Supervisor. It will be a decision that you will not regret. You will experience first hand, local government in action. You will understand that 99.99999 % of local officials really are doing their best for their constituents. We, as citizens need good people in office. We need rational, reasonable people to represent us. Don't just think about it. Just do it. In conclusion, I thank the people of Java for electing me as their Supervisor and giving me the opportunity to become Chairman of the Board. I thank all my good friends throughout New York State and I thank Cindy, Kevin, Colleen, Bridie and Mike for standing with me. From the bottom of my heart and for the last time I say.....

GOD BLESS YOU ALL !!!!!!!!!!!

Epilogue

ILLUSTRATIONS OF COURAGE

The following individuals are all Wyoming County Town Supervisors or former Town Supervisors, except Kevin but he has earned his place on this list. They have each earned a spot as true examples of courage. They fought for what they believed in. There are none better and they are true heroes:

- BOB BOWLES, Vice Chairman and Castile Town Supervisor
- JIM SCHLICK, Bennington Town Supervisor
- KEN LOWE, Covington Town Supervisor
- KEVIN DEFEBBO, County Administrator
- ROSS ROBERTS, Chairman and Perry Town Supervisor
- GUS PETRIE, Attica Town Supervisor
- HOWARD PAYNE, Arcade Town Supervisor
- DOUG BERWANGER, Arcade Town Supervisor
- PAUL AGAN, Attica Town Supervisor
- ANNE HUMPHREY, Perry Town Supervisor
- ALEX LANE, Warsaw Town Supervisor
- EARL DOMINESEY, Sheldon Town Supervisor
- IRENE GLAUS, Sheldon Town Supervisor
- NORM SMITH, Middlebury Town Supervisor
- SUZANNE WEST, Orangeville Town Supervisor
- MADONNA BARBER, Eagle Town Supervisor
- LARRY NUGENT, Genesee Falls Town Supervisor

WYOMING COUNTY ALL STAR TEAM

The following individuals are the members of the Wyoming County All Star Team. They have all earned a place on this team by their resolve to do the very best that they can do. They are not in any specific order and if I forgot anyone, I apologize. I thank them on behalf of all of us:

Suzie Aldinger
John Edwards
Frank Vitagliano
Cheryl & Dave Mayer
Dan Moran
Lucy Sheedy
Kathy Schwab
Joe & Mary Siler
John Meyer
Kathy Kuchler
John Bond
Mark & Becky Hopkins
David Dimatteo
Lum Zielinski
Willie Parmeter
Paul McQuillen
Dick Fisher
Maggie Dadd
Mike Griffith
Gerry & Esther Roberts
Bill Bruyere
Keith Kibler
Ed Conroy
Mark Balling
Richard Harrison
Rich Humphrey
Alex Dominick
Jack Fisher
Ed Redding
Bernie Hogan
Jeannette Wallace
Jim Wawrzyniak
Carl & Deb Heterbring
Suzie Wallace

Jim & Betty Hardie
Melane & Dick Spink
George Zielinski
Dave & Dorothy Hackett
Joe Heller
Doug George
Ron & Lori Falconer
Paula Parker
Pete Kline
Donna & Jay Schofield
Eric T. Dadd
Mike & Arlene Witkowski
Ron George
Gerry Stout
Norb Hoyt
John Hurst
Norm Effman
Bernie George
Charlotte Smallwood-Cook
Mark Dadd
Ray Barber
Ed Freyburger
Linda Williams
Jeff Gerde
Elaine Galligan
Jim Reger
Frank Conroy
Bill Horton
Suzanne Wheeler
George LaWall
Bill & Alice Becker
Patti Hughes
Stu Hemple
Pat & Dave Herrington

Bill Holt
Pat Harrington
Audrey Parmele
Rick Jensen
Mike Hogan
Sally Meegan
Dixie Perkins
Steve & Janet Beechler
Ron & Lucy Ely
Bill Close
Mike & Deb Zielinski
Steve Tarbell
Joe Mejak
Mike & Sandy Chassin
Jean Krotz
Mario Alaimo
Bob Kibler
Dennis Spink
Ron & Cyndy Smith
Rick Dean
Janet Coveny
Ray & Kathy Wilson
Jon Cooper
Terry Lowell
Donna & Mark Powers
Jim Pierce
Bud VanArsdale
Bill Streicher
Cheryl Miller
Dave Lindner
Don Almeter
Bob Grover
Jeff True
Jane Stephens
Judy Kessler
Lee Wishing
Madonna & Joe Barber
Arnold Cox
Larry Nugent

Marty Mucher
Chuck Kmicinski
Chuck Eley
Sue Ventresca
Bob Calmes
Sandy Boyd
Anne Herod
Ed Bartz
Brandon Beechler
Allen & Sally Capwell
Dan George
Cliff & Sue Stephan
Garry & Roxanne Ingles
Frank & Joan Minkel
Bill Thomson
Dave Davis
Mark Cali
Gary Weidman
John Copeland
Barb Shilling
Peter Humphrey
Brenda Copeland
Ed Till
Mary Rudolph
Richard Tindell
Sally Wing
Dick Clapp
Sam Gullo
Mike Quinn
Jason Mayer
Todd MacConnell
Dana Rudgers
Corky Upright
Eric Slocum
Pat Vadney
Nick Grover
Howard Miller
Hank Bush
Shirley Carr

Terri Halsey
Bob Conroy
Ron Herman
Buzz Comstock
Len Opanashuk
Gary Huff
Marcia Fladie
Dennis Halstead
Wendy Simpson
John & Gail Meyer
Don Joller
Peter Dueppengiesser
Diane Johnson-Jaeckel
Deb Lambert
Deanna Taylor-Thomson
Dave & Maria Hackett
Lori Tallman
Patti Yetzger
Cathy Bieber
Colleen Bean
Fred & Shirley Ingles
Kevin Bohn
John & Cris McLeod
Len & Holley Almeter
Pat Beechler
Bud Pleace
Tim McCutcheon
Tony Zielinski
Russ & Mary Potter
Ken & Marge Price
Jeff Rabey
Dave Reisdorf
Lucille Powers
Hank & Retta Bauder
Dennis Vergason
Gary Boorman

Paul Freyburger
Mike Ash
Frank Hollister
Toby Reh
Tim & Tammy Stafford
Beth Pond
Joe Lee
Beth Hildebrant
Ellen Grant
Larry & Wendy Rogers
Richard Harrison
Elaine Semlitsch
Brenda Brown
Kathy Murtha
Diane Green
Norm Metzger
Debi Owens
Del Sylor
Justine Ames
Dana Wright
Rocky Mitchell
Don & Bonnie Clark
Jim Keenan
Tony Almeter
Nick & Marcia Pleace
Florence Zielinski
Denny McCutcheon
John Zielinski
Frank Zielinski
David Kurzawa
Russ Reisdorf
Charlie Leone
Paul Ingles
Don Bowen
Mike & Sue Kozlowski
Father Ed Muerder

ALL STATE TEAM

The following is the All State Team that I have put together, again in no specific order and if I missed anyone, I apologize:

John McCain	Tom Reynolds	Dale Volker
George Pataki	George W. Bush	Newt Gingrich
Al D'Amato	Rick Lazio	Jimmy Griffin
Bill Paxon	Jeff Haber	Kevin Crawford
John Zagame	Bob Gregory	Nick Mazza
George Canon	Dennis House	Stan Dudek
Marcia Touey	Jay Gsell	John Walchli
Ed Burdick	John Margeson	Don Ninestine
Don Leysath	Larry Scott	Sean O'Connor
Gerry Meal	Jess Fitzpatrick	Mark Williams
Sandy Frankel	Jack Gilfeather	Chuck Swanick
Shawn Gray	Fran Leavenworth	Jimmy Keane
Mark Robinson	Dennis Gorski	Andy O'Rourke
Jerry Elicks	Brian Custer	Susan O'Rourke
Richard Hsia	Sue Meyers	Lynn Billings
Kathy Ahlberg	Molly Plant	Sharon Secor
Jan Griffin	Stoner Horey	Dan O'Donnell
Chris Kane	John LaPointe	Claude Faville
Bob Faville	Jon Stead	Jim Callery
John Callery	John Sackett	Dick Rudolph
Dennis Pelletier	Jack Doyle	Pat Knapp
Jake Essler	Marv Decker	Charlotte McLaughlin
Wanda Hudak	Art Shafer	Alice Alsworth
Ken Crannell	Kyle Tuttle	Nancy Calhoun
Matt Millea	Steve Aquario	Dale French
Barb Monohan	Tom Mazerbo	Ron Trybushyn
Mary Weinman	Gordon Hessell	Scott Schrader